Sally McKenna was born in Nairobi, Kenya, and was brought up on the Pacific island of Fiji. She is the restaurant critic for the Irish Independent, writing the weekly column "Guest Who's Coming to Dinner".

John McKenna was born in Belfast in 1959, and educated there and in Dublin. He has practised as a barrister and works as a journalist, writing principally on travel.

THE

IRISH FOOD GUIDE

A directory of sources
for lovers of good food and travel

Sally McKenna   John McKenna

With illustrations by Alwyn Gillespie

Anna Livia Press
1989

First published in 1989 by
Anna Livia Press Ltd
21 Cross Avenue
Dun Laoghaire
County Dublin

Text copyright © Sally McKenna and John McKenna 1989
Illustrations copyright © Alwyn Gillespie 1989

ISBN: 1 871311 04 7

Typeset and designed by Amadeus Publications Ltd
Cover by Bluett
Printed by The Leinster Leader Ltd

While every effort has been made to ensure that the information given in this book is accurate, the publishers do no accept responsibility for any errors or omissions.

For Almut, Kevin and Maureen
and John and Margie

ACKNOWLEDGEMENTS
Special thanks to Paula Buckley and Belinda Preston. Thanks also to John Brown, Andrew McElroy, Mary McDonnell, Malachy Keenan, Paddy Fay, and Cynthia Harrison.

CONTENTS

FOREWORD
by Mr John P. Wilson, TD, Minister for the Marine

IRISH FOOD — A TIME-HONOURED FEAST

I have always looked upon Ireland as the Garden of Europe. When I was Minister for Tourism I first met Sally McKenna and thought she was an ideal person to look into and assess that garden. Now I think she, and John McKenna, are ideally suited to assess the fruits of River, Lake and Sea.
Our lush pastures nurture fine cattle and our heather-strewn slopes provide excellent lamb and mutton.
Our crystal-clear seas, rivers and lakes are the most pollution-free in Western Europe and are teeming with a vast array of succulent seafood species.
This book will illuminate and inform the reader on the best traditions of the Irish culinary art.
Irish food figures greatly in our folklore and culture and salmon, for instance, was the piece de resistance at banquets given by the Kings of Ireland, often cooked on a spit after being flavoured with honey and butter.
Irish food has excelled over the years because it has been used and presented in a simple fashion which has been perfected over the centuries.
Many of our fine foods are valued abroad and our exports play a vital role in the country's economy. The raw materials both from land and sea are processed by the most sophisticated techniques to the highest quality standards.
The excellent basic foods in Ireland have hardly changed since an anonymous poet wrote in the ninth century:

I will choose and will not hide it:
Fragrant Leek,
Hens, Salmon, Trout and Bees.

May all who use this book partake of the "Bradán Feasa".

INTRODUCTION

This is a book about good food. It gives details of who produces good food, where and how you can find and buy it, and those places where it is best to eat it. It may surprise people that a book about good food in Ireland should be so large, but the book's size has not been gained at the expense of quality: The Irish Food Guide has many entries, but there are many, many more which have been left out because we felt that the standard of the food produced was not high enough. The criteria for inclusion is, simply, that the food is the best you can buy. We have not included growers, producers or restaurants only in order to criticise them: there is sufficient negative criticism in the food world already. Instead, we have searched for the good, and found it in abundance.

There is no reason why Ireland should not have a food culture as rich and varied as France or Italy, the two countries traditionally set up as benchmarks. We are an island where the western waters, at least, are famously unpolluted, and the North Atlantic produces a shoal of varieties of fish for us to enjoy. Combine this with the finest fishing lakes in Europe and we should have a fish cuisine second to none. That we do not, and sadly we do not, is a matter for regret.

Our pastures produce beef that is the envy of the world, yet frequently one hears tales of Irish folk holidaying abroad and marvelling at the quality of the meat they are eating. 'Oh yes' says the chef, 'It is wonderful, I get it from Ireland'. This often repeated story reveals the greatest weakness of Irish food; there are few good cooks, and the simple peasant cuisine on which our parents were reared has largely been lost. The Irish took up the cause of prepared, packaged food with a vengeance in the 1960's and the food culture that had sustained us for centuries vanished like snow off a ditch. It is slowly beginning to find its way back home, but in the meantime the cooks of today had begun to look abroad for guidance.

Most of them turned to France, and whilst nouvelle cuisine is not popular in this country (most people associate small portions with meanness) it has nevertheless reverberated throughout the catering colleges and the kitchens. This has been fine, up to a point, and the point where it stops being fine is the fact that the Irish almost always completely misunderstand the principles of nouvelle cuisine. They see it as something where taste comes secondary to appearance, which is in fact the wrong way around. From this fundamental error, countless miserable dinners continue to be born.

But the vogue for the new and the foreign also meant that we overlooked our native foods. Perhaps it is a part of our island mentality which means that we prize more highly those things which come from abroad. Modern tourism has developed this lack of self-confidence, creating folk who want to eat the ingredients they enjoyed on their holidays. The paradox of this, of course, is the fact that no group of the Irish population is more wedded to Irish food than the emigrant, tucked away in a flat in Kilburn, the Bronx or Sydney, waiting for a parcel of cooked ham and the local paper to arrive. Irish mothers continue to send food parcels to their sons and daughters, wherever they may be.

We have suffered from the fashions that beset the food world, but perhaps the time is right for the fickleness of fashion to work to our benefit. If we begin to look again at the foods we produce, then we will be doubly fortunate, for we solve not only many of the problems of health and wealth that have beset us over recent years, we also find that our food is amongst the finest produced anywhere in the world. A good Irish cheese, properly matured then brought to room temperature until it is just right, a fillet of beef cooked to allow the middle to remain moist and pink, a plate of early organic potatoes steaming with melted country butter, a tray of oysters and a bottle of stout, bright cherry tomatoes picked from the stem in the morning and fried with a smoked rasher, a big hunk of soda bread smeared with home-made jam along with a cup of tea, are just some of the things we do, inimitably.

The second benefit of eating local food is the fact that it is good fun to find it and buy it. No one ever had a memorable afternoon in a supermarket, but you can find and meet many memorable food producers by using this book, and see, understand, and appreciate the way in which food is produced. Above all you can get the food when it is at its best, without the needless intervention of transport, packaging, freezing and adulteration which threaten to rob so many foods of any vestige of taste — or nutrition.

Eating food in this way also helps you to avoid the dangers to health created by the various additives and preservatives which litter mass-produced food.

Everyone, these days, knows someone who has a child or a sister or brother or parent or friend who has health problems related to food allergies. If you know where to find good, hand-made food, food prepared without artificial sweeteners, added sugar and harmful chemicals, then you need not worry about whether or not food is doing you harm because it will only be doing you good. We must eat to live, so let us eat in a way that will allow us to live as well and as long as possible.

Eating good food means that you need not worry about weight as much as if you are eating prepared food which is filled with hidden salt and sugar. During the course of this book, which involved tasting hundreds of foodstuffs and numerous meals in widely varying establishments, we did not put on a single extra pound.

But the main problem with mass-produced food is that it owes nothing to the culture of Ireland and contributes nothing to it. A meal of junk food has no history, no folklore, no society, about it. It is eaten purely because one is hungry, and ironically it satisfies hunger only for a few moments. Good hand-made food is always individual, always different, always interesting. Above all it tastes good. It has tastes from the area in which it was made, it varies in tastes depending on the seasons, it varies depending on who makes it. Good food is, simply, interesting. Interesting to eat, interesting as an expression of personality, interesting to share. It adds complexity to the seasons, adds complexity to travel: a cheese made in Cavan is as good as a cheese made in Cork, but wildly different, a sausage made in Northern Ireland will often share little more than a name with a sausage from Galway, Kerry lamb is not the same as Connemara lamb. Ireland may be a small island, but its counties vary enormously one from the other. Eating the food from the counties allows you to savour the differences.

Using this book should allow the resident, the traveller and the tourist to avoid bad, badly prepared, boring food. Standards throughout the country vary enormously: the finest restaurant can sit beside the worst eating place, and the latter will not only not feel self-conscious, it will more than likely be the one with the more luxurious interior and the fancier prices. Good food can also, on occasion, go side by side with bad food — there are many restaurants where an excellent dish will be followed by one that is almost inedible. In part, this is the fault of snobbery. For many Irish folk, going to a restaurant is determined not by the food but by whether the restaurant is fashionable, luxurious or expensive. People are happy to spend money on bad food, if it is in the right place. This allows many cooks to get away with culinary murder. Add to this the fact that the Irish never complain — at least not until they get home, where they will abuse the meal and the restaurant for the next month — and you end up with restaurants that should not be allowed to open their doors doing very nicely indeed.

The happy reverse of this is that there are a handful of truly gifted cooks who use the finest of local ingredients and treat them with respect. They procure local meat and game, they fill their vegetable dishes with produce from people's back gardens, they line their cheeseboards with the best Irish cheeses and keep them until they are at their most luscious. These people, and the producers of the products they use, are the ones you will find in this book. Their food represents not only Irish cuisine, but also Irish culture, the culture of the land, the culture of rural life. They may add spice to it, they may even add European influences, but they remain determinedly, stubbornly Irish. This is why they are so valuable.

The principal section of the agricultural community we have detailed are those people who farm organically: the word 'organic' is used throughout the book to mean those folk who hold the symbol of the Irish Organic Farmers' And Growers' Association. The reason why they are dealt with in detail is simple: this is the part of the agricultural community growing for taste. Taste is the essential element of good food. Appearance is largely irrelevant, shelf-life something that should worry the grocer, not the eater. Organically produced food, particularly that most defiant symbol of Ireland, the potato, is more interesting, more pleasing, more enjoyable to eat. Good food must come from good ingredients and organic farming produces the best ingredients. The happy consequence of all this delicious fruit and those gorgeous vegetables is of course that organic farming is good for the land. Whilst conventional farming is slowly exhausting the soil and producing food that is good to look at but boring to eat, the organic growers are protecting the vital asset from which everything stems: the land. The last year has seen a dramatic shift in people's consciousness regarding the environment. It seems to us that anything which protects the environment should be applauded for that reason alone: the fact that we can also enjoy fabulous produce is a fortunate bonus.

Ireland continues to be distracted by the terrible famine of the mid-nineteenth century. We believe always in filling our bellies because tomorrow the food may not be there. Rural poverty also contributed to this asceticism towards food: the poor man has no money to spare for fancy foods. And yet it is one of our greatest losses that we have, in a time of relative plenty, relinquished the riches of the peasant diet in favour of insubstantial, imported, irrelevant food. In the past we may have been poor, but we were rarely hungry. Today, with increased wealth, we have plenty of people besotted with anorexia, bulimia and other food disorders which were unknown here only a generation ago. We have people who are constantly unhealthy because their diet is plentiful but harmful.

The Irish Food Guide is designed to be used as a tool to help people to eat well, and by eating well to live well. We do not need to leave our shores to find food of breathtaking quality, diversity and complexity. It is all here, just down the road, past the pub, left at the graveyard, third on the right past the sign for the disused creamery, but if you get to the church you've gone too far, so drive until you see a disused Morris Minor which is probably being used as a chicken coop. Then there it is, waiting to be enjoyed.

John McKenna, Sally McKenna
Dublin, September 1989

HOW TO USE THIS BOOK

The Guide is divided into the four provinces of Ireland: Connacht, Leinster, Munster and Ulster. It is then sub-divided into counties, and further sub-divided into townlands, peninsulas and towns. Finally the entries are recorded alphabetically.

Some counties are not included, simply because our search through them found no food of any particular merit.

Irish people are happy to give directions, but be warned, they are notoriously imprecise. Nevertheless most people in Irish towns and villages will be known locally. Don't be afraid to stop a complete stranger and ask, 'Do you happen to know of the whereabouts of the bicycling Germans who make cheese on the hill behind the forest?'. They will almost certainly know the answer, even if they've never eaten the cheese.

Ask about other local food. Look in small country shops. They will probably be attached to a post office, a funeral parlour and pub, and will sell free-range eggs, and good bacon, which you will find in a bucket of brine at the bottom of the fridge.

We have marked some entries with the symbol ➥ — these are producers, growers and shops that it's well worth going out of your way to visit, and restaurants that have reached a standard of technical and creative excellence. In addition to this there are a small number of entries marked with a star, ★. These are either the finest Irish ingredients, or the places where you will find Irish ingredients in the finest possible state, whether raw or cooked.

Added to this there is a directory at the end of each county which lists worthwhile addresses. To this section we have added restaurants that we didn't manage to visit, but which were recommended frequently by knowledgeable locals. These are marked 'Consistently Recommended'.

Finally, this book is not definitive, nor does it intend to be or want to be. A food culture is consistently expanding, contracting and developing. Do not be surprised if some of the entries vanish, and you find other fine foods which are not included. We hope to produce an updated edition of the Irish Food Guide whenever there are sufficient new entries to merit a new volume. Any producers, consumers or interested parties can contact us through Anna Livia Press.

POINTS OF ENTRY

The Shannon Duty Free shop is world famous. Irish duty free experts have been sent out as far as Russia and the Gulf to advise on the selling of goods without taxes, something which the Irish have practiced for years anyway.

If you're leaving the country via Shannon there are a number of good food items to look out for, so save a little change to spend after you've filled your bags with duty free whiskey and consumer durables.

Both Lir truffles and Butler's Irish chocolates are for sale, along with hand-made chocolates from 'Mrs Caffney'. You can buy a brown bread mix, along with biscuits from Bewleys and Kelly's. Cakes include a Porter cake from Clare as well as Barbara's Kitchen fruit cake.

If you want to take back some smoked salmon, then don't worry. Eamonn Holme's excellent wild smoked salmon 'Eagle Isle' is for sale along with Nolan's salmon from Dublin and Kealincha smoked trout.

You can buy tea bags containing brews concocted by both Bewleys and An Teach Ban.

Preserves come in the shape of Ownabwee jams, Lakeshore mustard, Eleonore's Irish salad dressing, and Mileeven and Healey's honey. There are marmalades from Oriel cottage.

There is freshly baked bread and scones which are made locally, and finally there are some farmhouse cheeses. You can buy the local sheeps' cheese, Cratloe, as well as St Martin's, and the flavoured cheddars made by Cahills.

If you want to have a meal soon after you arrive, we suggest you consult your map and try the following. We have included approximate (very approximate) times that it will take you to drive there after you have left the airport, boat, train, and cleared the customs. See individual entries for details and exact addresses.

If you're flying into Shannon you could drive to nearby McCloskey's restaurant in Bunratty (20 mins), but if you want to get some driving under your belt, head for The Mustard Seed in Adare, nearer Limerick (about an hour).

Coming by boat via Dun Laoghaire, head south for the Tree of Idleness in Bray (15 minutes). If this is too far try the Olive in Dun Laoghaire (5 minutes).

Unfortunately there is just nothing in the vicinity of Rosslare. Drive west across Wexford and cross via the ferry from Ballyhack to Passage East, where you will find Chez Flavien (an hour).

If you're landing in Larne you can shake off the rigours of the Stranraer ferry in the Ramore, Portrush (an hour), though you might prefer to head for Belfast in which case a casual, inexpensive meal can be bought at La Belle Epoque, a better, but more formal one at Roscoff (both an hour). These are also accessible for Belfast International Airport (an hour) and Belfast Harbour (fifteen minutes).

If you enter via Dublin's North Wall then drive down the quays to Pigalle (fifteen minutes). Otherwise cross over the toll bridge and head for The Park in Blackrock (twenty minutes).

Dublin airport is near to The Schoolhouse in Swords, where you can come off the plane and eat fresh fish and chips, as well as more exotic fare (twenty minutes). For something even more immediate stop off for a pizza at The Independent Pizza in Drumcondra, which is on the airport road (thirty minutes).

Connacht

COUNTY GALWAY

THE ARAN ISLANDS

Inis Mor, Inis Meain and Inis Oirr together make up the Aran Islands, a beautiful and distinctive trio where the quality of life, the wild flowers, the unpolluted waters, and the instinctive welcome of the islanders make it a place that no one should miss. Inis Mor is the largest island and its capital townland Kilronan can be reached by boat from either Galway or Rossaveal, or by plane, from Galway airport. Inis Oirr can be approached by boat from Doolin, in the Burren in Clare, and another boat ferries between the three islands.

Gaelic is the language of the islands, but English is more than tolerated. The islanders love visitors and make you feel most welcome — indeed, they encourage people to stay the night in the many bed and breakfasts. You can then see the rest of the island by minibus, hired bicycles, walking, or by the pony and traps — the gondolas of the Aran islands. The best way is probably on foot, for then you can listen to the cuckoos that serenade the islands, watch the skylarks rising and then parachuting back into the fields, admire the fabulous wild flora: Gentian violets, wild orchids and many many more varieties, and feel the effort that placed thousands of stones onto thousands more to make the miles and miles of dry stone walls that criss-cross the island. Everything on the island will amaze you: the walls, the flowers, the birds and the myriad of colours from grey windy days to the glorious aquamarine of the water in summer.

Cooking on the islands runs from simple Irish fare, as in Martina McDonagh's (the Garda's wife) restaurant on the seafront, or the Dun Aonghusa restaurant, Tel: (099) 61104, to the cosmopolitan and elegant (see entries for Joelle d'Anjou and Cliff House). There is a smoked salmon factory on Inis Mor, and when we visited Michael Gill of Cliff House he spoke of his experimental oyster beds. Over near Killeany there are various vegetable experiments being carried out to see what the island can produce. We saw vegetable marrow, sugar peas, wild strawberries and courgettes.

Be sure to buy the map drafted by Tim Robinson. It's a thing of beauty in itself, and very helpful in its detail of the islands. You can buy it in Galway and its environs as well as on the islands themselves.

3

KILRONAN

JOELLE D'ANJOU

Youth Hostel Restaurant
Kilronan Harbour
Inis Mor
Tel: (099) 61255
Contact: Joelle D'Anjou

Vegetarian smorgasbord and day-time cafe

Don't miss Joelle D'Anjou's vegetarian smorgasbord. Book during the day for 7pm sharp (otherwise the food just goes, and you'll be disappointed). Joelle cooks a feast of vegetarian dishes. You can bring your own wine and if you're staying a few days they will hold over what you don't drink for the next evening. They will also refrigerate white wine if you bring it before 7pm. During the day Joelle offers real coffee, home-made scones and lovely home-made brown bread, which he will make up into sandwiches along with vegetable soup. In the winter you may be lucky and catch Joelle's smorgasbord in Sligo town. Enquire at the White House Youth Hostel.

The restaurant looks out at the harbour, just below the youth hostel. Open seven days, from May to September.

CLIFF HOUSE

The Scrigeen
Kilronan
Inis Mor
Tel: (099) 61286
Contact: Olwen Gill

Restaurant attached to B&B

One of the best restaurants and a most comfortable B&B is to be found in Kilronan on Inis Mor island. Olwen Gill has a sophisticated style of cooking using fresh fish from the harbour or meat from the Galway butcher who delivers twice a week. To this she adds subtle sauces and glorious vegetable concoctions. Restaurant facilities are open to non-residents if you book.

On the Killeany road out of Kilronan. Open seven days.

MAN OF ARAN COTTAGES

Kilmurvey Bay
Inis Mor
Contact: Geraldine Dirrane
Day-time cafe

When Robert Flaherty made the film 'Man of Aran' he built two adjoining cottages that overlook Kilmurvey bay, a glorious beach for sunbathing or swimming. Geraldine Dirrane and her husband have renovated the cottages and turned them into a restaurant which offers tea, coffee and sandwiches to hungry passers by. She also cooks a reasonably-priced lobster lunch, and when we met her, was considering opening a one-room B&B where one couple could stay in a room overlooking the Atlantic.

Kilmurvey Bay.

4

AN tSEAN CHEIBH
(The Old Pier)
Kilronan Pier
Inis Mor
Tel: (099) 61228
Contact: Michael and Evelyn Muldoon

Restaurant and chipper

Kilronan boasts both a chipper and a gourmet restaurant side by side in The Old Pier building. Both of them are excellent. The chipper offers fresh fish, real chips and cakes and apple pie from the restaurant. The restaurant itself is a well- priced and well-prized location for anyone planning a special meal.

In the centre of Kilronan Open 11am-10pm Mon-Sat.

INIS MEAIN

DARA BEARG FLAHERTY, Creig Village, Inis Meain, Co na Gaillimhe. Dara grows vegetables in Inis Meain, and the last we heard he was experimenting with asparagus.

KILRONAN

Aran Salmon, Bradain Arainn Teo., Kilronan, Aran Islands, Co Galway. Tel: (099) 61240. Telex: 50137, Fax: (091) 61963. Contact: Michael Browne.

CLARINBRIDGE

There are two famous pubs in south county Galway, each within a few minutes drive of the other. Moran's Oyster Cottage (Morans of the Weir) in Kilcolgan is still in the hands of the Moran family (Contact Willie Moran, Tel: (091) 691113). They serve good quality standard pub food for most of the year, but during the months September to April it's worth going out of your way to visit them. This is the season when they serve oysters from their own oyster beds. You can call in any time during pub opening hours and taste that classic Irish combination: oysters and stout. This is the place to do it. Further up the road is Paddy Burke's in Clarinbridge. Run on the same lines, the difference is that Paddy Burke's will sell you Pacific oysters when the local shellfish are out of season. Not for purists, perhaps, but even Pacific oysters complement stout. (Contact: Ronnie & Rita Counihan, Tel: (091) 96107).

The Clarinbridge Oyster festival takes place around the 8th-10th September (check with Bord Failte for precise details).

BALLINASLOE

WILLEM & NICOLETTE DEN HEYER

Dromeyre
Kilimore
Ballinasloe
Co Galway
Contact: Willem and
Nicolette Den Heyer

Sausages, vegetables

Some aromas are irresistible, and one of them is the aroma of frying sausages as Willem Den Heyer cooks his home-made pork bangers on a little gas stove in the Saturday Market in Galway. Once you try a cooked one you will want a bag of them to take home. They cost about a pound for seven to eight. 'We started just for fun, and it's still fun', says Willem. The sausages are naturally produced, including natural skins. In winter the Den Heyers sell vegetables from their hot-house.

Contact the Den Heyers at the Saturday market in Galway from 8.30am.

CLAREGALWAY

GEAROID O MURCHU

Gra-Cre, Killeen
Claregalway, Co
Galway
Contact: Gearoid O
Murchu
Herbs, vegetables.

In season Gearoid O Murchu sells organically-grown vegetables, and the rest of the time he produces potted herbs which you can buy in the Galway Saturday market.

Contact Gearoid at the Saturday Market in Galway, from 8.30am.

CLIFDEN

SALMON & SEAFOOD

Specialites de
Saumons fumes
Sauvages Irlandais
Salt Lake Manor
Clifden
Co Galway
Tel: (095) 21278
Contact: Jean Jacques
Boulineau

Jean Jacques Boulineau and his wife Francoise came to Ireland with the intention of starting a fish farm. Both of them were biologists and have a daunting knowledge of the subject of fish. To their surprise, however, they found that stocks of wild salmon were still maintained and they were disgusted at the pollution, cruelty and bad taste of farmed salmon. Like true converts they now treat the wild salmon with a passionate zeal. They welcome visitors in the summer months and let you taste farmed and wild smoked salmon side by side to see for yourself the difference. 'One hundred percent of people prefer the

6

➥ Smoked wild salmon

wild'. If you rod- catch your own salmon they will smoke it for you for a fee, so you can take it back home in its preserved state. Otherwise they buy from the fishermen. You can see the whole process, gutting, bleeding, cutting, salting, and smoking, either as they do it, or in a series of presentation photographs. Ninety- five percent of M Boulineau's salmon is exported to France (Contact: 13 Rue E. Varlin, 75010, Paris, or 41, route de Rueil, 78150, Le Chesnay) but he's happy to sell it to you straight from the smoking room.

At the bottom of the hill in Clifden turn right, follow the road and Salt Lake Manor is signposted on the right hand side. Or ask directions in Clifden.

GALWAY

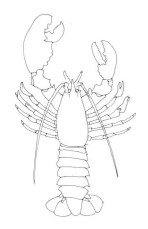

Galway city describes itself in a phrase that hints at brashness, 'The Capital of the West', but adds a touch of modesty, 'The Gateway to Connemara'. This is the duality of the seaside town, warm, carefree and cosmopolitan in season; wet, windy and needing an escape route out of it the rest of the year. But Galway has much to offer any time. Within the five contiguous streets, Quay Street, Cross Street, Middle Street, High Street and Shop Street, there are over twenty places to eat. The food offered varies from wholefood rolls, pizzas, Indonesian feasts to plenty and plenty of delicious fresh fish.

DRAGON COURT CHINESE RESTAURANT
Foster Street
Galway
Tel: (091) 65388

Chinese restaurant

Foster Street runs off the Great Southern Hotel side of Eyre Square. Half way along it, and up a flight of stairs is the Dragon Court, a light, sunny restaurant with disarmingly friendly waiters and waitresses (unusually, not all Chinese; we spotted an Italian). The menu of Peking Duck, Chow Mein, Fried Rice Sizzling dishes, and other commonly-spotted 'Western'- Chinese cooking, is made more indigenous by a confident and competent Chinese chef who refuses to

7

let these great Eastern dishes become bland at the behest of weak Western taste buds.

Galway city centre.

TIGH NEACHTAIN
Cross Street
Galway
Contact: Steve Kelly

➥ *Pub with specialist food*

This modest old pub contains great surprises. The first day we went there we missed lunch but noticed that the cook had not only produced Hungarian goulash, he had spelt it in Hungarian on the blackboard. When we returned, amongst the more obvious, but no less excellent foods, there was Indonesian Pork Satay; skewers of pork in a crispy peanut sauce. Steve Kelly, who looks after the food, tells of cooking Nepalese lamb one day, and having a Nepalese student come in for lunch. 'I asked him was it good?', said Steve. The answer was 'Yes, very authentic. The only thing missing is Yak Ghee'.

Tigh Neachtain is in the centre of Galway and is open for lunch each day.

GALWAY SATURDAY MARKET

Every Saturday morning, Galway market arranges itself around St Nicholas' Cathedral in the commercial centre of the town. Even though there are some well organised pitches, most of the market is impromptu, with eggs and cakes being sold from car boots, shrubs, plants and herbs plonked on the pavement, makeshift tables laden with vegetables. It is charming, and very continental: a good selection of interesting local produce, local endeavour and local ingenuity.

Naturally enough, every egg for sale is branded as free-range, but you will do well to get a true one — most of the genuine articles will have been pre-sold to people who know where they can find the real thing. But for cakes, fruit loaves and breads, you cannot do better than to buy from somebody's boot, patisserie is still one of Ireland's culinary weaknesses and the best sweet things are still made at home.

In season there are some true delights to be found: Angelica Rost presses her apples and adds nothing to the bottled apple juice she sells, a truly delicious drink. A number of stalls sell bread made either by the people themselves or by friends, but you can get excellent wholemeal, true sourdough rye and thick white plaited loaves. There is a wholefood van, craft stalls, spuds by the bucket, and a bustling sense of business to it all. For individual names see other entries in this section.

KINVARA

DIRK FLAK
Aughinish
Kinvarra
Co Galway
Contact: Dirk Flak

Organic vegetables

Dirk Flak's holding is right at the end of the Aughinish promontory — to the west there is nothing but the Atlantic. He sells his produce in the Galway market from the end of April to November. He stocks a full range of organically grown vegetables in season, and vegetable seedlings otherwise. He also sells to local restaurants. Holder of IOFGA symbol.

Drive to the Aughinish peninsula, turn left at the T-junction and you will see the farm on your right.

LOUGHREA

BREKISH DAIRY

Kylebrack
Loughrea
Co Galway
Contact: Hugo & Esther
Zyderlaam

*Farmhouse cheese,
yogurt, country butter*

One of the busiest stalls in the Galway Saturday market is Hugo and Esther Zyderlaam's dairy counter where you can buy yogurt, cheeses, country butter and bread. The Brekish Dairy yogurt is delicious: consistently smooth with a deep lemon taste. Their tangy soft goats' cheese is sold plain or herbed. There is also a rather ordinary cows' cheese, cut from a great big wheel right in front of you.

You can buy Brekish products either from the Saturday Galway market or from McCambridges' on Shop Street in Galway city centre.

MAAM

MAAM VALLEY CHEESE

Curr
Maam P.O.
Co Galway
Contact: Willem
Vanneman

Farmhouse cheese

Willem Vanneman and his wife make a Gouda-type cheese by hand on their farm in the Maam Mountains. They began farming with a Hereford cow who produced too little milk, ('She loved life', says Willem, 'but she wouldn't get pregnant'). They then bought a Fresian who produced too much milk, and so Maam Valley Cheese was born. Maam Valley comes in two sizes: three-quarters of a pound, and three-and-a-half pound wheels. It's a delicious cheese.

Travelling west from Galway turn off the N59, onto the R336. The farm is set well back off the mountain road. The best way to find it is to drive into the valley and ask the first person you see. You can buy the cheese from Sullivan's in Clifden, the Maam Cross craft shop, or from the farm.

MOYCULLEN

DRIMCONG HOUSE

Moycullen
Co Galway
Tel: (091)
85115/85585

Drimcong House manages to cook and serve sumptuous dishes in an understated fashion, a difficult task, aided by the tasteful decor and the capable staff, amongst whom Ivan, the wine waiter, is a treasure. Gerry Galvin's cooking reveals touches that would be beyond most chefs: confit of duck with

Contact: Gerry and Marie Galvin

➥ *Restaurant*

roasted duck breast, roast duck with roast rabbit, sole folded in filo with mango and melon, robust shellfish soup with tangy creamy rouille, rabbit terrine with a sweet mustard dressing. The table d'hote dinner is astonishingly good value at £14.95 (1989). A concern for the customer, the excellence of the food and the exceptional value of the table d'hote make Drimcong one of the finest restaurants in the country. Gerry Galvin also conducts cookery classes for six weeks up until Christmas, and there is a food fair of restaurant produce just a few days before December 25th.

Drimcong House is signposted on the N59 road from Galway to Clifden, about one mile north west of Moycullen. It is open From March to October Tues-Sat 7.30pm-11.30pm.

OUGHTERARD

EAMONN McGEOUGH

Oughterard
Co Galway
Tel: (091) 82351
Contact: Eamonn McGeough

Family butcher

Eamonn McGeough is a prize- winning butcher and a mighty raconteur. His shop is just off the main road running through Oughterard. He specialises in sausages, white pudding and beefburgers. He is everything a family butcher should be: knowledgeable about both his meat and his customers and a tonic to talk with.

Oughterard Town Centre.

TUAM

JOACHIM HESS

Newtown House
Abbeyknock Moy
Tuam, Co Galway
Contact: Joachim Hess

Organic vegetables, free-range eggs, organic beef, bread

Joachim Hess' stall in the Galway Saturday market is the first you come across if you enter the market via Shop Street. He sells eggs, excellent white bread, and organically-grown vegetables. On his farm he also raises organic beef, but you can only buy the whole animal. Holder of IOFGA symbol.

You can buy Joachim's produce at the Galway Saturday market.

CLIFDEN

DORIS' KITCHEN, Market Street, Clifden, Co Galway. Tel: (095) 21427, Contact: Doris and Helmut.

CONNEMARA

FIOR UISCE, Connemara Spring Water, Ballinafad, Co Galway. Water from the Twelve Pins mountains in Connemara. Bottled in Glenhoughan and sold in local shops.

GALWAY

BORD FAILTE, Aras Failte, Eyre Square. Tel: (091) 63081; Telex: 50170

FLEMINGS FISH SHOP, 29 Lower Dominick Street. A tiny fish shop with a large reputation. Tel: (091) 66673, Contact: Gay Fleming

CAFE NORA CRUB, Galway City. Tel: (091) 68376. Consistently recommended.

FULL MOON BAKESHOP, Lower Dominick Street, Galway. Tel: (091) 63853. Wholefood bakery baking such goodies as Berliners, Danish Corn Bread, Carob Cakes, Organic Rye Sourdough and Wholewheat. Consistently recommended.

MARY LAVELLE, Cloonamore, Inishbofin, Co Galway. Organic vegtetables sold on Saturday mornings outside the Church.

LEONIDAS CHOCOLATES, Corbett's Court, Williams Gate Street, Galway. Tel: (091) 67489. Contact: Breda.

McCAMBRIDGE'S DELICATESSEN, Shop Street, Galway. Tel: (091) 62259. Contact: Pat

McCambridge. Old world charm is still represented in McCambridges. There is a good dairy counter which gives prominence to Irish farmhouse cheeses.

McDONAGH'S FISH SHOP AND SEAFOOD BAR, 22 Quay Street, Galway. Tel: (091) 65001. McDonagh's is a large fish shop selling West Coast fish, country butter on occasion, and the Western speciality: salted mackerel. Beside it is a seafood bar where excellent fish is put alongside traditional Irish boiled vegetables.

MOVEABLE FEASTS, 5 Henry Street, Galway. Tel: (091) 67069, Contact: Deirdre Delap. Deirdre Delap will cater for any event, for numbers from one upwards. Her cooking is inspired by Elizabeth David and Jane Grigson. Suggested menus are available.

MOYCULLEN SEAWEED, Kylbroghlan, Moycullen, Co Galway. Tel: (091) 85112, Contact: Mr P Casburn. Mr Casburn supplies dilisk and carrigeen moss for shampoo and powder, as well as for edible use.

W. MULLINS BUTCHER, 27 Shop Street, Galway. Tel: (091) 64407, Contact: W Mullins. Mr Mullins is highly regarded by knowledgeable locals, and complies enthusiastically to all culinary requests.

O'GRADY'S SEAFOOD RESTAURANT, Clifden, Co Galway. Tel: (095) 21450, Contact: the O'Grady family. Open lunch 12.30am-3.30pm, dinner 6.30-10pm.

PASTA MISTA, 2 Cross Street, Galway. Good Italian cafe with fresh and dried pasta and beefy ragu sauces.

SEV'NTH HEAVEN, 25 Quay Street, Galway. Sev'nth Heaven is known for excellent pastries, both savoury and sweet. The restaurant is open all day until

13

9.30pm.

SILKE'S VEGETABLE SHOP, Munster Avenue, Galway. Tel: (091) 63363. Mr Silke's boast is that he will get you any vegetable you care for (as long as you have the necessary cash).

TAAFFES BAR, Shop Street, Galway. Taaffes is a normal pub both by day and by night, but is transformed from the mundane to the exotic each lunchtime where you can buy Indonesian-influenced food. Consistently recommended.

THE QUAY'S PUB, Shop Street, Galway. Pub serving good pub food.

COUNTY LEITRIM

On a damp day, driving through the hills of Leitrim, it becomes a county swollen with rain. The mountains sweep down to the sea and the landscape becomes grey upon grey upon grey. All the more delightful then to find such fine producers making the most of the hostile land.

MANORHAMILTON

CO-OP SHOP

Main Street
Manorhamilton
Co Leitrim
Contact: Dolores
Keegan, Rod Alston,
Eileen McCaughey,
Peter and Uli Steffan

Greengrocers with emphasis on organic veg, chutneys and pickles, jams, free-range eggs, quark

The Co-op Shop is fed by the members of the North Leitrim Vegetable Growers Co-op and offers a splendid variety of organic produce that changes with the seasons. There are free-range eggs, wonderful chutneys and jams and herbs from Eden Plants. You can also buy their excellent recipe booklet in the shop.

Manorhamilton Town Centre. Open 9.30-6pm.

NASOOL CREAMERY

Manorhamilton
Co Leitrim
Tel: (072) 55442
Contact: Bruno Reich

➥ *Farmhouse goats' cheese*

Bruno Reich produces a most surprising cheese from his holding near Manorhamilton. It looks like a Brie, has all the qualities of the better French cheeses, and yet is an Irish goats' cheese made with milk from the North of Ireland. Ninety percent of his cheese is exported, but if you get a chance to buy some, make sure you do. It's labelled 'Irish Goat'. 'I never saw a cheese like mine' says Bruno. Neither have we.

Available in Tir na nOg in Sligo, and supermarkets all over the country. Telephone for more details.

15

ROSSINVER

EDEN PLANTS

Rossinver
Co Leitrim
Tel: (072) 54122
Contact: Rod Alston or
Dolores Keegan

★ *Organic vegetables*
★ *Organic herbs*

On highly unpromising land, Rod Alston and Dolores Keegan have confounded local cynicism and produced a startling array of fresh herbs and fulsome organic vegetables. They are holders of the soil association symbol, and hold occasional open days to offer advice to herb growers. Their produce is simply astonishing. In look, taste, aroma and keeping qualities they outstrip anywhere else in the country.

Herbs can be bought by mail order or from the house 2-6pm each day. They distribute vegetables to the Co-Op Shop in Manorhamilton and Tir na nOg in Sligo. Rossinver is seven miles north of Manorhamilton. Go past the post office and shop, turn right immediately after the convent, where there is a sign to the herb farm. Eden Plants is the first turning on the left.

ARDVARNEY

EIBHLIN NIC EOCHAIDH, Ardvarney, Glenfarne, Co Leitrim. Member of Irish Organic Farmers' and Growers' Association, selling organic vegetables.

CARRICK-ON-SHANNON

MAUREEN McNALLY, Kilclare PO, Carrick-On-Shannon, Co Leitrim. Member of Irish Organic Farmers' and Growers' Association, selling organic vegetables and fruit.

KILTYCLOGHER

PETER'S HERB FARM, Meenagh, Kiltyclogher, Co Leitrim. Contact: Peter Nooley. Free-range eggs.

16

COUNTY MAYO

The landscape of Mayo is wide open bogland, but the food culture is private, and sporadic. Many houses, you will be told, have their own butter churn and their own granny to churn it, but as with many other things such as cheese and honey, it is not for sale. Occasionally you will stumble across a shop, like Ruddy Brothers, in the main street of Bangor, who keep a bowl of what they call 'country eggs': eggs of all sizes and shapes, from tiny white pebbles, to hulking great double-yolked hens' eggs, to sky-blue duck eggs.

Like Sligo and other western counties, it is a good idea to call into shops attached to pubs and post offices. Take a look at the locally-baked brown bread, it may be good; or try the bacon they might have at the bottom of the fridge and if you can, buy it from a brine-filled basin.

ACHILL ISLAND

Achill is less intensely picturesque than other parts of the West, but it has a definite rolling beauty of its own. It takes a while for the visitor to get a sense of the distinct Achill culture, the bridge that joins Achill sound to the mainland is short in every sense. Specialities of the area are mountain lamb and fresh fish.

ANNE FUCHS
Dugort
Achill Island
Tel: (098) 43233
Contact: Anne Fuchs

Goats' milk, goats' cottage cheese, kid meat

Anne Fuchs keeps up to fifteen lively goats on her mountain holding and for reasons that must stem from her grazing pastures, the milk from them is absolutely gorgeous. She also sells a very good cottage cheese, and kid meat according to season.

The house is near the hillside graveyard behind Keel, where you can ask for more detailed directions. Anne sells milk from the farm, and to Burke's in Castlebar and the Continental Cafe in Westport.

17

GERRY HASSET

Keem Bay Fish
Products
Pollagh
Keel
Achill
Tel: (098) 43265
Contact: Gerry Hasset

Smoked and fresh fish

Gerry Hasset's wild smoked salmon demonstrates beautifully his technique of catching and smoking fish using the least amount of refrigeration possible. He also smokes mackerel, trout and kippers and will smoke fish to order.

The house is on the hill past the church in Keel. Ask directions in the Chalet restaurant. You can buy from the house.

BALLINA

J. CLARKE & SONS

O'Rahilly Street
Ballina
Co Mayo
Tel: (096) 21022
Contact: M.J. Clarke

Fishmonger

Clarke's sell fish from as far away as Donegal and from just up the road in Killala. The Moy river, which flows through the town, provides them with fresh salmon in season which they smoke themselves. The salmon is deep blood red, and if you buy it fresh, try cooking it in Brendan Doherty's Country Butter which you can buy across the road.

Ballina town centre.

BRENDAN DOHERTY

O'Rahilly Street
Ballina
Co Mayo
Tel: (096) 21723
Contact: Brendan
Doherty

Grocer

The real discovery in this shop is lovely home-made butter which is sold in patterned slabs wrapped in grease-proof paper at the back of the shop. They also make their own brown and treacle breads, sell local preserves and a range of what they describe as 'health foods': nuts, seeds, pulses and multi-coloured caramalised fruit. God bless us, you can also buy altar wine and altar candles. The best time to visit Ballina is Friday, says the wise lady in the blue shop coat. 'It's pension day and it's pay day'.

Ballina Town Centre.

EAGLE ISLE SEAFOOD
Doohoma
Ballina
Co Mayo
Tel: (097) 86829
Contact: Eamonn Holmes

Fish smoker

Eamonn Holmes smokes only wild salmon and mackerel. He sells in Shannon Airport, and exports to France, Germany and Switzerland, and some hotels in Ireland buy his fish. The public can buy from the shop in between his smoking factory and his pub. He sells fish all year round by blast freezing the fish when it is in season. The shop also sells fresh salmon and grilse (small salmon).

From Bangor take the signs to Geesala and Doohoma. Continue until you see the sea (about ten-twelve miles); as you enter Doohoma there is a church on the right hand side. Eagle Isle seafood is the next building.

ETHEL'S HOMEMADE PRESERVES
Ballyholan House
Downhill Road
Ballina
Co Mayo
Tel: (096) 21853
Contact: Ethel Walker

Preserves

Ethel Walker makes dizzying concoctions of jams, chutneys and marmalades: rhubarb and fig jam, pineapple, marrow and whiskey chutney, three-fruit marmalade, and so on. 'All my ingredients are fresh and wholesome' she says, and the preserves are rightfully without preservatives.

Ring for details. You can buy the preserves from Brendan Doherty's in Ballina as well as in the Dunne's Stores arcade. You even see the jams in certain shops in Dublin, Castlebar, Westport and Clifden.

KILLALA

THE PIER FISHERMANS' CO-OP
Killala
Co Mayo
Tel: (096) 32099
Contact: Neil or Kevin

Fresh fish, crabs and crayfish

Unfilletted, ungutted fresh fish can be bought from the Co-Op shop at the end of Killala pier. You can buy them as soon as the boats have landed their catch. Availability depends on the weather, but it's usually around 5pm. There are boxes on the side of some of the boats for enormous live crabs and crayfish, which the fishermen are more than happy to pluck out and sell you. Expect to pay about £15-£20 for each crayfish.

The Pier in Killala, just north of Ballina.

WESTPORT

JOHN BOURKE & SONS
Western Freezer
Market
Bridge Street
Westport
Co Mayo
Contact: Vincent and
Ann Bourke

Delicatessen

Vincent and Ann Bourke's shop is misleadingly named the Western Freezer Market. Nothing in the shop is frozen and we believe the name will soon be changed. Look out for the painting of a salmon on Bridge Street. Vincent Bourke is a smoker of not only salmon but also hams and chickens. The salmon, which 'nine times out of ten' is wild salmon, is smoked for up to forty-eight hours. Ann also makes a wonderful liver pate.

Westport town centre.

CARROWHOLLY CHEESE
Kilmeenacoff
Westport
Co Mayo
Contact: Irma Van
Baalen

Farmhouse Cheese

Irma Van Baalen makes three types of cheese from cows' milk: a plain gouda, nettle and a pungent garlic. From goats' milk she makes a gouda cheese that is deliciously creamy. Fresh cheeses are also available and she is working on producing quark. Visitors are most welcome to view the farm.

Travel about three miles on the Leenane Road south from Westport: you will see a two storey house on the left. Take the lane opposite, keep to the left. After you cross the bridge it is the first house on the right. Look for a red Renault van. You can also buy the cheese at the Westport Thursday Market. It is open from 10am-6pm at the Octagon and is worth a visit. The Continental Cafe and Healthfood Shop also sells Irma's full range of cheeses.

RECIPE:
SMOKED CHICKEN AND POTATO SALAD

1 breast or 1 leg (meat carefully removed) smoked chicken; 1 lb potatoes, peeled and steamed until just cooked; small tin of sweetcorn; handful of cashew nuts (or you can substitute pumpkin seeds or other nuts); an overflowing tablespoon mayonnaise (or to taste); fresh coriander leaves. Chop the chicken into strips, and the potatoes into one inch cubes. Toss the potatoes in salt and pepper while still warm. Add the other ingredients carefully, and stir in the mayonnaise. Allow to go cold, and serve garnished with coriander leaves.

THE CONTINENTAL CAFE AND HEALTHFOOD SHOP
High Street
Westport
Co Mayo
Tel: (098) 26679
Contact: Uli & Chris
Steller Vorberg
*Restaurant and
wholefood shop*

A perfect lunch can be bought in the Continental Cafe: a bowl of excellent vegetable soup, a slice of homemade German sourdough bread, and a glass of hand- squeezed orange juice. Follow it with some Quark, or a cheesecake and a cup of Tanzanian coffee. You can also buy Halva, Irma Van Baalen's cheese, and general wholefoods. 'We see ourselves as a focus point, a place where people can meet and talk' they say. The shop can also supply free-range chickens. 'We've seen the farm, and those chickens have a whole mountain to themselves. They're only guarded by geese'.

Westport town centre.

CUILMORE BLUE
Westport
Co Mayo
Contact: Bob McArdle

*Farmhouse goats'
cheese*

You can find Bob McArdle's unusual blue goats' cheese for sale in a number of places in Westport. It's an intriguing cheese with strong, colliding flavours.

Ask directions to the farm from the Taylors at the Pottery shop on the Lenanne Road just south of Westport. You can buy the cheese at the Westport Thursday Market, at the Bourke's shop on Bridge Street, and selected other shops as far away as Dublin.

JOHN HENNESSEY
Revenue Road
Westport
Co Mayo
Tel: (098) 26661
Contact: John
Hennessey

Shellfish

John Hennessey farms shellfish in Clew Bay. One of his fish is the rarely sighted abalone, a white muscular shellfish that has to be tenderized before it is eaten. He also farms mussels.

Westport town centre.

21

MULLOY SHELLFISH LTD
Kilmeena
Westport
Co Mayo
Tel: (098) 41328
Contact: Padraic
Mulloy

Shellfish exporter

Mulloys produce lobsters, oysters, sea urchins, mussels, winkles, crayfish, salmon and clams. All are exported to Europe. They also co-ordinate sales for other western seaboard producers.

Telephone for details.

RARE FOODS
Karymara
Rosbeg
Westport
Tel: (098) 26224
Contact: Patrick
Percival

Food broker

Patrick Percival delivers specialist foodstuffs to restaurants in the Sligo, Mayo and Galway region, with occasional trips further east. He deals in veal, game (for which he holds a dealers licence), Irish farmhouse cheeses and assorted sundries.

Telephone for details.

CHRIS SMITH
Clogher
Westport
Co Mayo
Tel: (098) 26409
Contact: Chris Smith

*Organic vegetables
and herbs*

Chris Smith grows a complete range of herbs all year around, which he sells to hotels throughout Connemara, and which can be bought from the farm. You can buy his vegetables — courgettes, cucumber, tomatoes, spinach, everything except root vegetables. Chris is the only IOFGA symbol-holder in Mayo.

You can buy Chris Smith's veg. at the Thursday Westport Market outside the town hall, where he sells from 10.30am-1.30pm. He sells potted herbs to garden centres, and if you want to visit the farm ask directions at Westport Garden Centre, or ask anyone in Clogher.

QUAY COTTAGE
The Harbour
Westport, Co Mayo
Tel: (098) 26412
Contact: Kirsten
McDonough
Restaurant

Delightful quayside restaurant specialising in seafood, including John Hennessey's abalones. A good place to go for lunch.

Westport harbour. In summer open seven days, 12noon-11pm. Closed 24 December-1 February.

ACHILL

THE BOLEY HOUSE, Keel, Achill Island, Tel: (098) 43147, Contact: Tom McNamara. Open evenings. Straightforward cuisine, and we recommend you opt for fish, the restaurant's great strength.

THE CHALET, Keel, Achill. Tel: (098) 43157. Very good, simple restaurant specialising in fish and chips.

FISHERMANS' CO-OP, Opp Alice's Harbour Inn, Achill Sound. Tel: (098) 45123. Fresh fish is sold here six days a week, if the boats go out. The fish is landed at Cloghmore Pier.

O'GORMAN'S FISH SHOP, Keel, Achill Island. The O'Gorman's sell fresh fish from the shop attached to their house.

O'MALLEY'S POST OFFICE, Keel, Achill Island, Tel: (098) 43101/43125. Contact: Michael O'Malley. The shop is attached to the Post Office and stocks an interesting selection of wines.

BALLINA

T. McGRATH, O'Rahilly Street, Ballina. A good delicatessen stuffed from floor to ceiling with every imaginable product, sadly often imported. Free-range eggs, country butter, and
an excellent cheese counter as well as Moy river salmon in season.

SWISS BARN SPECIALITY RESTAURANT, Foxford Road, Ballina, Co Mayo. Tel: (096) 21117. Contact: Daniel Veillard. Tiny restaurant off the Foxford Road run by Swiss, Daniel Veillard. One of the few, if not the only, restaurant in Ireland where you can order a genuine Swiss Fondue.

BELMULLET

BEESEAS IORRA'S TEO, Bellmullet, Co Mayo. Tel: (097) 81101. Good boxty bread, available vacuum packed in shops throughout Mayo.

BOFEENAUN

RON YOUELL HONEY, Bofeenaun, Co Mayo. Contact: Ron Youell. Good honey, available in shops in Mayo and Sligo.

CASTLEBAR

HELENA CHOCOLATES, Main Street, Castlebar. Tel: (094) 22755/31270. Contact: Dirk Schonkeren.

WESTPORT

BORD FAILTE, The Mall, Westport, Co Mayo. Tel: (098) 25711; Telex: 53846.

COUNTY
ROSCOMMON

In the centre of Roscommon there is a hardware shop
that, back in 1962, was what many town centre
shops in the country would have been: P. Dolan & Co
Ltd, Main Street Roscommon. Phone Roscommon 15.
Paints, Oils & Colours, Wallpapers, Window Glass,
Electrical Ranges, Cookers, Fireplaces, Best Quality
Coal, Cement and Fireclay Goods, Artificial
Manures, Hardware, Timber, Ironmongery, Sanitary
Ware and Bathroom Equipment, Cut Glass, China,
Complete House Furnishers, Funeral Undertakers,
Grocery Provisions, Wines and Spirits.

Nowadays the telephone number of the shop is
(0903) 26135. The funeral service is defunct, as is
the grocery. All that remains from 1962 is the
Hardware and the Wines and Spirits. For in this
otherwise normal and sober shop, there is a small bar
with a slanty sink, selling various whiskeys, Piat D'Or
wine and bottles of beer and stout.

Just up the road in Market Square Seamus Hunt, of
Curry, Ballymurray, sells organic symbol fruit and
vegetables on Fridays and Saturdays. Along with his
own produce he sells that of Gerald Brown of 8, St
Patrick's Terrace, Roscommon. Gerald also produces
organic beef and will sell any surplus. Tel: (0903)
26596. Further details of the market stall from
Seamus Hunt at (0903) 7905.

The only other symbol holders in the county are Helga
and Henry Schedwill, Rainbowhill, Evikeen's, Boyle,
Co Roscommon, Tel: (079) 62114, who grow fruit
and vegetables.

COUNTY SLIGO

'Sligo is surprising': slogans quickly become meaningless because of over-use, but Sligo is, definitely, surprising. Beneath its self-denying exterior there is a wealth of local produce that exploits the resources of land and sea. And Sligo has resources in abundance. Inland lakes, proximity to the Shannon, the dark Ox Mountains, and the glorious views along the coastline stretching from Inniscrone to Donegal.

But it is the mountains Knocknarea and Ben Bulben that steal the show. With every change in the weather, and every change of angle that you view them the mountains cast different shadows. Myths, legends and tales of old come to mind if you look towards the cairn grave of Queen Medb, and the table top of Ben Bulben brings to mind the poetry of Yeats. Sligo is a mystical land.

BALLINAFAD

ROGER ELDRIDGE

Aughnafinigan
Knockvicar
Ballinafad
Co Sligo
Tel: (079) 67138
Contact: Roger
Eldridge

Organic beef

Roger Eldridge offers a freezer serrvice selling fore and hind quarters of organic beef. If you club together as a group, or have a very large freezer to accommodate the large quantity which he sells, this is a good chance to buy high quality competitively-priced beef.

Telephone first and ask directions.

BALLYMOTE

TEMPLE HOUSE

Ballymote
Co Sligo
Tel: (071) 83329

Temple House can accommodate up to nine guests at any time in wonderfully eccentric oppulence. Deb Percival cooks for guests only, using the organic produce from the farm. The land on the farm features

Contact: Sandy and
Deb Percival
Organic farmer, B&B

a secretive walled garden where even baby artichokes are grown. Any surplus produce is sold to callers, who can buy organic garlic, pick their own raspberries (by appoint.) or buy potatoes and Jerusalem artichokes. Huntin', shootin', fishin'! parties are specially catered for during the season.

Temple House is clearly marked on the map. Ring and ask for detailed directions to the house. See also the Hidden Ireland book, available from Bord Failte, which will give up to date details of prices etc.

CASTLEBALDWIN

COMMON GROUND
Annaghcor Common
Castlebaldwin
Co Sligo
Tel: (071) 65301
Contact: Jane
Thompson

*Environmental
magazine and
free–range eggs*

Jane Thompson is editor of the environmental magazine *Common Ground*. It has a readership of approximately 2,500, and incorporates the newsletter of the Irish Organic Farmers' and Growers' Association (IOFGA). Jane also sells free-range eggs. She has moveable hen houses and stocks only 120 birds in an effort to produce the best possible eggs.

The road to the house begins at the Castlebaldwin Post Office. Drive to the Post Office (in the centre of Castlebaldwin) and ask there.

CLIFFONEY

HANS AND GABY WALTER-WIELAND
Ballincastle
Cliffoney
Co Sligo
Tel: (071) 66399
Contact: Hans and
Gaby Walter Wieland

*Farmhouse cows'
cheese, farmhouse*

Hans and Gaby Walter-Wieland began to make cheese because they had cows' milk left over. They now make and sell both a cows' cheese and a paler goats' cheese, quark, and some varieties of soft, fresh cheeses, all of which they sell in Sligo. They also bake a delicious cheesecake, a great provoker of gluttony amongst all those who encounter it.

Take the road turning right just before the village of Cliffoney coming from the Sligo direction. Go past three houses and theirs is the next cottage on the left. You can buy the cheese from the house. Otherwise each cheese is

goats' cheese
➡ *German baked*
cheesecake

for sale in Tir na nOg, Grattan St, Sligo (fresh cheese every Thurs), and the cheesecake at the Cottage Restaurant, also on Grattan St, Sligo.

RECIPE: DILISK BREAD

Into a conventional brown soda bread mixture of 12oz wheatmeal, 2 oz white flour, 1oz oatmeal, 1 tsp salt, 1tsp bicarbonate of soda (There is an excellent basic soda bread recipe in Myrtle Allen's cookbook 'The Ballymaloe Cookbook' Gill & McMacmillan Ltd 1984, from which this recipe is adapted) add a small handfull of washed, finely chopped dilisk and mix into the flour with buttermilk (half to three-quarters of a pint) until it is accommodated in a moist ball of dough. Place on a greased baking tray, and bake in a hot oven (Gas 7, 425° F, 200° C) for about 35-40 mins, until the bread comes out clean and sounds hollow when you tap it. Very attractive looking loaf, and a good accompaniment to cheese.

COOLANEY

CABRAGH LODGE
Coolaney
Co Sligo
Tel: (071) 67706

Fiona and Ian MacMahon opened their doors to visitors in 1986. Their house, an old shooting Lodge, is, they believe, the highest house in County Sligo. The view is staggering. The food in Cabragh Lodge is strictly vegetarian. Don't go there expecting an 'Irish

Contact: Fiona & Ian
MacMahon

Vegetarian guesthouse

breakfast'. They offer dinner to their guests and can accommodate approximately six people. It's preferable to book in the summer, essential in winter.

Last road on the right before you turn left over the bridge into Coloorey (approaching from the Sligo/Dublin road). Travel straight up this road for about three miles. It's the highest house in sight on the right hand side.

INNISCRONE

ANTHONY KILCULLEN
Sea View House Farm
Corballa
Inniscrone
Co Sligo
Tel: (096) 36255
Contact: Anthony and
Bridie Kilcullen

★ *Organic farm shop*

The Kilcullens have an organic farm shop in the yard of their elegant farmhouse, and from it sell the superlative produce of their farm: beef, pork and lamb, mustardy-yolked free range eggs and a selection of vegetables that change with the seasons. Eating their meat is a revelation: it is full of taste and texture and in a different world entirely from that of conventionally-reared animals. Prices are also very reasonable, and the Kilcullens are the only people we know of to sell organic meat in a prepared state. Anthony Kilcullen also delivers in the locality and his excellent flour, milled at the farm, is made into bread by Garveys of Ballina.

Sea View House Farm is about one mile down the R298 which runs off the main Sligo/Ballina road, and is clearly signposted. The shop is open Fri, 6-10pm; Sat, 2-6pm, or by telephone appointment.

RATHLEE

MELVIN'S SEAWEED
Cabra
Rathlee
Co Sligo
Tel: (096) 49042

Carrigeen moss and dilisk

Frank and Betty Melvin collect and package Carrigeen and Dilisk from the stones near their home. Irish cookbooks often give recipes for these sea vegetables, which are known for their medicinal qualities.

Telephone for details. The seaweed is available from Tir na nOg, and Moody's, both on Grattan St, Sligo, as well as many more healthfood shops throughout the country.

29

SLIGO

HARGADON'S PUB

O'Connell Street
Sligo
Tel: (071) 42974
Contact: Pat Lee Doyle

Pub

You can do no better than stroll into Hargadon's legendary pub where the shelves sag stylishly even before you drink a pint. Darkened snugs, a pot-bellied stove, and old Guinness artefacts give Hargadon's an atmosphere that was once widespread, but is now, sadly, unique.

Sligo town centre.

KILFEATHER'S

34 Market Street
Sligo
Tel: (071) 43564
Contact:Gary Kilfeather

Fish and fruit

Gary Kilfeather not only sells excellent wild salmon in season, his is also one of the few places where you can find a decent choice of fruit, in particular apples. In season he will often have up to half a dozen varieties.

Sligo town centre.

REVERIES

Rosses Point
Sligo
Tel: (071) 77371
Contact: Damien Brennan or Paula Gilvarry

Restaurant

Reveries is an elegant and astute restaurant that manages to mix creative cuisine and comfort food, modernity and formality, innovation and tradition into its own pleasing concoction. A well- informed wine list, a prize- winning cheeseboard and hospitable welcome complete the place. Add a few of Damien Brennan's hilarious stories and you have a perfect night out.

Overlooking the sea at Rosses' Point, just north of Sligo town centre.

TIR NA nOG

Grattan Street
Sligo
Tel: (071) 62752
Contact: Mary and John McDonnell

★ *Wholefood shop*

Some wholefood shops are 'live'; others, those musty collectors of dehydrated, non-perishable, capsuled 'health' food, are what Mary McDonnell would call 'dead'. Tir na nOg fits into the living, breathing category. It's a vital and powerful magnet for all the best produce in the Sligo area and beyond. Go in during the summer and you'll find fresh vegetables, fresh herbs, fresh cheeses. In winter there's freshly-made peanut butter. Soon they will be investing in a

30

grain mill so you can mill your own flour on the premises. You will also find shampoos, soaps and healthy beauty products, wholefoods and homeopathic medicines. Tir na nOg is everything a shop can, and should, be. The McDonnels have a commitment to their shop, their suppliers and their customers.

Sligo Town Centre.

TRUFFLES RESTAURANT
The Mall
Sligo
Tel: (071) 44226
Contact: Bernadette O'Shea

Restaurant

Bernadette O'Shea has recently opened an excellent restaurant selling wholefood during the day, pizzas in the evening. Everything is supervised efficiently by Bernadette O'Shea who knows her pizzas beat everything for miles. But don't overlook the food during the day, which is genuine and good value.

Sligo town centre.

STRANDHILL

NOEL CARTER
Primrose Hill
Strandhill
Co Sligo
Tel: (071) 61644
Contact: Noel Carter

Clams

Noel Carter's clam production is in its nascent stage, but when available it will be possible to buy them from his door. Aside from the clams, the view from the house, after you negotiate the road, open and shut the gates, and drive across Sligo airport, is beautiful. Pick a clear day to go, but telephone first.

Ask directions on the telephone.

PADRAIG McLOUGHLIN
Coolenamore
Strandhill
Sligo
Contact: Padraig
McLoughlin

Mussels

Padraig McLoughlin gathers mussels which you can buy from him at the house.

The house is the last inhabited bungalow before Bree's pub on the Strandhill road.

N WOODESON
Coolenamore
Strandhill
Co Sligo
Tel: (071) 68127
Contact: N. Woodeson

Oysters

Other inhabitants of Sligo tell you 'you must try Noelle's oysters, she looks after them like children'. Indeed they are very good, and you can buy them from the house.

First right after the swimming-pool sign on the road travelling from Strandhill to Ballisodare. Telephone first.

CRIMLIN CHEESE
Chaffpool
Tubercurry
Co Sligo
Tel: (071) 85615
Contact: Claudia and
Volkmar Klohn

Farmhouse cows' cheese

Claudia and Volkmar Klohn buy the unpasteurised milk of fresian cows to make Crimlin cheese. It is a tilseter type cheese which is not pressed, but is treated with a culture each day, and allowed to mature for two months. It won first prize at the 1989 Dublin Spring Show, and you can buy it direct from the farm. The cheese is also exported to England and Germany.

Telephone for directions if you want to buy from the farm. Otherwise it is for sale in Sligo at Tir na nOg, Cosgrave's and Kate's Kitchen.

LISSADELL

LISSADELL SHELLFISH
Lissadell
Co Sligo
Tel: (071) 63563
Contact: Kevin O'Kelly

Spawning shellfish

Kevin O'Kelly operates a shellfish hatchery where the spawn produced by clams is carefully treated and nurtured until it reaches a size of about one millimetre, at which time it is taken to the sea. He also spawns other shellfish.

Follow signs to Lissadell House. When you come to the estuary take the second turn on the left and follow to the sea.

SLIGO AQUACULTURE LTD
Lissadell
Co Sligo
Tel: (071) 42990
Contact: Charlie Kelly

Clams

Charlie Kelly produced and exported about seventeen tons of clams in 1988 and the same in 1989. Sligo Aquaculture has been in operation for four years, growing the Japanese species of clam to maturity, a process which takes three years.

Follow signs to Lissadell House. When you come to the estuary take the second turn on the left and follow to the sea.

SLIGO

JOELLE D'ANJOU, White House Youth Hostel, Sligo. Joelle occasionally cooks his famed vegetarian smorgasbord during the winter at the White House Youth Hostel (see Aran Islands for details). Book through the hostel or through Tir na nOg.

BORD FAILTE, Arras Reddan, Temple Street, Sligo, Co Sligo. Tel: (071) 61201; Telex: 40301.

COSGRAVES, Market Street, Sligo. This is a lovely old delicatessen selling cheese, boxty bread, and china amongst many other things.

COTTAGE RESTAURANT, Grattan St, Sligo. Coffee shop and cafe. Look out for the Walter-Wieland's German baked cheesecake.

KATE'S KITCHEN, Market St, Sligo. Delicatessen and cafe serving home-made soups, salads, snacks and sandwiches at lunchtime.

ELIZABETH & DICK WOOD-MARTIN, Woodville, Sligo. Tel: (071) 62741. Delicate free-range eggs, for sale in Tir na nOg, Grattan St, Sligo

Leinster

COUNTY CARLOW

County Carlow is a place outsiders often know little about. The capital town has a grand courthouse, but the locals will happily tell you that, in fact, it should not be there at all — it was meant for somewhere else. Otherwise, the town is quiet. A shop like the Cigar Divan on Dublin Street seems especially attractive because there are now so many plain, boring facades and dull, barn-like shops. Across from the Cigar Divan is Brennan's Butchers, long well-known for their sausages and bacon. They have a second branch on upper Tullow Street.

Elsewhere on Dublin Street do look into the shop attached to The Beams restaurant. Here Peter O'Gorman has an excellent stock of wines — expensive, but tasteful. There is also a good cheese counter, which unfortunately is not graced by a cheese made in Carlow — there are none. The Beams Restaurant is open for dinner from Tuesday to Saturday, Tel: (0503) 31824.

Around the corner on Tullow Street, there is a good off-licence at number 148 — Tully's wine shop.

A few miles away in the village of Borris, is The Step House Tel: (0503) 73401/73209, Contact: Breda Coady, a member of the Irish Country Houses and Restaurants Association. It's a pleasant place, with dowagers who talk too loudly, breezy tourists and silent couples.

At the Clashganna Mills Trust, in Ballykeenan in Borris (Tel: (0503) 73441), Philip Tirard holds the IOFGA symbol and grows fruit and vegetables which you can buy across the border in Roots and Fruits of Kilkenny: firm peppers, healthy lettuce and scallions. The other symbol holder in the county is Laurence Kinsella in Curran, Borris, Co Carlow. There are plenty of stalls set up at farm gates throughout the county; often these are worth trying, but do ask about how the produce has been grown. If you come across someone who is selling their surplus, then that is the time to buy. Even if you have to stop a few times to find this, the crack will be worth it.

DUBLIN

Dublin was once the second city of the English empire. Since independence its importance has faded along with its grandeur, but thankfully it still retains a unique spirit and its population has a boisterousness rarely found amongst Northern Europeans.

As soon as the sun shines Dubs reveal themselves to be Mediterranean in spirit, shedding their clothes, disporting themselves as if they were born to a more luxurious climate. Even the rain rarely dampens the exuberance of the young population, an exuberance that manifests itself each evening in the pubs for which the city is still famous.

Dublin is a city in terms of population, but a town in terms of atmosphere. You can cope with it on a bicycle, and it remains an easy city to live in.

No one in Dublin is anonymous, whether you're a busker, have been seen on the Late Late Show, or are just known in your local shop. It is a friendly place.

The visitor, reared on James Joyce's masterpiece 'Ulysses', would find it difficult nowadays to navigate using that book, but the irreverence Joyce captures in his dialogue can be heard every day of the week. Much of the architecture of the city may have changed, most of it for the worst, but the nervous self-confidence of the Dub is eternal.

DUBLIN RESTAURANTS

Eating out in Dublin is not a pastime practised by its citizens as a matter of course. Each evening cars spill away into the suburbs, and city centre restaurants are more often than not visited by those who have more than their fair share of loose change.

In the suburbs a few restaurants are busy, because they're perceived to be cheap. But even though they may cost slightly less than their inner city alternatives, they rarely represent better value for money.

This bestows an atmosphere of indulgence on many Dublin restaurants. They're there to fill the faces of the better off, and they're used to prove status — food is the very least of their customers' concerns.

It's really quite difficult in Dublin to enjoy a good casual meal. Only ethnic restaurants offer a cheap, relaxed evening; the pseudo-French/Irish restaurants are often stilted and over-serious.

As with many towns and cities, it's in the vegetarian restaurants that the best value in food is to be found. In Dublin, Cornucopia is the place to go for a filling, wholesome meal that avoids predictable vegetarian slush. The potato salad, the pies, and the rich soups are quite addictive. Another excellent vegetarian restaurant is Blazing Salads in the Powerscourt Townhouse Centre.

Lebanese, Japanese, Chinese, Russian and Indian food are all on offer at reasonable prices for good cooking. Of these the Imperial Chinese Restaurant, the China Sichuan Restaurant, the Ayumi-Ya Japanese restaurant and the Rajdoot Tandoori are essential viewing.

One of the best restaurants in the country, let alone Dublin, offers gourmet Greek Cypriot cooking. This is the Tree of Idleness in Bray, an exotic bacchanalian experience that lives up to the lyricism of its name.

Dublin is certainly well endowed with French restaurants. Restaurant Patrick Guilbaud has been bestowed with more honours than others, but Freres Jacques, Le Relais des Mouettes and Restaurant Pigalle all have their moments.
The standard of cooking of Dublin's more exclusive restaurants: The Park, Blackrock, and Whites on the Green, is usually high, though it's also high in price, which makes one entitled to be a little more critical.

Another of Dublin's exclusive restaurants is, unusually, owned by the Railways. Restaurant na Mara is a lovely fish restaurant, expensive, but consistently good.

Fashion plays its part too, and one of the trendier restaurants that manages to mix very good cooking with designer dynamism is Shay Beano. If you want a meal late at night, then the character and atmosphere of The Trocadero, overwhelms the unimaginative cooking.

High Street Italian is to be found in Nico's and Del Monaco, but the best of the genuine article is to be found in the Kapriol if you don't mind paying high prices for what is, essentially, a simple peasant cuisine.

The best chips in town come from Leo Burdock's, and Dublin is well placed for pizzas at the Independent Pizza Company. If you want a pizza delivered to your home then ring Pizza Time on Richmond Street.

The Powerscourt Townhouse Centre is a shopping and restaurant centre that looks the way of Covent Garden in London. All the restaurants here have something to offer, from good sandwiches, to good fish to salads. Sandycove is the suburb to visit if you want a reasonable collection of alternatives, many positioned on the seafront.

Good 'Irish' cooking — though definitely as much Gallic as Gaelic, can be found in the Soup Bowl in Molesworth Street and Clarets. There are only two indigenous Irish restaurants, the clever Gallagher's Boxty House, and Oisins. That there are only two is a matter for regret.

DUBLIN RESTAURANTS

- Abbey Tavern, Howth, Co Dublin. Tel: 390307
- Buttery Brasserie, Royal Hibernian Way, Dawson Street, Dublin 2. Tel: 778611
- The Colony, Johnson's Court, off Grafton Street, Dublin 2. Tel: 712276
- The Carriage, William Elliot Centre, Dublin 2. Tel: 794056
- Coq Hardi, 35 Pembroke Road Dublin 4. Tel: 684130
- Digby's Restaurant, 5 Windsor Terrace, Seafront, Dun Laoghaire. Co Dublin. Tel: 804600
- Ernie's Restaurant, Mulberry Gardens, Donnybrook, Dublin 4. Tel: 693300
- Gallery 22, 22 St Stephen's Green, Dublin 2. Tel: 616669
- Glenasmole Restaurant, Glenasmole, Dublin Mountains, Dublin 24. Tel: 513620
- Cafe Klara, 35 Dawson Street, Dublin 2. Tel: 778111/778313
- Locks Restaurant, 1 Windsor Terrace, South Circular Road, Dublin 8. Tel: 538352
- Mahler's Restaurant, Powerscourt Townhouse Centre, 52 South William Street, Dublin 2. Tel: 794056
- The Park, Main Street, Blackrock, Co Dublin. Tel: 886177
- Red Bank Restaurant, 7 Church Street, Skerries, Co Dublin. Tel: 491005
- Saddle Room, 7/8 Ely Place, Dublin 2. Tel: 761751
- The Shelbourne Hotel, St Stephen's Green, Dublin 2, Tel: 766471
- Soup Bowl, 2 Molesworth Place, Dublin 2. Tel: 618918

• The Westbury Hotel, Clarendon Street, Dublin 2. Tel: 791122

VEGETARIAN

• Blazing Salads, Powerscourt Townhouse Centre, Dublin 2.
• Cornucopia Wholefoods, 19 Wicklow Street Dublin 2. Tel: 777583
• Coffee Bean, 4 Nassau Street, Dublin 2. Restaurant and vegetable shop.

ITALIAN

• Le Caprice, 12 St Andrew Street, Dublin 2. Tel: 716043
• Coffee Inn, 6 Ann Street South, Dublin 2. 770107
• Del Monaco, 1 Fade Street, Dublin 2. Tel: 773915
• Kapriol Restaurant, 45 Camden Street Lower, Dublin 2. Tel: 751235
• Nico's, 53 Dame Street, Dublin 2. Tel: 773062
• Pasta Fresca, Unit 4, Chatham Court, Chatham Street, Dublin 2. Tel: 792402
• Pasta Pasta, 22 Exchequer Street Dublin 2. Tel: 792565
• Pavani's Restaurant, 2 Cumberland Street, Dun Laoghaire, Co Dublin. Tel: 809675
• Unicorn Restaurant, Merrion Court, Off Merrion Row, Dublin 2. Tel: 762182

FISH, BURGERS AND CHIPS

• Beshoff Ocean Foods, 14 Westmoreland Street, Dublin 2. Tel: 778026 and 7 Upper O'Connell Street, Dublin 1. Tel: 724899
• Burdock's, Werburgh Street, Dublin 2.
• Cafolla's, 75 Mespil Road, Dublin 4. Tel: 603127

FRENCH

• Bon Appetit, 29 Pembroke Road, Dublin 4. Tel: 606140
• La Vie En Rose, 6a Stephen's Street Upper, Dublin 2. Tel: 781771
• Le Relais Des Mouettes, Marine Parade, Sandycove, Co

Dublin. Tel: 809873
- Les Freres Jacques, 74 Dame Street, Dublin 2. Tel: 794555
- Pigalle, 14 Temple Bar, Merchant's Arch, Dublin 2. Tel: 719262
- Restaurant Patrick Guilbaud, 46 James Place, Baggot Street Lower, Dublin 2. Tel: 764192
- Shay Beano, 37 Lower Stephen's Street, Dublin 2. Tel: 776384
- Whites On The Green, 119 St Stephen's Green, Dublin 2. Tel: 778466

JAPANESE

- Ayumi-Ya Japanese Restaurant, Newpark Centre, Newtownpark Ave, Blackrock, Co Dublin. Tel: 831767

LEBANESE

- Cedar Tree, 11 St Andrew's Street, Dublin 2. Tel: 772121

WINE BARS

- Dobbins, 15 Mount Street Upper Mews, Dublin 2. Tel: 764679
- Mitchell's Cellars, 21 Kildare Street, Dublin 2. Tel: 680307
- Rudyard's Restaurant and Wine Bar, 15-16 Crown Alley, Dublin 2. Tel: 710846
- The Sandbank, Westbury Hotel, Grafton Street, Dublin 2. Tel: 791122
- The Wine Epergne, 147 Upper Rathmines Road, Dublin 6. Tel: 976130

RUSSIAN

- The Grey Door, 23 Pembroke Street, Dublin 2. Tel: 763286
- The Old Dublin, 91 Francis Street, Dublin 8. Tel: 542028

Liberties Vocational School
BULL ALLEY STREET
DUBLIN 8

INDIAN

• Eastern Tandoori, 34 South William Street, Dublin 2. Tel: 710506; The Old Parish Hall, Kill Lane, Deansgrange, Co Dublin. Tel: 892856
• Rajdoot Tandoori, 26 Clarendon Street, Westbury Centre, Dublin 2. Tel: 794274

CHINESE

• Fans Cantonese Restaurant, 60 Dame Street, Dublin 2. Tel: 794263
• Imperial Chinese Restaurant, 12a Wicklow Street, Dublin 2. Tel: 772580
• Orchid Szechuan, 120 Pembroke Road, Ballsbridge Dublin 4. Tel: 600629
• China-Sichuan Restaurant, 4 Lower Kilmacud Road, Stillorgan, Co Dublin. Tel: 884817/889560.

AMERICAN, MEXICAN AND AMERICAN PIZZA

• Bad Ass Cafe, 9 Crown Alley, Dublin 2. Tel: 712596
• Chicago Pizza Pie Factory, St Stephen's Green Centre, Dublin 2. Tel: 781233
• 18th Precinct, 18 Suffolk Street, Dublin 2. Tel: 718000
• Fat Freddies, 20 Temple Lane, Dame Street, Dublin 2. Tel: 796779
• FXB's, 1a Lower Pembroke Street, Dublin 2. Tel: 764606/767721
• Judge Roy Bean's, 45 Nassau Street, Dublin 2. Tel: 797539
• Independent Pizza Co, 46 Lower Drumcondra Road, Dublin 9. Tel: 302957 and a new restaurant in South Anne Street, beside Keogh's pub.
• Pizza Time, 30 Richmond Street South, Dublin 2. Tel: 751762
• Poor Mouth Cafe, Abbey Mall, Middle Abbey Street, Dublin 2. Tel: 734491

IRISH

- Gallagher's Boxty House, 20 Temple Bar, Dublin 2. Tel: 772762
- Oisin's, 31 Upper Camden Street, Dublin 2. Tel: 753433

DAY-TIME RESTAURANTS

- Balcony Restaurant, Top Floor, Powerscourt Town House Centre, Dublin 2
- Kilkenny Kitchen, Nassau Street, Dublin 2, Tel: 777066

BISTROS AND INFORMAL RESTAURANTS

- Fitzers Restaurant, Point Depot, East Link Bridge, Tel: 365977; 41 Lower Camden Street, Tel: 753109, Fitzers also run the restaurant in the National Gallery.
- George's Bistro, 29 South Frederick Street, (Rere Setanta Centre), Dublin 2. Tel: 797000
- The Old Schoolhouse, Coolbanagher, Swords , Co Dublin. Tel: 402846
- Trocadero, 3 Andrew Street, Dublin 2. Tel: 775545

FISH RESTAURANTS

- Ante Room Seafood Restaurant, 20 Lower Baggot Street, Dublin 2. Tel: 604716
- King Sitric Fish Restaurant, East Pier, Howth, Co Dublin. Tel: 325235
- The Lobster Pot, 9 Ballsbridge Terrace, Dublin 4. Tel: 680025
- Lord Edward Seafood Restaurant, 23 Christchurch Place, Dublin 8. Tel: 542420
- Periwinkle Seafood Bar, Powerscourt Townhouse Centre, William Street South, Dublin 2. Tel: 794203
- Restaurant Na Mara, Harbour Road, Dun Laoghaire, Co Dublin. Tel: 806767

THE ASIA MARKET

30 Drury Street
Dublin 2
Tel: (01) 779764
Contact: Helen Pau

Eastern food store

The Asia Market is an indispensible shop for buying anything other than Irish food products. From fish gravy to bok choy, chopsticks to woks, the Asia Market may be small in size but it carries a wealth of products. Helen Pau, who has an equally invaluable sense of humour, will give sage advice to those who want it.

Dublin city centre. Open on Sundays also.

AYUMI-YA

Newpark Centre
Newtownpark Avenue
Blackrock
Co Dublin
Tel: (01)
831767/944396
Contact: Mrs Akiko
Hoashi

Japanese restaurant

The quiet success achieved by Mrs Hoashi over the last six years has allowed the Ayumi-Ya, for most of its existence the only Japanese restaurant in Dublin, to expand and introduce the tappan-yaki, a custom-made table with a hot plate on which the chef cooks right in front of the diners. You can kneel on large cushions to eat in the Ozashiki Room, or eat Western-style. A good tip is to allow the staff to select a menu for you. If you are lucky, this can become a seamless experience of delicious food.

South of the City Centre, near Blackrock. Open: Tues-Sat 7-11pm, Sun, 6-10pm.

JAMES BEST & CO
Arbour Hill
Dublin 7
Tel: (01) 773704
Contact: Kieran Best

Natural sausage casings

The sausage casings produced here in Arbour Hill are mainly for export, but Mr Best assures us that if you turn up he might be able to sell you the casings in small amounts. All the skins are natural.

Telephone for more details.

BEWLEY'S CAFES
• 12 Westmoreland Street, Dublin 2
Tel: (01) 776761
• 78 Grafton Street Dublin 2
Tel: (01) 776761
• 13 South Gt George's Street Dublin 2
Tel: (01) 776761
• Dundrum Shopping Centre Dublin 14
Tel: (01) 4985185
• Stillorgan Shopping Centre, Co Dublin
Tel: (01) 880484
• Dun Laoghaire Shopping Centre Co Dublin
Tel: (01) 800165
   Shop only
• Ilac Centre Henry Street Dublin 1
Tel: (01) 729034
   Shop only

Cafe and specialist coffee shops

The Bewley's Restaurants have introduced significant changes in recent years in an attempt to counter their difficulties, but often the changes have only diminished the unique character of these tea rooms. The city centre rooms are best observed from a deep-red seat. They are still very much part of Dublin and just as unsure of themselves as the city is. The shops sell tea, cakes and bread. They roast coffee on the premises and their brews are available all over the country. There are Bewley's Cafes in Galway and Limerick.

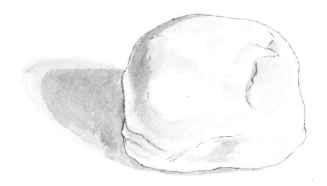

BUCKLEYS
4 Chatham Street
Dublin 2
Tel: (01) 771149
Contact: Paddy Buckley

Butchers

Buckleys have branches all over Dublin, including 8 Lower Camden Street, which is where the meat is prepared, and where you can find some of the more unusual cuts. One of Buckleys' specialities is Dublin spiced beef.

Branches all over Dublin.

LEO BURDOCK'S
Werburgh Street
Dublin 2
Contact: Brian Burdock

➥ *Fish and chips*

Burdock's chipper is a Dublin institution, and deservedly so. It sells only fish, chips and soft drinks, and joining the ever-present queue to order your supper is one of Dublin's finest experiences. The food is cooked in a coal-heated fryer, and should be eaten as soon as possible, preferably sitting on the St Patrick's Cathedral benches.

Dublin city centre, behind Christchurch Cathedral. Closed Sunday and Tuesday.

BRETZEL KOSHER BAKERY
1A Lennox Street
Dublin 8
Tel: (01) 752724
Contact: Morgan
Hackett

➡ *Continental bakery*

Popularly known as the Jewish bakery, the Bretzel's bread can be found in a variety of shops around Dublin city centre. Nothing however, can beat queueing up on a Sunday morning for freshly baked rolls, bagels, onion bagels, and the best croissants North of the English Channel.

Portobello Bridge, near the Grand Canal.

RELIGION AND FOOD IN IRELAND

One of the largest meat processing companies in Ireland is owned by a Pakistani Muslim, Sher Rafique. The name of the company is the Halal Group (Clare Road, Ballyhaunis, Co Mayo Tel: (097) 30555) and it describes simply the product that the plant supplies. Irish meat is slaughtered according to Muslim custom, processed, and exported, and it earns the company well over three hundred million punts in annual sales.

Muslims visiting Dublin may visit the Halal Meat Shop on Grantham Street (Dublin 2, Tel: (01) 780054), where raw, halal slaughtered meat is sold along with vegetables, spices, and the occasional filled, fried filo pastry.

Kosher food is also quite easily obtained in Ireland. The Bretzel Bakery (see Dublin entry) adds a final prayer to the already excellent dough, and Kosher meat can be found in Erlichs (35 Lower Clanbrassil Street, Dublin 8, Tel: (01) 542252, Contact: Bertha Erlich) and Swissas (31 Lower Clanbrassil Street, Tel: (01) 540249). Both butchers are pleasingly old-fashioned shops, the lack of modernisation unfortunately revealing a decline in the Dublin Jewish community.

Over in J. Fine (81 Terenure Road North, Terenure, Dublin 6, Tel: (01) 907649, Contact: Mrs White) you will find a full range of Kosher groceries: gefilte fish, matzo bread, kosher wine and cheese and unleavened bread. This, however is the only Kosher grocery shop in Dublin.

The Hare Krishnas used to run a good restaurant in Dublin, but it's been closed for some time. Members of the Clergy are usually to be found in either Wynn's or the Clarence Hotel, depending on which station, Connolly or Heuston, they may be arriving from, or departing to, the country.

BUTLER'S IRISH
Unit 5
Enterprise Centre
Pearse Street
Dublin 2
Tel: (01)
710599/710480
Contact: Mairead
Sorenson

Handmade chocolates

Butler's Irish make a very full range of handmade chocolates. Their fillings run the gamut using both fresh cream and hard centres.

Telephone for more details.

CAVISTON'S DELICATESSEN
59 Glasthule Road
Sandycove
Co Dublin
Tel: (01)
802715/809120
Contact: Stephen
Caviston

Delicatessen, fish monger

As well as fresh fish, Irish cheeses and a wide variety of smoked products, including wild salmon that they smoke themselves, Caviston's are interested in selling any good food made by small Irish producers. The shop is characterised by cheerful friendliness even during the lunchtime queues for their made-up sandwiches. In the fish shop at the back they will happily advise you on recipes for the wide variety of fish they sell.

Main Street of Sandycove.

THE CHEESEBOARD
6 Johnson's Court Mall
Clarendon Centre
Dublin 2
Tel: (01) 791422
Contact: Monica
Murphy

Cheese and wine

The Cheeseboard has a fine selection of cheeses, including an almost full complement of Irish farmhouse cheeses. They are now concentrating their resources on exporting Irish cheese. They also import wine.

Dublin city centre.

CHINA-SICHUAN RESTAURANT
4 Lower Kilmacud Road
Stillorgan

This unprepossessing restaurant is a State-owned enterprise of the Sichuan Province People's Republic of China. This allows them easy access to authentic ingredients which, in the hands of their quartet of

Co Dublin
Tel: (01)
884817/889560
Contact: Sichuan
Catering Service
Company

Chinese restaurant

chefs can produce a meal that is both magnificent and mystifying.

Just off the Stillorgan by-pass. Open Mon-Fri, 12.30-2.30pm & 6-11.30pm. Sat 1-2.30pm & 6-11.30pm Sun 1-2.30pm, 6-11pm.

CORNUCOPIA WHOLEFOODS
19 Wicklow Street
Dublin 2
Tel: (01) 777583
Contact: Neil & Deirdre McCafferty

Restaurant and wholefood shop.

A constant menu that customers never tire of is the hallmark of Cornucopia's success. Vegetarian soups, pies, salads and rolls are not only fresh and delicious but extremely good value. Seating arrangements are cramped due to the restaurant's popularity. The shop area at the front sells a wide variety of wholefoods and organic vegetables. The restaurant is not open in the evening.

Dublin city centre.

THE DUBLIN FOOD CO-OP
St Andrew's Centre
Pearse Street
Dublin 2
13 Christchurch Place
Dublin 8.
For membership Tel:
(01) 544480

Food co-op and market

The Dublin Food Co-Op is a consumer's wholefood co-op begun in 1983 with the aim of making shopping an amiable communal experience, and to provide for its members, organically grown and natural wholefoods at wholesale prices. A co-ordinating body manage the scheme and use purchasing power transfers — a system which relies on prior orders to enable goods to be purchased at the best possible price. You become a member by buying a £1 share, paying an annual subscription and by offering to help. The upshot of all this is a marvellous market held each second Saturday from 9am-5pm in the St Andrew's Centre on Pearse Street which is bounteous with organic vegetables, mouthwatering cakes, mountains of good bread, herbs, pulses and everything you could imagine. A truly imaginative venture which it is a great pleasure to attend.

A prominent red brick building on Pearse Street, near the IDA Centre.

51

THE COUNTY DUBLIN ORGANIC PRODUCERS

The best source of information about organic symbol producers in Dublin is Nicky Kyle, the treasurer of IOFGA. Contact her at Springmount, Ballyboughal, Co Dublin, Tel: (01) 433031. The produce of many of the growers can be found in the Saturday market of the Dublin Food Co-op, and some also sell to Organic Foods which means the fruit and vegetables can be found in the Dublin supermarkets of Superquinn and Quinnsworth, as well as various wholefood shops. Amongst the other growers are William Browne of Ashfield, The Green, Garristown, Co Dublin, Tel: (01) 354527, (after 6pm) who specialises in organic fruit, Kathy Marsh of Tobersool, Balbriggan, Co Dublin, Tel: (01) 411863, who sells some produce in the Balbriggan Country Market on Friday mornings in the Town Hall, 9.30am, Deirdre Keogh, Willow Cottage, Ballycoras Road, Kiltiernan, Co Dublin (vegetables, fruit, herbs and flowers), Marcus McCabe, All Hallows Garden, Dublin 9 (fruit, herbs, bedding plants and vegetables). Brennan's Bakery in Dublin, Tel: (01) 513933 hold the organic symbol for the bread they make using Josef Finke's flour from Ballybrado farm. Laura Turner organises the organic gardening courses run at Crannagh Castle, Tipperary, Tel: (01) 453853.

DUNN'S
95 Manor Street
Dublin 7
Tel: (01) 773156
Contact: Mr Gerard Dunn

Fish, game and smoked products

Dunn's wholesale from their shop in Manor Street, and retail at 6 Upper Baggot Street, Tel: (01) 602688. They smoke all types of fish, including cod's roe, but their speciality is salmon. They also sell a range of what they call 'gourmet foods' which includes roast duck. In season, the shop is lined with game birds as they hold a game licence. They also sell all types of fish including Dublin Bay Prawns.

Telephone for more details.

FITZERS
41 Lower Camden Street
Dublin 2
Tel: (01) 753109
Contact: Sharon Fitzpatrick

Vegetable shop, restaurants

In addition to the shop on Camden Street, the Fitzers organisation also run the Diner next door, the National Gallery Restaurant, and the Point Depot Restaurant. But it is the shop that has long been a staple for wholefood devotees. Fitzers is excellent for fruit and vegetables and the back of the shop contains giant hessian bags of beans, legumes, spices, dairy products, as well as specialist items from olive oil, to vanilla pods.

Dublin city centre

FOTHERGILLS
141 Upper Rathmines
Road
Dublin 6
Tel: (01) 962511
Contact: Terry and
Breda Lilburn

Delicatessen

Fothergills is one of those shops which is always occupied by both customers and glorious aromas. Excellent breads, a good cheese counter which includes Croghan fresh goats' cheese from Wexford, good cooked meats and a full range of groceries including honeys, McCambridges bread and ice cream.But it is the desserts and cakes that take the biscuit: effervescent meringues, spongy chocolate bombs and gorgeous cakes. Backing all of this up is a full catering service run by the Lilburns from which you can choose from half-a-dozen starters, a range of quiches and soups, main courses such as carbonade of beef, lamb biryani, pheasant Vallee d'Auge, and a dozen puddings. Friendly, helpful staff make shopping a pleasure. If you bring your own crockery — pudding bowls etc — they will fill them for you. A perfect deceit for the timid cook.

On the right hand side of the Upper Rathmines Road as you drive out of Dublin.

FRERE JACQUES
74 Dame Street
Dublin 2
Tel: (01) 794555
Contact: Jean Jacques
Caillabet

French restaurant

The elegant French cuisine of Frere Jacques, when on song, is one of the city's better French restaurants. The food is cooked by Michael Rath, and is a pleasing mix of nouvelle ideas and bourgeois ingredients. There is a fairly decent wine list.

Dublin city centre. Open Mon-Fri 12.30-2.30; 7-11pm. Sat 7-11pm. Closed Sunday.

THE GALLIC KITCHEN
Christchurch Market
40-48 Back Lane
Dublin 8
Tel: (01) 761872
Contact: Sarah Webb

➥ *Patisserie*

Sarah Webb is, quite simply, an excellent cook. Her quiches are full with flavour, her hand-made chocolates deliciously dreamy, her bread rolls packed with taste. She sells her food from a shop at the front of the Christchurch Market, across the road from the Cathedral, beside Mother Redcaps' Tavern, on Fridays, Saturdays and Sundays from 10am-6pm. The rest of the week she cooks for functions of any and every description.

Opposite Christchurch Cathedral. Open 10am-6pm Fri, Sat,

53

Sun. You can also buy Sarah's food from Browne's in Sandymount, Marron's of Donnybrook, Mother Redcap's Tavern in Christchurch, Bites in Pembroke Road, Millers at Mespil Road, Sheehans pub in Chatham Street and the Garden Cafe on the Rathmines Road.

THE GOURMET SHOP
Rathgar
Dublin 6
Tel: (01) 970365
Contact: Thomas
Cronin

Delicatessen

An old-style delicatessen with old-style virtues such as good service and helpful knowledge of their wares from the staff. The Gourmet makes an excellent, clean-tasting coleslaw, amongst other salads, has organic tomatoes from a local greenhouse in season, and pretty much every delicatessen product you can think of and a judicious selection of wines.

Bordering on Terenure, at the top of the Rathgar Road.

GOURMET SMOKED FOODS
Unit 4 C
St Margaret's Industrial Estate
Dublin 11
Tel: (01) 424318/428242
Contact: Adrian Sweeney

Smokery

Adrian Sweeney smokes fish, fowl and meat, including chicken, duck breast, pork, and beef. At the moment he is concentrating his efforts for the larger outlets: restaurant and catering establishments, but he has plans to sell his products retail via delicatessens.

Telephone for more details.

GREEN ACRES
9 Fleet Street
Dublin 2
Tel: (01) 710880
Contact: Helen Heapny

Wholefood shop

The speciality of Green Acres is cooked vegetarian lunches to take away. These include spicy nut burgers, exotic spring rolls, and wholewheat pies. You can also buy Bananas-breads, free-range eggs and general wholefood products.

Fleet Street runs parallel to the river Liffey, on the South side.

HERE TODAY
25 South Anne Street
Dublin 2

The shop on South Anne Street is an invaluable repository of unusual fruit, herbs, local and imported vegetables. There is less choice in the smaller

Tel: (01) 711454

Powerscourt Townhouse
Centre
Dublin 2
Tel: (01) 794079
Contact: Declan
Tiernan/ Pat Treacy

Greengrocers

Powerscourt stall, but both shops act as major
suppliers to restaurants all over the city.

Dublin city centre.

HICK'S
Woodpark
Sallynoggin
Tel: (01) 854430
Contact: Jack Hick

➡ *Pork butcher*

Hick's is a small butchers set back off the Sallynoggin
Road. Jack Hick specialises in pork and has trained in
Germany, as has his son Donal. Here you can buy
North German Bratwurst, Italian sausages, French
Garlic sausages, Swiss sausages, magnificent thinly
sliced kassler, chorizos, black and white puddings
and rarities like Nusschenken and Dutch Frikadel.
Jack Hick is currently breeding Wessex Saddlebacks
which he is crossing with the white pig in order to get
the best pork. One of the few places where you can
get real pancetta, which is invaluable in Italian
cooking. Jack Hick's son, Donal is opening a similar
shop in Dalkey. Details from the Sallynoggin shop.

Just off the Sallynoggin road facing the Park.

HOME BAKERY
22 Little Mary Street
Dublin 1
Contact: Margaret
Murphy

Bakery

Tiny bakery where Mrs Murphy will sell you her
delicious home-made cakes, including real Dublin Gur
cake.

Just off Capel Street at the North end.

HOWTH PIER
Howth
Co Dublin
Tel: (01) 393396 (Mon
& Fri)

The larger trawlers arrive at Howth on Tuesday and
Thursday nights, but there is no selling direct from the
boats. Go instead to the shops on the pier,
particularly the unmarked McLoughlin's, whose fish
are guaranteed to be fresh. Michael Wright's is also

Contact: Pat O'Regan,
Area Officer, Bord
Iascaigh Mhara (Irish
Sea Fisheries Board)

Fish

excellent, with a wider selection that doesn't come straight from the boats, including salmon and scallops. The best time to go to the harbour is on Thursday evenings.

Go as far as you can through Howth until you come to the pier.

THE IMPERIAL
Wicklow Street
Dublin 2
Tel: (01)
772580/772719
Contact: Mrs Cheung

Chinese restaurant

The speciality of the Imperial, a discreet pair of rooms situated at the end of a corridor, is Dim Sum, steaming little dishes that they serve every day from 12.30 to 5.30. Don't go on either Friday or Saturday, the days when the dim sum chef takes time off. The best day to go is on Sunday and let these endlessly ingenious concoctions tantalise your palate. One of the best meals in town.

Dublin city centre.

THE KAPRIOL
45 Camden Street
Dublin 2
Tel: (01) 751235
Contact: Giuseppe and
Egidia Peruzzi

Italian restaurant

The Kapriol can turn out to be an expensive restaurant despite the fact that the food is simple. The reason so many are prepared to pay is because of the individual attention given to each dish by Egidia, who is a natural Italian cook. Go for the best Zabaglione north of the Alps, and you will find the best atmosphere of any restaurant in town.

Top of Camden Street where the road divides.

KILTIERNAN COUNTRY MARKET
Golden Ball
Kiltiernan
Co Dublin

Country market

Kiltiernan Country Market is a wonderful institution that goes beyond its two-and-a-half hour opening time to organise social meetings, barbeques etc. The market itself brings together a display of free-range chickens, jams, cakes, chutneys, flowers, free-range eggs, buttermilk and made-up savouries all under one roof every Saturday morning.

Kiltiernan Village. The hall is on the left hand side as you approach from Dublin.

LEONIDAS CHOCOLATES
16 Royal Hibernian Way
Dawson Street
Dublin 2
Tel: (01) 795915
Contact: Michelle

30 Mary Street
Dublin 1
Tel: (01) 733066/733914
Contact: Sharon

Belgian chocolates

In the run up to St Valentine's day, Mother's Day and Easter the queues outside the Leonidas shops are gargantuan. Their chocs are not only gorgeous but very good value — often cheaper than a box of vegetable fat commercial chocolates.

Dublin city centre.

LIR CHOCOLATES
IDA Enterprise Centre
East Wall Road
Dublin 3
Tel: (01) 787800
Contact: Mary White

Truffles

Mary White and her team produce the most exquisite truffles. They come in milk, dark and white chocolate, and they have a particularly delicious fruit range including cherry, kiwi fruit and strawberry.

You can buy the truffles in Superquinn in Blackrock, and Brown Thomas on Grafton Street amongst other outlets. Telephone for details.

LITTLE ITALY
68 North King Street
Dublin 7
Tel:(01) 725208/733935
Telex: 90603
Contact: Marisa Rabbitte

Importers, distributors and retailers of all types of Italian food.

Little Italy is both a wholesale and retail supplier, and as a result quite unusual Italian goods can be bought at a fraction of the price that a city centre delicatessen would charge. Good Italian table wines come in two litre bottles, there is a good selection of dried pasta, and you will also find anchovies, Italian sun-dried tomatoes, and three varieties of good strong Lavazza coffee.

The market area of Dublin city centre — at the North end of Smithfield market.

MacCONNELL'S
38 Grafton Street

MacConnell's smoked salmon is good, and their fish is reliably fresh. When they sell out, that's it, no

57

Dublin 2
Tel: (01) 774344
Contact: Sean Nelson

Fishmongers

unearthing more fish from the freezer. Not a place to find exotic seafood, but good for fresh fish from the Irish sea.

Dublin city centre

MAGILLS
14 Clarendon Street
Dublin 2
Tel: (01) 713830
Contact: Brendan
Condon

German delicatessen

The attitude of the staff, and the elderly exiles who make up a large section of their customers, slowly selecting their careful way through the smoked meats, sausages and cheese in their rich East European accents, make Magills one of Dublin's more characterful shops. The theatre doesn't take from the produce, which includes wonderful black olives and an excellent liver sausage amongst many other indispensible items.

Dublin city centre.

RESTAURANT MAHLER
Powerscourt Townhouse
Centre
52 South William Street
Dublin 2
Tel: (01) 795046
Contact: Andrew
McElroy

Restaurant

Joe Kerrigan maintained a remarkably high standard through the years he worked with Andrew McElroy in The Carriage Restaurant. It was a place where you could always be certain of an excellent lunch at a decent price. The move to Restaurant Mahler should allow greater scope for his undoubted talents and combined with Andrew McElroy's flair, it should be an exciting new restaurant.

Basement of Powerscourt Townhouse Centre. Opening November 1989. Open all day and each evening, six days a week. Closed Sunday.

MARDI CONFECTIONERY
Unit 9 Deansgrange
Industrial Estate
Dun Laoghaire
Co Dublin
Tel: (01) 892202
Contact: Raymond
McDonagh
Specialist patisserie

Mardi Cakes are quite easy to spot around the town, they are used in a number of smart restaurants, as well as not a few delicatessens. They are often fruit filled flans, made from soft sponge, creme anglaise and glazed fresh fruit. Some of their cakes are fantastic to look at, and they taste good to.

Telephone for more details.

THE MARKET WINERY
George's Street Arcade
Dublin 2
Tel: (01) 779522
Contact: Tony Ecock

Wine merchant

High excise taxes mean that selecting any wine in Dublin can be fraught with risk —there is no such thing as a bargain, though you can come across a good buy. In the Market Winery, Tony Ecock has distinguished himself by his willingness to instruct and guide customers through his small but interesting range. His knowledge goes far beyond his own stock. Details of the Ecock Brothers Wine Importing and Distributing Company can be obtained from Tony.

Dublin city centre

MOORE STREET AND CAMDEN STREET MARKETS

You will find lots of prams in Moore Street, but their primary function as child carriers has long been abandoned in favour of their use as portable stalls. Other, more settled traders in Moore Street line the street permanently, selling vegetables, fruit and fish, each day of the week apart from Sunday. The market is interesting for its sharp repartee (there is even a book on the subject) rather than for its produce, which is often cheap, but tired.

A smaller street market is held daily in Camden Street, with permanent stalls and the familiar mix of staples plus fish, and more fish is to be found in the Iveagh market behind Christchurch.

If these markets could bottle their character, it might prove to be their most desirable product.

THE MARKETS
Chancery Street
Dublin 2

Fruit and vegetable market, next door to fish market.

Both the fish and vegetable markets open at 7am, and this is the time to see them at their best. Most of their business is wholesale, but some stallholders sell to the public; 'Jaysus, I'd sell to the divil himself' said one fish-husband. 'We just don't refuse money' said the man at J. Boggan & Sons, a stall that marks the area where the public can buy produce in small amounts. The occasional horse and cart can still be seen: time has not stood still here, but it does move less quickly than in the rest of the city. In the centre of the vegetable market is a restaurant, open all day, serving Dublin coddle and Irish stew in the winter; pork chops, shepherd's pie, steak and onions etc in the summer. Best time of all to go is in the morning for a breakfast of bacon sandwiches and a mug of tea.

The restaurant is called Paddy's Place, Tel: (01) 735130.

Just north of the River Liffey Between Capel Street and the Law Courts.

MARRONS
51 Donnybrook Road
Dublin 4
Tel: (01) 698031
Contact: Des or Pat
Marron

Delicatessen

Marrons is an old style delicatessen where you find delicacies like flavoured vinegars, freshly squeezed orange juice, Sarah Webb's patisserie and other exotica.

The far side of Donnybrook as you leave Dublin city centre.

RECIPE: DUBLIN CODDLE

The secret of this recipe, like most others, is ingredients. If you have sausages wrapped in plastic, stuffed with rusk, water and preservatives; bacon that boils in its own water when you fry it; spuds that have been sprayed and spray you when you peel them and onions that exude nothing, then you won't have Dublin coddle.

If, however, you have any of the following: Willem Vannemann's, or Lavistown's or Gillian Boazman's or Vicky Heslop's sausages; bacon from Noreen Curran in Dingle, Burke's of Clonmel or the Kilcullen's of Sligo; and potatoes from Rory Allen in Ballymaloe, John Hoey in Newtownabbey, Wendy and Michael Miklas of Kilkenny or any of the organic producers, then you will have what once tasted like Dublin coddle.

If so, take 2lbs potatoes, 1lb onions, 12 oz sausages, 8 oz bacon, a scant 2 pints of water. Cut half of the potatoes into 1cm cubes, and the other half into large chunks (quartered if they're large, halved if they're small). Quarter the onion and separate the layers. Chop the bacon into chunks, the sausages into thirds. Put water onions, sausages, bacon and the small cubed potatoes into a large saucepan. Cover and bring to the boil. Remove any scum as soon as it forms. Then add the large chunked potatoes and simmer uncovered until they are soft. By this time the small potatoes will have disintegrated to give a thick soupy sauce. This is adapted from a recipe given to us by Joe Kerrigan of Restaurant Mahler. He suggests that you garnish it with a sprig of parsley and some triangular croutons. Serve in bowls. Coddle is traditionally a breakfast dish.

C. MORTON AND SON LTD
15 Dunville Avenue
Dublin 6
Tel: (01) 971254
Contact: Mr Morton

Supermarket

A supermarket that is of interest both to the serious shopper and students of architecture and design. Morton's supermarket is a beautiful example of modernist art, and they have had the good sense to stock it with fine foodstuffs. Many of the most worthwhile products from all over the country are to be found here.

Between Rathgar and Rathmines.

MULLIGAN'S
8 Poolbeg Street
Dublin 2
Tel: (01) 775582
Contact: Mr Cusack

Pub

Mulligan's has the reputation of serving the best pint of Guinness in Dublin, and with a good pint there is, as they say, eatin' and drinkin' in it, so this is the ideal place for a liquid lunch. Mercifully, the pub has not become self-conscious on account of its reputation, it's still stocked with real life regulars.

Dublin city centre.

THOMAS MULLOY LTD
12 Baggot Street Lower
Dublin 2
Tel: (01) 766133
Contact: Mr Mulloy

Game fish and seafood

Mulloy's have three shops, this one in Dublin, one on the pier in Howth and a stall in the Corporation market. They are licensed game dealers and smoke only wild salmon, as well as selling the usual sea fish.

Dublin city centre.

NOLAN'S
29A Stoneybatter
Dublin 7
Tel: (01) 770656
Contact: Mr Moore

Grocer

A pleasant old grocery shop usually staffed by pleasant old gentlemen, Nolan's is notable for excellent free-range eggs and chickens, and delicious home-cooked hams, cooked in the shop and sliced while still on the bone. You can also find good cakes of brown bread and decent vegetables.

North of the river.

OISIN'S
31 Upper Camden Street
Dublin 2 Tel: (01)

Oisin's is just the type of restaurant you hope to find when visiting a foreign city. It serves indigenous food: Irish Stew, Ham and Cabbage, Cockle Soup, Spiced Beef and puddings made from Carrigeen and Baileys

753433/691610
Contact: Feargal O
Huigin

Irish restaurant

Irish Cream. Each guest is given a little concoction involving Poitin as they arrive, and the atmosphere is genuine Dublin in its casual homeliness. This is one of the few places where you can get a bowl of real Dublin coddle: and they add 'sour apples', or cooking apples.

At the southern end of Camden Street near the junction with Harcourt Road.

RECIPE:
FRESH FETTUCINI WITH SMOKED SALMON

1oz butter; four button mushrooms, sliced thinly; four large but wafer-thin slices of smoked salmon, cut into strips; quarter of a pint of cream; 3 whirls of Pasta Fresca fettucini. Gently fry the mushrooms in the butter for about five minutes. Add the salmon, and immediately pour in the cream. Boil vigorously until the cream reduces by a third (this should take a minute if you have a good sized frying pan and intense heat). The cured salmon will 'cook', but will retain its smokiness. Meanwhile cook the pasta, this also takes just a minute if you want it al dente. Have ready a heated bowl. Tip in the pasta and smother with the sauce, serve at once with freshly ground black pepper. (Serves two people)

PASTA FRESCA
Unit 3/4
Chatham Street
Dublin 2
Tel: (01) 792402
Contact: May

Fresh pasta shop

A small variety of high quality fresh pasta, gnocchi and pastries can be bought in Pasta Fresca along with all the trimmings: freshly grated parmesan, wine and some sauces. Five high tables allow you to eat and drink on the premises, or you can take the food away. Salami, olives, olive oil, bread and many Italian specialities weigh down the shelves.

Dublin city centre. With the move into the premises next door, Pasta Fresca are changing their opening times and will stay open all day, until 12pm.

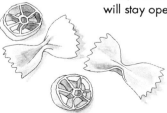

RESTAURANT NA MARA
Dun Laoghaire
Co Dublin
Tel: (01) 800509/
806767
Contact: Head of Irish
Rail Catering: Tom
Mythen

Restaurant

Restaurant na Mara is unusual in that it is owned by the Irish Railways and is situated in one of their gorgeous buildings over the DART station in Dun Laoghaire. The restaurant specialises in fish and seafood.

RESTAURANT PIGALLE
14 Temple Bar
Dublin 2
Tel: (01) 719262
Contact: Lahcen Iquani

French restaurant

A variety of establishments came and went from these unprepossessing premises before Lahcen Iquani arrived and quickly stamped his personality on the place. Excellent value and solid, but delicate food, the place is often packed with lawyers turning lunch into the longest meal of the day. A short but interesting wine list with good house wines.

Dublin city centre, just south of the river at the ha'penny bridge. Open for lunch 12.30-2.30; dinner 7-10.30.

LA POTINIERE
Unit 2
Powerscourt Townhouse
Centre
South William Street
Dublin 2
Tel: (01) 711300
Contact: Mary Leung

Sandwiches

La Potiniere is the best place to buy sandwiches in town. Many combinations have been dreamt up by the regular lunchtime clientele, and many more are possible. The shop also sells cheese, muesli and yogurt.

Powerscourt Townhouse Centre is signposted from Grafton Street in Dublin's city centre.

THE RAJDOOT TANDOORI
Westbury Centre
Dublin 2
Tel: (01) 794274
Contact: Miss Gill
Restaurant

The ugly exterior of the Rajdoot conceals a cool, dimly lit, fragrant interior. Part of the chain of restaurants which began in England, the Rajdoot has maintained its high standards, and in the process picked up a selection of awards.

Dublin city centre Open Mon-Sat, 12-2.30, 6.30-11.30.

T P REYNOLDS & CO
50 Pembroke Road
Dublin 4
Tel: (01)
600246/600091
Contact: Pedro
Reynolds

Wine importer

Pedro Reynolds imports a modest selection of
Portuguese wines into Ireland. They are all reliable,
but look out especially for the excellent CRF wines.

Telephone for more details.

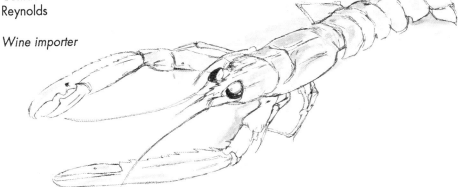

SAWER'S
3 Chatham Street
Dublin 2
Tel: (01) 777643
Contact: Michael
Reynolds

Fishmongers

Sawer's usually has the widest selection of fish to be
found in Dublin, it's rare to be unable to get almost
anything and everything here: shark, tuna, lobster,
oysters, and so on. They also sell game in season,
ducklings, chickens, chicken livers and smoked
salmon.

Dublin city centre.

SHAY BEANO
Lower Stephen's Street
Dublin 2
Tel: 776384
Contact: Eamonn O
Cathain

Restaurant

Shay Beano is an up-to-date French Bistro, all
designer plates and black and white wall prints, filled
more with innuendo than content. But this is not a
restaurant where design triumphs at the expense of
the cuisine. The cooking is daring, but excellent, with
a challenging wine list. The standard is always high,
and the sophistication backed by an understanding of
both style and basic techniques.

Dublin city centre.

DUBLIN PUBS

In James Joyce's 'Ulysses' Leopold Bloom finally, after much circumlocation, opts for a simple lunch of gorgonzola cheese and a glass of claret in Davy Byrne's pub in Duke Street. The visitor to Dublin is best advised to follow a similar course. In food terms the wise eater will savour the atmosphere of Dublin's drinking houses, and leave it at that. If it's eatin' and drinkin' you want, take a spoon and fork to a pint of stout.

Everybody, but everybody, will tell you differently, of course. The world and his wife always know of a place where the coddle is only mighty, the beef and spuds the best in the country, the lasagne the juiciest you can find outside Rome. Like most Dublin rumours, these stories tend to sink faster than a souffle when you prod them. The coddle will be a collection of slatternly bangers in a soup of salt and stock cube, the beef will be a fatty mush toasted under a torchlight, the sandwiches will be a triumph of food engineering: just how can you get so much air and water into two bits of bread and a whack of ham?

The suburban pubs, which often do a healthy lunchtime trade, are the worst, featuring curries that weren't curried, shepherd's pie that no shepherd would recognise and soups that are guaranteed to be fresh from the packet.

If you can't get some gorgonzola and a glass of claret, opt instead for a liquid lunch and digest the unbeatable atmosphere.

THE STAG'S HEAD

Dame Court
Dublin
Tel: (01) 793701
Contact: Peter
Callaghan

Pub, serving food.

Simple pub food of bangers and chips, ham and cabbage and so on is well cooked and properly handled at the Stag's Head. It is cheap, and thankfully reliable. The clientele are an exhibition in themselves: briefless barristers, boisterous Dubs, courting office couples. The good plain food is matched with the unbeatable atmosphere of an old Dublin pub.

Dublin city centre.

SUPERQUINN

Head Office
Enterprise House
Blackrock
Co Dublin
Tel: (01) 883222
Contact: Managing

Superquinn's approach to both customers and suppliers goes beyond the simple profit-margin motive. Many of their stores demonstrate the finest examples of Irish produce, from fresh fish to handmade chocolates, with careful wine shops and thoughtful design. All the the supermarkets feature products of many of the smaller Irish producers.

Director Feargal Quinn
Chief Buyer: Damien
Carolan

*Supermarket featuring
many of the products
mentioned in this book.*

Stores: Ballinteer Avenue, Dublin 14, Tel: (01) 898181;
Blackrock Shopping Centre, Co Dublin, Tel: (01)831511;
Blanchardstown Shopping Centre, Dublin 15, Tel: (01)
210414; Castle Street, Bray, Tel: (01) 867083; McKee
Avenue, Finglas, Dublin 11, Tel: (01) 434975; Knocklyon
Road, Templeogue, Dublin 16, Tel: (01) 942421; 9 North
Main Street, Naas, Tel: (045) 76666; Northside Shopping
Centre, Coolock, Dublin 5, Tel: (01) 477111; 116 Sundrive
Road, Kimmage, Tel: (01) 961335; Sutton Cross, Sutton,
Dublin 13, Tel: (01) 323180; Superquinn Shopping Centre,
Dublin Road, Swords, Co Dublin, Tel: (01) 406222;
Walkinstown, Dublin 12, Tel: (01) 505951.

TRADITIONAL CHEESE

Limekiln Lane
Walkinstown
Dublin 12
Tel: (01) 509494
Contact: Eugene Carr

Irish farmhouse cheeses

Traditional Cheese was set up five years ago and on
its first pricelist had eleven products. It now carries
one hundred and sixty different product lines and
turnover has doubled in the last eighteen months.
Eugene Carr distributes Irish farmhouse cheeses all
over the country and exports to England and the
Continent.

Telephone for more details.

WHAT ON EARTH

255 Harold's Cross
Road
Dublin 6
Tel: (01) 965111
Contact: Jim Dempsey

Wholefood shop

A neat wholefood shop on the left side of the road in
Harold's Cross as you drive up to Terenure.
Vegetables from Organic Foods can include luscious
cherry and beef tomatoes as well as crunchy carrots
with their stalks on. Also fine fresh cheese from the
Copsewood goats' farm in Co Wicklow.

On the left side of the road as you drive up to Terenure.

THE WINDING STAIR BOOK CAFE

40 Lower Ormond Quay
Dublin 1
Tel: (01) 733292
Contact: Kevin Connolly or Eileen Connolly

Bookshop and cafe

Exquisite second-hand bookshop where leather-bound volumes are the backdrop for the best place in town to have coffee, and a slice of Mrs Connolly's fruitcake.

Overlooking the Ha'penny Bridge on the North side of the River Liffey.

THE WINE GALLERY

Brookfield House
Brookfield Terrace
Blackrock
Co Dublin
Tel: (01) 833500
Contact: Brendan Quinn

Wine merchant specialising in organic wines

Brendan Quinn stocks a comprehensive list of organic wine, including a Premier Cru Champagne from Yves Ruffin; a Bordeaux Superieur from Yvon Dubost, Chateau Bossuet; a Pomerol, also from Yvon Dubost, Chateau Lafleur du Roy; a hefty Chateauneuf-du-Pape, Chateau de Beaucastel and many other unusual and special wines, not all of which are organic.

Opposite the Blackrock shopping centre is the road leading to Brookfield Terrace. You can buy directly from Brendan Quinn if you telephone first. Otherwise his wines are available in Superquinn.

DUBLIN

ACADEMIE DU VIN, 43 Belgrave Square, Monkstown, Co Dublin. Tel: (01) 843394, Contact: Tom Doorley. Wine courses.

THE ADAM SALESROOM, St Stephen's Green, Dublin. Tel: (01) 760261. Regular Vintage Wine Auctions.

ALEXANDER'S IRISH WHISKEY MARMALADE, P.O. Box 2239, Dublin 24, Contact Malcolm Alexander, Tel: (01) 525777, Fax: (01) 526412

ARANMORE BROWN BREAD, 16a Tubermore Avenue, Dalkey, Co Dublin, Tel: (01) 852468

BAILEY'S IRISH CREAM, Gilbeys of Ireland Ltd, Naas Road, Dublin 12, Tel: (01) 561111. The most popular liqueur in the world, adopted from the old Irish practice of dampening down whiskey with a little cream. Baileys now uses the cream from the milk of seventy-thousand cows *daily*, and some thirty-six million bottles are sold worldwide annually.

BALLYGOWAN SPRING WATER CO LTD, 90 St Stephen's Green, Dublin 2. Tel: (01) 540360

BANANA'S BREADS, Tel: (01) 972163, Contact: Paul and Nanette. Paul and Nanette were known in Dublin for their wholefood restaurant, Bananas. Now they confine their talents to the making of bread and cakes. You can buy these in Cornucopia, Wicklow Street and Green Acres of Fleet Street.

CAIS, Irish Farmhouse Cheesemakers Association, c/o National Dairy Council, Grattan House, Lower Mount Street, Dublin 2. Tel: (01) 619599

EIREFORCE, 5 Auburn Road, Dublin 4, Tel: (01) 838340. Alfalfa sprouts.

GUINNESS A SON & CO (DUBLIN) LTD, St James's Gate Brewery, Dublin 8. Tel: (01) 536700

HANLON LTD, 20 Moore Street, Dublin 1. Tel: (01) 733011. Good for game.

LIFEFORCE FOODS, 4 Halston Street, Dublin 7. Tel: (01) 724204/726184. Wholefood importers.

ALEX GARDNER'S COOKERY SCHOOL, St Mel's, Grove Park, Lower Rathmines Road, Dublin 6. Cookery School, and Gourmet tours of Ireland, learning about Irish food and eating in the very best

Irish restaurants.

LE GOURMET, Unit 1, Adelaide Court, Adelaide Road, Dun Laoghaire. Tel: (01) 808608. Importers of Middle Eastern foods, olives, pitta bread, humous, plus a few specialities like truffles and caviar.

McCAMBRIDGES LTD, 35 Ranelagh Main Street, Dublin 6. Tel: (01) 976755. Bread and Ice cream.

SWEENEY'S, 20 Lower Dorset Street, Dublin. Tel: 749808. Very good off licence in charming old grocer's shop on Dorset Street.

WHOLEFOODS WHOLESALE, Unit 2A, Kylemore Industrial Est, Killeen Road, Dublin 10. Tel: (01) 262315/6. Contact: Quentin Gargan.

WINE IMPORTERS

BOLANDS WINE MARKET, 169 St Mohbi Road, Dublin 9. Tel: (01) 373220. Wine Importers

CALLAGHAN VINTAGE WINES, 19 Maywood Lawn, Raheny, Dublin 5. Tel: (01) 311369 (after 5pm). Wine importers.

CASSIDY WINES LTD, 56 Sandyford Industrial Estate, Sandyford, Dublin 18. Tel: (01) 945157, Telex: 90900, Fax: 954477. Wine importers.

ECOCK WINES & SPIRITS, Unit 3, Newpark Centre, Newpark Avenue, Blackrock, Co Dublin. Tel: (01) 831664

EDWARD DILLON & CO. 25 Mountjoy Square, Dublin 1. Tel: (01) 364399. Wine importers

FEBVRE & CO LTD, 14 Highfield Road, Dublin 6. Tel: (01) 973953. Importers of wine, cooking chocolate, oils, spice mills, etc.

FINDLATER LTD, 149 Upper Rathmines Road, Dublin 6. Tel: (01) 976130. Off licence and wine importers.

A&C RICHARDSON, 8 Monaloe Way, Blackrock, Co Dublin. Tel: (01)886239/886615. Direct shipments from Burgundy.

FITZGERALD & CO, 11 Bow Street, Dublin 7. Tel: (01) 725911. Wine importer.

GILBEY'S OF IRELAND, Naas Road, Dublin 12. Tel: (01) 561111. Wine importers, and spirit manufacturers.

GRANTS OF IRELAND, St Lawrence Road, Dublin 20. Tel: (01) 264455. Wine importers.

GREENHILLS WINES & SPIRITS, P.O. Box 1470, Greenhills Road, Dublin 12. Tel: (01) 504601. Wine importers.

HOUSE OF WINE, 78 Woodlawn Park Grove, Dublin 23. Tel: Tony Maguire at 519952, Rory Considine at 980898, Fax (01) 97834. Specialists in importing Spanish wine.

HOTEL AND RESTAURANTS SUPPLIERS, 62 Middle Abbey Street, Dublin 1. Tel: (01) 730298. Importers of wines, pastas, olive oil, spirits, and other related products.

IBER WINES LTD, 25 Lower Hatch Street, Dublin 2. Tel: (01) 611533, Telex: 32748, Fax: (01) 76837. Wine importers.

KELLY & CO LTD, Tel: (01) 732100, Independent Wine Wholesaler.

McCABES, 51/55 Mount Merrion Avenue, Blackrock,

Co Dublin. Tel: (01) 882037. Wine importer.

MITCHELL'S, 21 Kildare Street, Dublin 2. Tel: (01) 760766. Wine Importers.

O'BRIENS FINE WINES, 30-32 Donnybrook Road, Dublin 4. Tel: (01) 693033. Also Sandymount, Blackrock, Dun Laoghaire, Dalkey, Bray, Vevay, Greystones. Wine importers, and off-licences.

T.P. REYNOLDS & CO LTD, 50 Pembroke Road, Dublin 4. Tel: (01) 600246/600091. Portuguese wine importers.

SYRAH WINES, 11 Rowanbyrn, Blackrock, Co Dublin, TEL: (01) 893670. Wine importers, specialising in the Rhone valley.

TASERRA WINE MERCHANTS, Hogan House, Grand Canal Street, Dublin 2. Tel: (01) 613022, Fax: (01) 613130, Telex: 91293

WEST END WINE CO LTD, 134 James' Street, Dublin 8. Tel: (01) 718897, Telex: 30224, Fax: (01) 720821

WOODFORD BOURNE LTD, 139 Francis Street, Dublin 8. Tel: (01) 536063, Fax: 537854. Wine importer.

COUNTY KILDARE

The county of stud farms and sheikhs suffers from having too many towns situated on main roads. Kildare town itself is little other than a wide spot in the road, while Naas is still, slowly, recovering from the many years in which its famous traffic jams made everyone's heart sink.

The county gives the impression of being both settled and moneyed, but there is no evidence that this has built up a taste for good food. Moyglare Manor in Maynooth, on the Moyglare road, a few miles out of the town is a grand country house with accommodation, which serves dinner, and Sunday lunch (Tel: (01) 28635 Contact: Norah Devlin). Otherwise one can eat at the rather eccentric Doyle's Schoolhouse in Castledermot (on the lefthand side of the road to Carlow as you go through the village, Tel: (0503) 44282, Contact: John Doyle), a restaurant where a dish of true inventiveness can be followed by one of rigorous dullness.

There are only two organic growers in the county. Enda Kiernan of Ovidstown, Straffan (Tel: (01) 288450. Approximately four miles past Celbridge, ring for precise directions) produces on a small scale, while Pat Murtagh (Tel: (01) 288278 Glyndale, Maynooth Road, Celbridge) produces herbs and light vegetables in a glasshouse and, he says, won't see anyone disappointed if they want to buy vegetables.

The truly bright light amidst this gloom is the excellent fresh goats' cheese made by Mary Morrin a few miles from Kilcock. Mary's goats are a cross between Anglo-Nubians and British Saanens and from their milk she makes one cheese with fresh herbs and one which is coated in dried herbs. You can get it at the Friday Country Market in Naas or from the house. (Tel: (01) 287244). You will find the house on the Kilcock to Naas road. Coming from Kilcock, go past

72

the Powers' Seeds factory, take the next turn on the right and go for half a mile up the road until you see a green gate on the left hand side.

COUNTY KILKENNY

Though the town of Kilkenny typically turns its back on its river it is, says the Shell Guide To Ireland, "one of the most attractive, as it is one of the most interesting, of Ireland's inland towns".

This is a fine understatement. Kilkenny is a beautiful town which is pleasing in almost every way. Its ancient vaulted buildings are complemented by aesthetic shopfronts from many years ago which have been lovingly preserved. The total harmony means that the occasional blunder is of little importance: unlike many Irish towns, Kilkenny allows you to bask in beauty.

It is also a festive place and, if you go during the Arts Week, a busy one, festooned with foreigners. Its scale, its river, its castle all conspire together to give it a huddled, inviting air. There are oodles of decent pubs and decent people.

The county compliments its capital. On a good day, the chequerboard fields dappled in sun and the lazy roads shadowed by mature trees, it is a mighty place. Even a small town like Castlecomer, which in other parts of the country might be pinched and mean, has a grand sweeping centre to it. This is a majestic county.

CASTLECOMER

CLAIRE COOGAN'S CHEESE
Rathkyle
Castlecomer
Co Kilkenny
Tel: (056) 41105
Contact: Claire Coogan

Farmhouse cows' cheese

You rarely see Claire Coogan's cheese for sale — most of it is exported and the rest is sold locally to restaurants. A pity, because this soft cheese with its distinctive orange rind is most pleasing and interesting.

The only way to get the cheese is to arrange a private delivery through the post — ring Claire at the above number.

FRESHFORD

KEN CUMMINS AND LYNN VENABLES
Ringwood
Freshford
Co Kilkenny
Tel: (056) 32188
Contact: Ken and Lynn

Organic fruit, flowers and vegetables.

Along with Clare Mooney of County Meath, and Denis Healy of Wicklow, Ken and Lynn are one of the major suppliers to Organic Food. They produce vegetables, herbs, fruit and flowers.

Telephone for more details.

KILKENNY

SHORTIS WONG
74 John Street
Kilkenny
Co Kilkenny
Tel: (056) 61305
Contact: Mary Shortis
or Chris Wong

Food shop

Splendid small deli with all the local products including Lavistown cheese, sausages and country butter, and excellent Ennisnag cheeses. Mary Shortis and Chris Wong cook their own hams and make excellent brown soda bread using Kell's wholemeal flour which, sadly, is only sold in twenty-five kilo bags at present. They also sell wholefoods.

Kilkenny City Centre.

75

THE WINE CENTRE

John Street
Kilkenny
Co Kilkenny
Tel: (056) 21687
Contact: Maureen and
Eamonn O'Keeffe

Wine merchant

This is an excellent off-licence with a varied and interesting selection of wines, some of which are quite rare. Decent prices mean this is a good place to look for something unusual.

Kilkenny City Centre.

LAVISTOWN

LAVISTOWN FOODS

Lavistown
Co Kilkenny
Tel: (056) 65145
Contact: Olivia
Goodwillie

Cheese, pork
➡ *Sausages*

"We are happy to sell cheese from the farm, because that is how you get it at its best" says Olivia Goodwillie, a succinct summary of the attitude that makes Lavistown foods so good. As well as an excellent semi-hard cheese with a pleasing depth of taste and good texture, Olivia also makes wonderful sausages. "Ingredients" says the label: "Pork, spices, salt, garlic", and that is all you get. To eat the bangers at their best, grill them for about six to eight minutes in total — if you fry them make sure you prick them first, and they are also good in Irish pot dishes such as Dublin Coddle. Another pork venture is the Lavistown Pork Circle: you join by sending your name, address and telephone number to Olivia and within about two to three months when your name comes up to the top of the list you will be contacted about how you would like the meat cut and delivered. Half a pig will weigh approximately fifty pounds and as of September 1989 the price was 90p per pound. The pork is antibiotic free and the pigs are naturally reared. As if all this was not enough, Olivia and Roger also run the Lavistown Centre for Environmental

76

Studies and courses include Lavistown Cookery, Kilkenny Flora, Exploring The Burren and many others. They take place over various weekends.

Lavistown is three miles outside Kilkenny. To buy cheese etc, it is wise to telephone for details. There will usually be somebody at home.

LEYRATH

MAEVE BRENNAN
Woodside
Leyrath
Co Kilkenny
Tel: (056) 65588 (056) 59852 (after 8pm)
Contact: Maeve Brennan

Fruit and vegetables

Six miles from Kilkenny on the roadside you may see a notice announcing organic vegetables for sale — this is where Maeve Brennan sells from, though she also delivers to local restaurants. Sweet tomatoes, crisp purple beans, hearty corn and good spuds as well as salad vegetables are just some of the things you can find, and do ask about the full-flavoured apples. Some of Maeve's produce is sold in Roots and Fruits in Kilkenny. Maeve hopes to apply for the IOFGA symbol.

Two miles from Kilkenny on the N10 road to the east.

PILTOWN

WENDY AND MICHAEL MIKLAS
Raheen
Piltown
Co Kilkenny
Tel: (051) 43519

Vegetables, herbs, beef, cheese

You can find the vegetables grown by Michael and Wendy in Over The Rainbow in Clonmel. They are just starting with a new generation of Kerry Cows, and hope to sell the beef — at the moment they have a small herd of Hereford cows, and when the animals are slaughtered they will sell some of the surplus to those who come quickly enough. Their herbs are quite delicious, and in the spring of 1990 they hope to start making a gouda-type cheese from the milk of their Kerry cows. They hold not only the IOFGA symbol but a symbol to prove they farm bio-dynamically.

Visitors are welcome at the farm, telephone for details and with orders.

MILEEVEN LTD

Owning Hill
Pilltown
Co Kilkenny
Tel: (051) 43368
Contact: Eilis Gough

*Honey, cider and
honey vinegar*
Beeswax polish

Mileeven was set up in 1987, and all their products are based on honey. You can buy jars of honey (bees of more than one nationality), and a liqueur of honey and Irish mist, furniture polish made from beeswax and, best of all, their Honey and Organic Cider Vinegar, which makes just the best French dressing.

Telephone for more details.

RECIPE:
GREEN SALAD WITH HONEY DRESSING

3 tabs olive oil; 1 full tab Mileeven's Honey and Cider Vinegar; salt and pepper ;1 head lettuce or a mixture of different lettuce leaves; 1 green pepper; 1 stick celery; 3 roots of spring onion; 1 avocado (optional); any leaf of fresh green herb: parsley, fennel, dill etc. In the base of a salad bowl mix together the oil, vinegar, salt and pepper. Shred the lettuce, sliver the green pepper, cut the celery into the thinnest slices possible. Sliver the onion, and cube the avocado. Tip the ingredients into the bowl with whatever herb you might have. Toss and serve immediately.

TEAGASC

Kildalton Agricultural
College
Piltown
Co Kilkenny
Tel: (051) 43105
Contact: TEAGASC

*Government
agricultural advisory
service*

TEAGASC is the Government's agricultural advisory service. Details of what the college produce can be obtained from the office. (NB This department used to be known as ACOT)

Telephone for details.

STONEYFORD

KING'S RIVER COMMUNITY
Ennisnag
Stonyford
Co Kilkenny
Tel: (056) 28234
Contact: Dieter
Gerhardt

Vegetables and eggs

If they have any surplus of their organic vegetables or eggs at the King's River Community, they will sell it from the farm. Holders of the IOFGA symbol.

Telephone for more details.

KILKENNY

BORD FAILTE, Shee Alms House, Rose Inn Street, Tel: (065) 21455 (Feb-Nov)

THE GOOD EARTH, St Kiernan's Street, Kilkenny. Health Food Shop.

KELL'S WHOLEMEAL FLOUR, Kell's, Co Kilkenny. Tel: (056) 28310 (Mill) (054) 35800 (Office). Contact: Billy Mosse

KILKENNY DESIGN WORKSHOPS, Castle Yard, Kilkenny. Tel: (056) 22118. There is a coffee shop attached to the workshops.

KILKENNY SPRING WATER COMPANY LTD, Smithland's North, Waterford Road, Kilkenny. Tel: (056) 63136

LACKEN HOUSE, Dublin Road, Kilkenny. Tel: (056) 61085/65611. Open for dinner. Chef is Eugene McSweeney, whose name is always prefixed by the words "award-winning". Consistently recommended.

EDWARD LANGTON RESTAURANT AND BAR, 69 John Street, Kilkenny. Tel: (056) 65133. Winner of the Pub of the Year competition, and bar catering award winner. Open for lunch and dinner. Consistently recommended.

ROOTS AND FRUITS, St Kiernan Street, Kilkenny. A fine greengrocers where you can buy Maeve Brennan's produce, and produce from the Clashganna Mills Trust of Ballykeenan, Borris, Co Carlow, who are Organic Symbol Holders.

E. SMITHWICK & SONS, St Francis' Abbey Brewery, Kilkenny. Tel: (056) 21014

COUNTY LOUTH

There are lots of hotels in County Louth. They litter the N1 road from Newry to Dublin as it runs through the county, either grand old Victorian hulks with battlements and balustrades, or sixties slab blocks with acres of net curtains.

They have huge menus, and confidently announce starters such as 'Grapefruit Surprise'. And what a surprise it is! Firstly, it is surprising that anyone would have the cheek simply to empty a can of grapefruit segments into a bowl. Secondly, it is surprising that they then had the cheek to plop a cherry on top of it. The biggest surprise of all is the fact that they will charge you a price that would be more suitable to an exotic concoction involving a fresh grapefruit and some culinary expertise.

Away from the hotels there are occasional trailer-trucks servicing the multitude of drivers who blaze between Dublin and Belfast and other roadhouses that shout: 'Hot Food Served All Day'. This, of course, means that they have both a deep freeze and a microwave oven, and they are expert in placing an item from the former into the latter.

Combine this dispiriting array with a stroll around Dundalk — surely the fast-food capital of the country — and Louth can seem like a county you would want only to by-pass if you are in search of good cooking. But, happily, whilst there is relatively little to detain you, there are some shops and eating-houses that are worth not merely a detour, but worth a pilgrimage.

CARLINGFORD

FERGUSON'S SHELLFISH

Greenore Road
Carlingford
Co Louth
Tel: (042) 73350
Contact: Ambrose
Ferguson

Oysters

If you want to buy oysters in this locality try Ambrose Ferguson. Like most of the members of the Carlingford Lough Aquaculture Association, he's a producer of pacific oysters and, like most others, supplies to Cuan Sea Fisheries for their Shore To Door service. However you can still buy oysters here, usually all year around, and get details of other producers.

Ferguson's are easily found in Carlingford.

COLLON

FORGE GALLERY RESTAURANT

Collon
Co Louth
Tel: (041) 26272
Contact: Desmond
Carroll

Restaurant

In the metropolis of Collon, the Old Forge is a spruce, well designed restaurant, pleasantly informal in every way. Portions are large and whilst ambition is sometimes greater than ingredients, everyone works hard to make an evening enjoyable. A decent wine list, full licence, lousy music.

On the main street in Collon. Open: Tues-Sat 7-10.30pm.

DROGHEDA

THE BUTTERGATE

Millmount
Drogheda
Tel: (041) 34759
Contact: Fidelma
MacAllister

Restaurant/wine bar

The Millmount Craft and Cultural Centre was once a Military Barracks. Now there are eight craft units and a restaurant/wine bar. The cooking of the restaurant is the inimitable Northern mixture of plain food embellished with more daring sauces. The menu usually features Kieran's Brothers Kassler, or Turf smoked bacon as it's called in this part of the world. The desserts are a clever whisper of various liqueurs added to concoctions of cream, plus wholesome looking crumbles and pies. The centre is easy to get to and worth detouring from the Dublin-Belfast road.

Cross the river Boyne leaving Drogheda on the N1 to Dublin. Quarter of a mile later you will see a signpost, and

50 yards later you turn right onto Mary Street (the Ashbourne Road) which leads you to another right onto the road that takes you into the centre.

KIERAN'S BROTHERS LIMITED
15 West Street
Drogheda
Co Louth
Tel: (041) 38728/9
Contact: Mark Kierans

Delicatessen

Just opposite the cathedral is Kieran's Brothers inspiring deli. 'We lead . . . others follow' is their motto, and it is disappointing that more shops don't follow more closely. The honey-baked ham, prepared and sold here is truly superb: crusty, scored and singed on the outside, filled with flavour throughout; you cannot do better than to pack a few slices between two hunks of the brown bread made for Mark Kierans by a lady in nearby Dunleer. There is also delicious smoked turkey and, made to order, smoked rack of lamb. Their smoked salmon comes from Clarke's in Ballina, and no 'paint' is used to colour the barbecued chickens. Kierans also have a nifty tea shop and restaurant at the back of the shop.

Drogheda town centre.

ONLY NATURAL
Corner of Stockwell Street
and Dyre Street
Drogheda
Co Louth
Tel: (046) 24302 (home)
Contact: Elizabeth Hughes

Wholefood shop

Mainly of interest for the organically-grown vegetables sold here which come from Cathy Marsh in Balbriggan, and can include rarities like gypsy peppers and big yellow marrows.

Drogheda town centre.

MANNA FOODS
Unit 2
Workspace Centre
Mayorality Street
Drogheda

Eleonore Nowack's two salad dressings — Irish Dressing and Natural Garlic Dressing — made their debut in early 1989 and the former quickly won a prize as Best Irish product for that year. They are expertly made and look delicious, with the sort of

83

Tel: (041) 34624
Contact: Eleonore
Nowack

Salad dressing

handmade freshness of taste that means you can pass
them off as your own work.

Widely available through supermarkets. Telephone for
details.

DUNDALK

**THE
CONTINENTAL
MEAT CENTRE**
20 Clanbrassil Street
Dundalk
Co Louth
Tel: (042) 32829
Contact: Ann and Alo
Putz

Continental meats

The variety of cooked meats which Ann and Alo Putz
produce in their little shop is eye-opening. The array
of delicately marbled, fat-speckled sausages and
salamis is nirvana for lovers of charcuterie.
Beautifully-balanced Pastrami, which American
customers happily tell Ann Putz is better than anything
you can buy in New York, smoked beef sliced paper-
thin and suffused with flavour, spicy chorizo, soft
rotwurst and a powerful garlic and rum salami, the list
goes on, and in each item the expertise is clearly
apparent. None of the sausages or salamis or meats
are other than perfectly prepared, with an equal
balance of flavour and texture. Many of them can be
kept for many months. Their list also includes
Hungarian salami, Westphalian ham, speck, Italian
sechi, and raw meats too. You can also buy goats'
milk and country butter, made nearby by Caroline
Meegan.

Dundalk town centre.

KNOCKBRIDGE

TARA CHEESE
Dunbin
Knockbridge
Co Louth
Tel: (042) 35654
Contact: Caroline
Meegan

Farmhouse cheese

Recognisable by its red plastic coat, Tara is a semi-
soft, mild cheese made by Caroline Meegan on the
family farm a few miles from Dundalk. Caroline
trained in Holland and has been making Tara cheese
since the beginning of 1988. As well as this smooth
Edam type, which she matures for a month, Caroline
also makes quark. One attraction of Tara for the
weight-conscious is the fact that it has only eighteen
percent fat content — the cream is taken out and used
to make butter which is sold in the Continental Meat

Centre in Dundalk town. Tara cheese is sold in Quinnsworth supermarkets amongst other shops. You can also buy from the farm.

Telephone first for directions.

OMEATH

SEACO LTD
Omeath
Co Louth
Tel: (042) 75159
Contact: James
McQuaid

Oysters

Seaco Ltd is one of the nine oyster producers located on Carlingford Lough, where you will find more oysters than anywhere else in these islands. Most of the produce is exported, James McQuaid of Seaco sends all of his production of flat oysters to Cuan Sea Fisheries of Strangford, but, he says, 'If you want oysters we will never see you stuck'. Some growers supply local hotels and pubs, and if you contact any of the members of the Carlingford Lough Aquaculture Association, you should have no trouble finding something to go along with a bottle of Guinness.

Telephone for directions.

ARDEE

THE GABLES RESTAURANT, Dundalk Road, Ardee, Co Louth. Tel: (041) 53789. Contact: Michael Caine. Consistently recommended.

CARLINGFORD

JORDANS PUB & BISTRO, Newry Street, Carlingford, Tel: (042) 73223. Consistently recommended.

DROGHEDA

THE COUNTRY GARDEN, Drogheda Shopping Centre. Contact John Collier. Good greengrocer, and while you're there look out for Connolly's Deli, also in the shopping centre, which has a good cheese counter.

DUNDALK

BORD FAILTE, Market Square, Dundalk, Co Louth, Tel (042) 35484

GERMAN SALAMI CO, Tenato, Avenue Road, Dundalk. Tel: (042) 34758. Contact: Mr Albrecht. Wide range of salamis, available throughout the country.

McARDLE MOORE & CO LTD, The Dundalk Brewery, Dundalk. Tel: (042) 35441.

RAVENSDALE

TRISTA'S KITCHEN, Ballymackellet, Ravensdale, Co Louth. Tel: (042) 71168. Range of excellent mayonnaise, both plain and flavoured, distinguished by their colourful tubs. Widely available, especially in Superquinn supermarkets.

Fish can be bought from stalls on the main street in Dundalk every Thursday.

COUNTY MEATH

Drive into and around County Meath and the horizon, magically, seems to disappear. You are confronted with an endless vista of sky and air. According to some Dubliners this drives the locals insane, but it is always impossible to encounter all or any of the lunatics.

Instead of going mad, the good people of County Meath are busy pottering away on their holdings. This is the land of the small producer, growing enough for home and family and selling the surplus. Such a one is Eleanor D'Eyto of The Old Presbytery, Churchtown, Dunderry (Tel: (046) 21730), a tireless campaigner on behalf of the Organic Growers, and yet a woman who describes herself as a 'gardener'. When she has a surplus, Eleanor sets her sign out in front of the house, like many others. Unlike other counties, where 'alternative' people moved in and began to grow, Meath has no alternative folk — the land is well settled and expensive. But this does not mean that you need be doomed to a diet of well-sprayed food — Eleanor has details of the other small growers in the county, who include William Brown, Ashfield, The Green, Garristown, Kieran Cummins of Trammon, Rathmoylan, Thomas Harrington of Knightsbrook, Trim, Liz Lyons of The Cottages, Seabank, Bettystown and Dave Robinson of Rathbeggan, Dunshaughlin. All are holders of the organic symbol. Dave is also associated with the Sonairte Ecology Centre at The Ninch in Laytown, a scheme which has another site at Balbriggan (Tel: (01) 413586, contact: Tom Simpson). Sonairte is a charity, a company limited by guarantee which, it is hoped, will become a centre for alternative energy, organic gardening and energy conservation. They currently have eighteen people on government schemes and any surplus production is sold from the centre on Sunday afternoons, from 3-6pm — Sonairte is exactly one mile from Julianstown in County Meath. Drive east from Julianstown to the sea and you will see an old farmstead on the right hand side. Sonairte, by the way, means 'positive strength'.

Elsewhere Pat and Mary Stanley at Meadstown, Dunderry, will sell any surplus of their vegetables, fruit, herbs, buttermilk and jams, Tel: (046) 31174, while Gordon Evans produces worm compost at Clontall, Drumconrath, Navan under the title Leinster Earthworm Technology. Possibly the biggest producer in the county is Claire Mooney of Ashbourne (Tel: (01) 350225), who is one of the members of Organic Foods. The secret of County Meath, the way to find out who is making country butter, who has free-range eggs, that are real free-range eggs, is to ask, and you will receive.

DUNDERRY

DUNDERRY LODGE
Dunderry
Navan
Co Meath
Tel: (046) 31571
Contact: Nicholas and Catherine Healy

★ *Restaurant*

Ireland has copious resources to draw on for the capable chef. There are numerous varieties of game, the island is surrounded by rich Atlantic sea beds, inland rivers produce exquisite fresh water fish, the land is lush and the finest herbs, fruit and vegetables can easily be grown. Put all of this, plus a careful supply of some of the best of France, into the hands of chef Catherine Healy, and you have an unbeatable combination of tastes, textures, aromas and sensations. Bricollages of just-picked herbs and leaves lifted slightly with a dressing based on Provencal olive oil, raunchy game, flavourful terrines, and light delicate desserts are put together, often using produce from their own garden, where the Healy's grow an imaginative range of herbs. Added to all this is an interesting wine list, some of which Nicholas Healy imports himself. Whether or not you stay for a meal you can also purchase some imported French goods, including flavoured mustards, tapenade, anchoiade, Provencal olive oil, Dunderry home made preserves, and a selection of imported wine, including: Vins de Savoie: Chignin Bergeron, Coteaux de Tomery;

88

Chignin, Coteaux de Tormery (both white) and Mondeuse, Coteaux du Tomery (red). Ask about other rare wines.

Going from Dublin, drive to Navan. From Navan take the Athboy road. Drive for four and a half miles and you will come to a crossroads. Turn left. Dunderry Lodge is well signposted from there on.

GORMANSTOWN

KEENOGUE CHEESE
Gormanstown
Co Meath
Tel: (041) 29060
Contact: Eileen McCullough

Farmhouse cheese

Keenogue is a Caerphilly-type cheese made from the raw milk of Fresian cows. Eileen McCullough ages the cheese for between six to eight weeks which allows the complex crumbliness of a Caerphilly to develop. You can find the cheese in the Connolly's shops in Navan, Dundalk and Drogheda, and also the Cheeseboard in Dublin. Eileen also sells from the farm.

Going south from Drogheda drive one and a half miles past Julianstown. There is an ESSO station on the left hand side and the farm is the first entrance on the right hand side down from the garage.

KELLS

MARTRY MILL
Tallon's Mills
Martry
Kells
Co Meath
Tel: (046) 28800
Contact: James Tallon

Stoneground wholemeal flour

It can be difficult to find the excellent, coarse Martry Mill flour, but worth the effort. Production at Tallon's Mill has changed little over the centuries and the flour is very different from the commercial flours we export today. You can buy from the mill in Martry, and the flour can be found in some wholefood shops in Meath and Westmeath.

Telephone for directions.

RATHMOYLAN

DE BRAAM MINERAL WATER

Rathmolyan
Co Meath
Tel: (0405) 55082
Contact: Ms Dorian de Braam

The mineral water revolution in Ireland which was begun by Ballygowan, has seen the birth of many local waters, but few are as interesting as de Braam. Sold in a tall glass bottle, there are both still and sparkling varieties, and the latter is particularly pleasing.

De Braam water is now quite widely available in good food shops. Telephone for more details.

KILMESSAN

THE STATION HOUSE HOTEL, Kilmessan, Co Meath. Tel: (046) 25239/25588. Contact: The Slattery family. Consistently recommended.

COUNTY OFFALY

The county of Offaly is characterised by the tentacles of the Grand Canal that writhe their way from near Kilbeggan in the north, way beyond Tullamore in the centre and across Mountmellick and Portarlington in the south over to Dublin.

In the county's heyday the canal was full of craft taking linen and turf to Dublin, and even though the waterway is no longer used, the county still reaps the benefits through strong sturdy buildings, and elegant tidy towns, the remnants of great wealth. There are some aspects of Offaly that almost look English: village greens, water pumps and extenuated fields are not features of the neighbouring counties.

However the feeling of affluence as you drive through is not matched by good food. Apart from one cheesemaker and one good sausage maker, the county is quite bereft.

BALLYCOMER

BALLYARD FOODS
Ballair Estate
Ballycumer
Co Offaly
Tel: (0506) 36113
Contact: Ballyard Foods

Farmhouse cows' cheese

Mont Belair is a Gouda type cows' milk cheese, made by Ballyard Foods and distributed by the Traditional Cheese Company.

Telephone for more details.

BIRR

ANITA BULFIN
Derrinlough House
Birr
Co Offaly

Anita Bulfin grows a wide variety of fruit and vegetables, everything from red cabbage to cherry tomatoes to fennel, on a one acre site using a polytunnel. She sells them in the Harvest shop in the

91

Tel: (0509) 33094

Organic grower

Market Square, Birr, as well as to the Fox's Den Restaurant in Cloughjordan, amongst other local shops and restaurants. Holder of IOFGA symbol. The only other holders of the symbol in the county are George and Walburga va Ow of Raheenbeg, Geashill, Co Offaly.

Telephone for more details.

MONEYGALL

RUDDS'
Busherstown House
Moneygall
Co Offaly
Tel: (0505) 45206
Contact: David Rudd

Sausages, black pudding, bacon and pork pies

David Rudd left his Dublin job in advertising and took his family to Moneygall to make sausages. They bought a large Georgian house, and set about the business of turning it into a cottage industry. Now they sell antibiotic-free sausages and bacon, made to old-fashioned recipes, as well as a delicious black pudding. Best of all, though, are their wonderful pork pies.

Look out for Rudd's products in the Midlands, and you can also find them in Superquinn, in Blackrock, Ballinteer, Bray, Knocklyon, Sutton and Swords; Nolan's, Clontarf; and Super Value, Mount Merrion.

COUNTY WESTMEATH

The lakes of County Westmeath give the first geographical suggestion that the east is behind you and the west just beginning. Drive from Dublin westwards and it is the first glimpse of Lough Owel and Lough Errel along with the ending of the Grand Canal which signals that one has entered into another culture, another view of life. By the time you reach Athlone, the consciousness of the River Shannon is suddenly everywhere.

James Joyce once described Mullingar as the most boring town in Ireland, a sentiment which is always uppermost in the minds of visitors and makes the locals defensive. You get the impression of a town which is trying hard to be characterful, and yet not quite managing to succeed. Athlone, a more confident place altogether is, in fact, less colourful.

MOATE

ARDNURCHER GOAT FARM
Horseleap
Moate
Co Westmeath
Tel: (0506) 35112
Contact: the Temperli family

Goats' milk ice cream

This is a new company that makes a most delicious goats' ice cream. It's made from pasteurized goats' milk, and they also sell a cows' milk ice cream to restaurants. Flavours are vanilla, chocolate and strawberry.

Take the Galway road from Dublin and go through Horseleap. Look out for a large garden centre, and there is a road opposite (next to the Post office) signposted to Clara. The house is a large Georgian rectory on the left — phone for precise details. You can buy the ice cream in some branches of Superquinn as well as Nolan's of Clontarf and Cavistons in Sandycove.

MULLINGAR

GOKI'S MEATS LTD

Streamstown House
Streamstown
Mullingar
Tel: (044) 26340
Contact: Volker
Gonserowski

German butcher

At the rear of the splendid Streamstown House is Gokis Meats. Here you can buy the myriad and magnificent German meats Volker Gonserowski prepares. Volker was a butcher in Germany for over twenty years before coming to Ireland, and his expertise shames the victuallers of his new country. Meat-filled frankfurters, the best pork pate you can get north of France, lemony smoked hams — there is a feast here for the carnivore. Look out especially for Tower Meat, an expensive but unique meat, cut paper thin, but laden with diffuse tastes. It's a recipe that Volker has created himself.

The shop is open Mon 9-6pm, Tues 9-6pm, Wed 2-6pm, Sat by appointment, but Volker stresses that if there is someone in the house it will always be possible to buy meat. Streamstown House is half a mile from Streamstown which is off the road from Mullingar to Athlone. The house has fine white gates — you can't miss it — turn left at the pub in Streamstown. Goki's Meats all have a drawing of a monk on their wrapping.

GIGGINSTOWN CHEESE

Gigginstown
Collinstown
Mullingar
Co Westmeath
Tel: (044) 72143
Contact: Thomas Drumn

Farmhouse cows' cheese

Gigginstown is a dancing cheese — locals pronounce it Jig-instown and a well handled piece of this mature territorial cheese should have you dancing. Sue Farrell makes this cheese from the raw milk of fresian cows. It has a natural rind and is aged for between four to six months. Like a good territorial it has a distinctive taste peculiar to the area in which it is made.

You can buy the cheese from the farm, but it is extremely difficult to find. Ring for detailed directions. Otherwise the cheese is widely available throughout the country.

MULTYFARNHAM

MULTYFARNMHAM DEER FARM
Clonbugh Farm
Multifarnham
Co Westmeath
Tel: (044) 71117
Contact: Chris Burley

Deer farm

Driving on the main N4 road out of Mullingar you can see frisky deer scampering about. This is The Multyfarnham Deer Farm, who have about twelve hundred fallow deer in total. Chris Burley supplies his venison to good restaurants and sells privately from the farm, the season running from September to January. He also arranges for some of the venison to be smoked. Callers are welcome to the farm, and if you telephone first orders can be made up before you call.

Drive six miles out of Mullingar on the main N4 road to Longford/Sligo. You will pass the Covert pub on the right-hand side. Three quarters of a mile further on there is a gate lodge with white windows. This is Multyfarnham.

TYRRELLSPASS

DAVID G COUPER
Inse Riada
Tyrrellspass
Co Westmeath
Tel: (044) 23114
Contact: David G Couper

Organic beef and lamb

David Couper produces organic beef and lamb, arranges slaughtering and preparation by a local butcher and will deliver the prepared meat anywhere within a sixty to eighty mile radius. The smallest order he takes is usually for about thirty pounds of meat, but as his cattle are Dexter cattle a side of beef will tend to be quite small, about one hundred and fifty pounds. You can ring with an order, David will prepare the meat and hang it: two weeks for beef, ten days for lamb, and you can then either collect or arrange delivery.

Telephone for more details.

ATHLONE

BORD FAILTE, 17 Church Street, Athlone, Co
Westmeath, Tel: (0902) 72866

MULLINGAR

BORD FAILTE, Dublin Road, Mullingar, Co
Westmeath,. Tel: (044) 48650

CROOKEDWOOD HOUSE, Mullingar, Co
Westmeath, Tel: (044) 42165. A restaurant highly
spoken of by locals and much prized by German
visitors. Open Dinner 7-10pm, and Sunday lunch.
Consistently recommended.

NUTS AND GRAINS, Dominican Place, Grove Street,
Mullingar, Co Westmeath. Tel: (044) 40238, Contact:
Rita McKeown. You can order country butter, place
orders for Multyfarnham deer, get Compsey yogurt,
and Martry Mill flour, along with the usual pills and
pulses.

COUNTY WEXFORD

Wexford is the county of honey. Drive anywhere throughout it after a good summer and you will be urged by numerous signs to buy honey direct from the producer. There are many large scale producers also, but their honey is often the produce of more than one country, never mind one county. Much better are the folk who simply keep a few hives at the bottom of the garden — the bees are never fed on sugar and the honey can be clean rather than cloying. Look out especially for the faintly-green clover honey.

Wexford town itself is dominated by its main street, a narrow thoroughfare that never makes the town seem claustrophobic. The other streets in the town scramble quickly upwards from the sea, but the main street waddles and winds its way lazily from end to end. During the Wexford Opera festival folk throng to the town and put up in White's Hotel and for ten days the place is dizzy.Then everything settles back down again and the town becomes a normal rural place, quietly going about its business.

BALLYHACK

NEPTUNE RESTAURANT
Ballyhack
Co Wexford
Tel: (051) 89284
Contact: Pierce and Valerie McAuliffe

Restaurant

The best way to approach this lovely restaurant is to jaunt across on the ferry-boat from Passage East in Co Waterford — the short journey sharpens the senses and the appetite. There is a neat glass-cased verandah which is perfect for lunch, though it is the sort of intimate setting that makes Irish eaters extra diffident. Stick to fish, which they serve simply and confidently.

Open lunch and dinner, Ballyhack village.

CROSSABEG

INNISGLAS TRUST

The Deeps
Crossabeg
Co Wexford
Tel: (053) 28226
Contact: Anthony and
Eve (the Mill), Thomas
(the cheese) Emla (pork,
and vegetables), Derek
(the bakery) or Jeanie
(honey)

*Farmhouse cheese,
bread, flour, tree
nursery, organic
vegetables, honey*

The Innisglass community produce flour — they buy local wheat and Anthony Kaye grinds it in their mill — nettle cheese, made by Thomas Grimm, organic symbol-standard vegetables, which they grow for the South East Organic Growers and free-range pigs — they can take orders for large amounts. They also bake bread at the bakery, and produce jars of honey.

A lot of Innisglass produce is sold in Humble Natural Foods in Wexford town, otherwise you can find the cheese all over the country, and the bread gets as far as Dublin — you can buy it in the fortnightly Co-op market. Visitors are welcome at the farm, Take the Crossabeg road from Wexford. Turn left at the sign post to Killerin, and it's one and a half miles on the left.

ENNISCORTHY

CROGHAN CHEESE

Ballynadrishogue
Blackwater
Enniscorthy
Co Wexford
Tel: (053) 29331
Contact: Luc and Ann
Van Kampen

Farmhouse cheese

Luc and Ann Van Kampen make the creamy soft Croghan cheese in three flavours: plain, parsley and chive, green and black pepper and garlic. They make a semi-hard cheese which is aged for two months. If you have the plain cheese, smear it on a hunk of bread, dot it with slivers of sun dried tomato and toast it under the grill.

The cheeses are distributed by the Traditional Cheese Company, and can be found in Fothergills in Dublin and Humble Natural Foods in Wexford amongst other places. Telephone for more details.

DAVID HASSLACHER

Clonhaston
Enniscorthy
Co Wexford
Tel: (054) 33147

Asparagus grower.

Telephone for more details.

Contact: David
Hasslacher

Asparagus

ST KILLIAN &
EMERALD IRISH
BRIE
Adamstown
Enniscorthy
Co Wexford
Tel: (054) 40560
Contact: Patrick and
Juliet Berridge

*Farmhouse cows'
cheeses*

St Killian, a soft, hexagonal shaped camembert-type cheese, is perhaps the cheese you will see for sale most often in Ireland. Patrick Berridge is the largest producer amongst the farmhouse cheesemakers, making Emerald brie, which comes in a large wheel, as well as St Killian. Try to eat both when they are beginning to weep.

Telephone for more details.

GOREY

MARLFIELD
HOUSE
Gorey
Co Wexford
Tel: (055)
21124/21572
Telex: 80757
Fax: 21572
Contact: Mary Bowe

Country house
➥ *Restaurant*

Marlfield House is a regency house that has been extended with a conservatory and a new wing of fine luxury bedrooms. The latest asset of the organisation is chef Stephen Doherty, former Head Chef of Le Gavroche in London. It's expected that the new chef will continue the excellent cooking that earned him three Michelin stars in London, but as this book went to press he had only been in the restaurant a matter of days.

Telephone for details, reservations are essential. Open for lunch 1-2pm, dinner 7.30pm-9.30pm.

99

MURRINTOWN

HERENFORD FARM

Kilmannon
Murrintown
Co Wexford
Tel: (053) 39412
Contact: Tom and Lise
Anne Kearns

Organic fruit and vegetables

Holders of IOFGA symbol, growing fruit and vegetables which they sell locally to shops, hotels and restaurants. In the long term Tom and Lise Anne hope to grow kiwi fruit to add to their raspberries, strawberries and blueberries.

Telephone for directions and details.

NEW ROSS

MURT AND LIZ FLYNN

Poulmaloe
Whitechurch
New Ross
Co Wexford
Tel: (051) 88454
Contact: Murt and Liz

Organic growers

IOFGA symbol holders, Murt and Liz supply some local hotels and restaurants with vegetables, fruit and herbs and some of their produce goes to Organic Foods. They are members of the South East Organic Growers' Group, and have details of other members.

Telephone for more details.

DESMOND AND OLIVE THORPE

Knocknoe House
New Ross
Co Wexford
Tel: (051) 24557
Contact: Desmond and Olive

Organic growers

Holder of the IOFGA symbol, growers of cereals and vegetable. Produce also lamb and beef.

Telephone for more details.

RICHARD AND IVAN WARD

Fortagusta

Holders of the IOFGA symbol — growers of cereals which they supply to Ballybrado farm and also lamb which can be found in Superquinn supermarkets.

100

Arthurstown
New Ross
Co Wexford
Tel: (051) 89113
Contact: Richard and
Ivan

Vegetables from the South East can be found in the L+N supermarket in Wexford town. Also in Pettits supermarket and Humble Natural Foods, in Wexford.

Organic growers

SLIEVECOILTE
The Goat Farm
Terrerath
New Ross
Co Wexford
Contact: Aine Kent

Slievecoilte cheese is made by Aine Kent in New Ross. Write to her for more details.

Write for further details.

Farmhouse cheese

WEXFORD

HUMBLE NATURAL FOODS
Lower Rowe Street
Wexford
Tel: (053) 24624
Contact: Catherine
Reilly and Heike
Weiehagen

A tiny little shop just off the main street in Wexford. Here you can find cheeses and bread from the Innisglass Trust, a fine country butter made by Mr Carr and splendid clover honey, from Curracloe. Contact DJ Deasy Tel: (053) 37145. Also local yogurts and organic vegetables from the South East Growers. Catherine and Heike are both friendly and knowledgeable about anything and everything going on in Wexford, so this is a good place for information too. Don't miss the jars of pickled cucumber, and the apple date cakes.

Just off the Main Street in Wexford Town.

101

LETT BROTHERS LTD
Batt Street
Wexford
Co Wexford
Tel: (053) 22811
Contact: Maurice
Roche

Mussels

Lett and Company are the largest single producer of processed mussel dishes in Ireland. They use bottom dredged mussels, unlike fishermen on the west coast where most of the mussels are rope cultured.

Telephone for further details.

WEXFORD HONEY
At the end of a good summer, like 1989, Wexford is abuzz with honey. Some of the better ones to watch out for are Jim Kenny's Golden Hive, Enniscorthy; Bolgers honey made by the Bolger family in Enniscorthy and, widely available, Walshe's Honey from Carrickbyrne. There is also honey from the Innisglas Trust, and, best of all, Clover Honey from Curracloe, made by DJ Deasy — Tel: (053) 37145.

BALLYCOGLEY

KEVIN CARR, Littletown, Ballycogley, Co Wexford. Tel: (053) 35313 organic vegetables

ENNISCORTHY

JOHN MAGEE, Coolroe, Clonegal, Enniscorthy, Co Wexford, organic vegetables

DAVID STOREY, Bleachlands, Oylegate, Enniscorthy, Co Wexford. Tel: (053) 38147. Organic vegetables and fruit.

FOULKSMILLS

HORETOWN HOUSE, Foulksmills, Co Wexford. Tel: (051) 63663/63706. Open for dinner Tues-Sat 7-9pm and lunch by advance booking. Telephone for details. Consistently recommended.

GOREY

MICHAEL O'CONNOR, Rathpierce, Gorey, Co Wexford. Producer of organic cereals and vegetables

ULRICH ROESLER, Wells Ho, Gorey, Co Wexford. Producer of organic cereals, beef and vegetables

TAGHMON

PAULINE STAFFORD, Ballyhurst Street, Taghmon, Co Wexford. Tel: (053) 34191. Organic vegetables.

WEXFORD

BORD FAILTE, Crescent Quay, Wexford, Co Wexford. Tel: (053) 23111.

THE CELLAR RESTAURANT, Wexford Arts Centre, Cornmarket. Tel: (053) 23764. Contact: Heidi Funder. Heidi also runs a catering service cooking for private parties. Tel: (053) 39404.

LA CUISINE DELICATESSEN, 80 North Main Street, Wexford. Tel: (053) 24986. Contact: Philip and Brigid Doyle. Good deli with selection of local products.

JAMES MEYLER, Fishmonger, The Bull Ring, Tel: (053) 22339/41990. Good wholesale and retail fish shop with salmon smoked on the premises. Fresh fish is also sold on the coast at Curracloe and Fethard-on-Sea.

WEXFORD PRESERVES, available in La Cuisine Deli, North Main Street. A range of excellent fruit preserves — telephone them at (053) 24353 for more details.

WEXFORD COUNTRY MARKET, The Bull Ring, Friday, 9.30am.

COUNTY WICKLOW

The proximity of Wicklow to Dublin has robbed it of a sense of true independence, and left it something of an adjunct to the capital; a place where commuters return in the evening, and where weekenders keep houses that are empty for most of the year.

The county is a strange mixture of the genteel and the brash: remaindered ladies almost rub shoulders with noisy offspring in places like Bray. There are gentle villages with bellicose day trippers, polite tea rooms and boisterous fast food bars. Overall, there is no Wicklow character to set it apart as a county and a community: you have to take the old with the new, and make what you can of it.

BRAY

THE TREE OF IDLENESS
Seafront
Bray
Co Wicklow
Tel: (01)
Contact: Akis and
Susan Courtellas

➥ Greek Cypriot
restaurant

Akis Courtellas has won stars for his cooking and for his wine list including the coveted Egon Ronay Wine List of the Year for Great Britain and Ireland. But though his wine list may be a truly awesome selection of vintages and varietals, it is for his cooking that he is more often feted. Combining rusticity with culinary flamboyance, Akis Courtellas has redefined simple Greek cooking with outlines drawn from the nineteen eighties. The elegant strictures of modern cuisine refuse to be coy under his hands as he lavishes Mediterranean abundance on every offering. A meal here is always a marvellous indulgence.

The South side of the Seafront at Bray. Open for dinner from 7.30-11pm, Sunday 7.30-10pm, Closed Monday.

ENNISKERRY

THE POWERSCOURT ARMS HOTEL
Enniskerry

After a thirst-creating stroll around Powerscourt Gardens, take yourself off to the public bar of this picturesque hotel in the square of Enniskerry and drink a pint of their Guinness. For some reason it

105

Co Wicklow
Tel: (01) 863507
Contact: The Manager

Pub

tastes creamier and better than most pints you will come across. We don't know how they do it, but we're glad they do.

Facing the square in Enniskerry.

KILCOOLE

NORTH WICKLOW COUNTRY MARKET
St Patrick's Hall
Kilcoole
Co Wicklow
Tel: (01) 874317
Contact: Mrs Jackson

Food market

Beautiful cut flowers, fine free-range chickens from Newcastle, fresh cream, country butter and fine baking mean that the North Wicklow Country Market doesn't last very long. It starts at 10.30am on Saturday and make sure you are early otherwise the cute local folk will have snapped up everything.

10.30am Saturday. The hall is signposted as you drive into Kilcoole — look for the sign, on the right hand side of the road as you drive from Dublin.

KILPEDDER

MARC MICHEL
Tinna Park House
Kilpedder
Co Wicklow
Tel: (01) 819726
Contact: Marc Michel

Organic grower

Some of Marc Michel's produce is sold to Organic Foods, but he also operates a unique organic delivery service ranging from Grafton Street in Dublin to Ashford to Kiltiernan and down to the coast. If you place an order in the spring you can receive a steady stream of excellent vegetables as they come into season. Marc will supply a variety box weekly and any other particular orders.

Telephone for more details.

KILTEGAN

DENIS HEALY
Talbotstown
Lower Kiltegan
Co Wicklow
Tel: (0508) 73193
Contact: Denis Healy

Denis Healy is one member of Organic Foods, an organisation of organic growers which arranges supplies of produce into seven Quinnsworth supermarkets, all of the Superquinn supermarkets and to Fitzers on Camden Street in Dublin, and What on Earth in Harold's Cross in Dublin. Other producers in

106

Organic grower

Organic Foods are Clare Mooney of Killegland, Ashbourne, Co Meath (Tel: (01) 350225) and Ken Cummins and Lyn Venables of Ringwood, Freshford, Co Kilkenny (Tel: (01) 32188).

Telephone for more details.

UTE LANGE
Ballinroan
Kiltegan
Co Wicklow
Tel: (0506) 73278
Contact: Ute Lange

Organic grower

The Langes grow carrots and leeks organically, as well as broccoli, french beans, beetroot and cabbage. Much of their produce is distributed by Organic Foods (Denis Healy is their neighbour). You can find some of it in the Dublin Co-op.

Telephone for further details.

KILMACANOGUE

COPSEWOOD YOGURT
Kilmacanogue
Co Wicklow
Tel: (01) 862081
Contact: Edward Drew

Goats' and cows' milk yogurt, soft goats' cheese

Freda and Connie Baker must be the longest-established makers of yogurt in Ireland. Sadness was felt throughout the country when Connie Baker died of cancer in January 1987. But the traditional making of yogurt still continues. The cow's milk yogurt, plain or flavoured, the Greek-style strained yogurt, and the goats' milk yogurt, for which they are famed, all come from their pedigree herds and unpasteurized milk is used. They also make country butter which is hand churned, and a variety of soft cheeses. None of their products contain any preservatives or additives which gives their cheese a lovely, earthy, yellowish colour, unpalatable to those who prefer their cheese bleached white. Everything they make is constructed with dedication to a passing tradition.

Drive through the village of Kilmacanogue and go through the first gate on the left as you drive towards Greystones. The yogurt-making room is at an entrance to the right.

ROUNDWOOD

ROUNDWOOD SUNDAY MARKET
Parish Hall
Roundwood
Co Wicklow
Contact: The Committee

Market

Mountains of good home baking, delicious lemonades, country butter, fresh herbs and flowers fill the Parish Hall in the centre of Roundwood every Sunday from March to December. The volume of business tends to put the helpful ladies into a tizzy, so be patient.

Roundwood town centre.

BALLYSHEMANE DEER FARM
Near Roundwood
Co Wicklow
Tel: (0404) 46114
Contact: Franz
Waldburg

Farmed deer

Franz Waldburg is one of a tiny handful of farmers producing venison. He sells to hotels and restaurants in the area and as far away as Rosslare. The farmed venison is available all year around. Franz sells only the complete carcass.

Telephone for more details.

ARKLOW

I.D.A.S. LTD, Woodenbridge, Arklow, Co Wicklow. Tel: (0402) 5233. Excellent smoked trout available in supermarkets, especially Superquinn.

ASHFORD

WENDY NAIRN, The Arches, Glanmore, Ashford, Co Wicklow. Organic Grower.

BRAY

THE NUT KEG, Quinsborough Centre, Tel: (01) 861793 Contact: Roger White (also in Swords) Bread, home-made dips, organic vegetables, Copsewood Cheese and Yogurt

GLEN OF THE DOWNS

OLD MacDONNELL'S FARM, Glen of the Downs, Co Wicklow, Tel: (01) 828992. Widely available yogurts.

ENNISKERRY

POPPIES RESTAURANT, Enniskerry, Co Wicklow. Home baking, jams.

TALLON'S DELI, Enniskerry, Co Wicklow. Organic veg, goats' cheese

KILMACANOGUE

BALLYMACAD FARM, Kilmacanogue, Co Wicklow, Tel: (01) 868964. Goats' milk — you can buy it in the Nut Keg, Bray.

NEWTOWNMOUNTKENNEDY

DRUMBAWN FARM, Newtownmountkennedy, Co Wicklow. Tel: (01) 819794. Contact: Tom Dolan. Free-range egg producer.

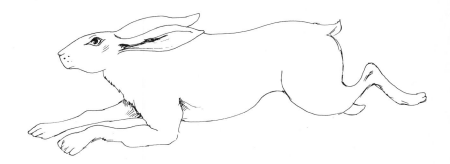

Munster

COUNTY CLARE

Nowhere is as beautiful, and as harsh, as the Burren in County Clare. Striated rocks dominate the landscape, with pockets of pasture that appear to have been afterthoughts in the formation of the land. The word boireann means a rocky place, and the wending hills and valleys are suffused with limestone. This gives the Burren its abiding sense of mystery _ how, and why, did it all come about, you ask as you look down from the top of Corkscrew Hill. The densely detailed map of the area produced by Tim Robinson shows not only 'Holy Wells', known for toothache cures, but also a 'Blessed Bush, and marks of St Brigid's Knees', and even 'a strange field'. In truth, everything about the Burren is strange and mesmerising.

THE BURREN

AILLWEE CAVE CO LTD
Ballyvaughan
Co Clare
Tel: (065)
77036/77067
Contact: Roger or Ben
Johnson

*Burren Gold Cheese,
Burren Natural
Preserves, Gleninsheen
Spring Water,
Christmas hampers,
restaurant,
kitchenshop, home-
made salami*

Alongside the spectacular caves the Johnson family have built up quite an industry of food production. The Gleninsheen water is natural spring water from the caves. They bottle it and sell it uncarbonated. They also make rich fruit jams and marmalades (including a bitter sweet Wild Damson Jam), and put together Christmas hampers of quality Irish foodstuffs. The kitchenshop sells china, and you can also buy wine. In the cave they have designed an imposing restaurant, selling teas, cakes and coffees throughout the day, soups, pies, sandwiches and such at lunchtime. All the produce in the restaurant is home-made. Burren Gold cheese also comes from this eclectic organisation. Ben Johnson, who also makes good salamis, is happy to show you around the cheese-making room, and sells three gouda-type cheeses: plain, black pepper, and garlic with chives. All are made from unpasteurised milk, and are another good reason to visit the caves.
The caves are signposted throughout the county. The farmshop is the first building you come to, the restaurant is up inside the caves. Both are open all day.

RECIPE: GARLIC CHEESE POTATO GRATIN

2lbs potatoes; three quarters of a pint of milk; salt and pepper; 4oz grated garlic farmhouse cheese; cream; butter. Slice the potatoes as thinly as possible, preferably using a mandolin. Butter a gratin or casserole dish. Put in a layer of potato, sprinkle with a little salt and pepper, and cast on a thin sprinkling of cheese. Repeat this until all the potatoes are used up. Warm the milk in a saucepan. Pour over the dish until you reach a level with the top of the potatoes. Pour some cream on top, and dot with knobs of butter. Bake in a hot oven (400F, 200C, Gas 6) for about one hour. The top should be crisp and browned, the potatoes melded to a creamy completeness.

ANNALIESE BARTELINK

Poulcoin
Kilnaboy
Co Clare
Contact: Annaliese
Bartelink

Farmhouse cows' cheese, farmhouse goats' cheese

Annaliese Bartelink is a Dutch woman living in the lunar landscape of the Burren. Her house perches on the side of a steep hill, a collection of rounded buildings with sweeping windowed, thatch roofs, thatched by her husband Harry. The cheese is made from both cows' and goats' milk, all from animals from the farm. At its best her cows' cheese matures to a melting creamy texture, throbbing with taste. If you can arrange to buy a fully mature cows' cheese by post, you will receive one of the best cheeses in the country. Annaliese makes the cows' cheese in four flavours: celery and cumin, garlic, pepper and thyme and, best of all, the plain. The goats' cheese is a

114

harder cheese, which is usually made plain, though sometimes flavoured varieties are available.

Annaliese will send cheese in the post, which is cheaper than you would imagine. She also delivers in the locality. The cheese is available in Hylands of Ballyroughan, The County Lane, Ennistymon, McMahons, Kinvara and occasionally in The Iona wholefood shop in Hollywood, Co Down.

GALWAY BAY OYSTER FARMS
Pond House
Burren
Co Clare
Tel: (065) 78126
Contact: Mark Hellmore

Shellfish exporter

Mark Hellmore produces all his shellfish for the export market with the exception of supplying a few local hotels. The area in which he works has one of the greatest varieties of marine life in the world, and he exports spider and brown crab and clams along with the better known types of shellfish. All his produce is transported live, in seawater.

Telephone for more details.

GERRY HOWARD
La Verna
Lisdoonvarna
Co Clare
Tel: (065) 74032
Contact: Gerry Howard

Butcher

Gerry Howard is best known for his sausages, which are widely available around Lisdoonvarna, but he is careful to oversee the entire cycle of production of the meat he sells and thus maintain the quality.

Lisdoonvarna town centre.

KILSHANNY FARMHOUSE CHEESE
Derry House
Lahinch
Co Clare
Tel: (065) 71228
Contact: Peter and Janette Nibbering

Five flavours of Gouda-type cheese are produced here in Lahinch: plain, cumin, garlic, garden herb, and green pepper. They are made by Peter and Janette Nibbering. The rind is waxed and the cheeses mature well. Raw milk is used from the farm next door. If you want to stay the night in a cheese factory, they do B&B as well.

Telephone for precise directions if you want to buy cheese

115

Farmhouse cows' cheese

from the house. Otherwise you can buy it at the Limerick Saturday market.

REDBANK SHELLFISH
New Quay
Burren
Co Clare
Tel: (065) 78105
Contact: Gerry O'Halloran

Shellfish

You can buy local and Pacific Oysters direct from the Redbank premises. They also sell lobsters, crayfish and sea urchins. Any amount, large or small, will be accommodated.

The Company buildings are situated behind Linnane's Bar at New Quay.

ROADSIDE TAVERN
Lisdoonvarna
Co Clare
Tel: (065) 74084
Contact: Peter Curtin

Smoked salmon and trout

'It's got to do with the socio-economics of around here' said Peter Curtin who not only runs a characterful wood-panelled pub, but operates a smoking house too. He produces smoked trout and cold smoked salmon.

Lisdoonvarna town centre. You can buy the salmon from the pub.

ENNIS

INAGH FARMHOUSE CHEESES
Inagh
Co Clare
Tel: (065) 26633
Contact: Meg and Derrick Gordon

★ *Farmhouse cheeses*

Meg and Derrick Gordon live in a picture book farmhouse with dogs, cats, cockerels, chickens and two haughty guinea fowl who strut around the farmyard inspecting everyone and everything. The love that Meg exudes towards her exquisite goats is reflected in the quality of the cheese, which is unsalted, and sold as a hard cheese with a developing flavour and maturity (Lough Caum), and two soft cheeses: a log and four-ounce 'crottins' (St Tola), all with natural rinds.

You can sometimes buy cheese from the farm, though Meg is usually cleaned out of everything by cheese shops from Galway (McCambridges) to Dublin (The Cheeseboard). The Gordon's free-range eggs and plenty of their cheese are

116

used in The Cloister restaurant on Abbey Street in Ennis, Tel: (065) 29521, Open: 10.30am-10pm.

AN TEACH BAN
Newhall
Ennis
Co Clare
Tel: (065) 36792
Contact: Sigrid Gilger
or Jean Ready

Herb teas

This is a herb and spices company that makes a delicate and delicious series of herb teas. Look out particularly for their agrestic Slimmers' Lemon Leaf Tea.

Telephone for more details.

ENNISTYMON

COUNTRY LANE
Main Street
Ennistymon
Co Clare
Tel: (065) 71138
Contact: Catherine
Lane

Wholefood shop

Amidst the predictable batches of wholefoods in Catherine Lane's shop you can find excellent sourdough bread, real free-range eggs from hens and ducks, a delicious chocolate fudge from Ennistymon, and all the local cheeses.

Ennistymon town centre.

KILRUSH

SAINT MARTIN CHEESE
Carnanes
Kilrush
Co Clare
Tel: (065) 51320
Contact: Eileen
O'Brien

Farmhouse cows' cheese

Eileen O'Brien uses the raw milk of her fresian cows to make Saint Martin Cheese. Of all the goudas produced in Ireland this is the most unusual: a close textured cheese with a dusted orange rind. Eileen ages the small cheese for a month and distributes it herself in the locality.

The cheese can be found in the Supervalu in Kilrush, Mortell's in Limerick, Shannon Duty Free, and the Cheeseboard in Dublin. You can buy from the farm. Telephone for directions.

THE SHANNON REGION OF CLARE

BUNRATTY MEAD & LIQUEUR CO
Bunratty Winery
Bunratty
Co Clare
Tel: (061) 62222
Contact: Oliver Dillon

Mead

Mead has a reputation for giving one powers of fertility and virility, and rumour has it that bride and groom drank this honey liqueur every night for a month after the wedding. Thus: the honeymoon. Mead is still made in Ireland at the winery beside Bunratty Castle. It's a scrumptious brew made from honey, grape juice and herbs, and it's strengthened to 14.5 per cent vol.

Drive on behind Durty Nelly's Pub where you will see the signs to the Winery.

CRATLOE HILLS CHEESE
Brickhill
Cratloe
Co Clare
Tel: (061) 87185
Contact: Sean &
Deirdre Fitzgerald

Farmhouse sheeps' cheese

The only Southern Irish sheeps' cheese is made in Cratloe, just outside Limerick. Following a great Mediterranean tradition Sean and Deirdre Fitzgerald take milk from their Friesland Ewes and make it into a mild white cheese. The milk is pasteurised and the cheese ripened for up to eight weeks.

Leave the Ennis/Limerick dual carriageway at the sign for Knappogue Castle (there's a Maxol Station on the corner). Follow the road through Cratloe village until you get to the 'Cratloe' sign indicating the end of the village (facing away from you). Take the next road on the left over the little hump bridge. The road leads to the farmhouse. The cheese is sold throughout the country, especially in Limerick and Shannon Duty Free. They also sell from the farm.

MacCLOSKEY'S RESTAURANT
Bunratty House Mews
Bunratty
Co Clare
Tel: (061) 364082
Contact: Jerry and
Marie MacCloskey

Restaurant

MacCloskey's is an excellent restaurant. Understated and efficient, its experiments are cautious but effective, and the five courses of the table d'hote form a seamless symphony of tastes which complement and applaud one another. The vegetables come crisply al dente, the lamb meltingly tender, the free-range chicken filled with flavour. They also use more crockery per serving than any other restaurant — do leave a tip for the dishwasher.
Signposted from the centre of Bunratty. Open 7pm-10pm Tues-Sat.

118

WHITEGATE

HELGA FRIEDMACHER
Dereney
Whitegate
Co Clare
Tel: (0619) 27105
Contact: Helga
Friedmacher

Organic farmer

Helga sells all types of organic vegetables. Look out especially for her organic beef tomatoes. Her vegetables are available between mid-April and Christmas.

Helga is just off the road between Scariff and Portumna. Ask directions in Whitegate, or telephone. You can also buy her produce at Eats of Eden in Limerick city centre.

ENNIS

MULQUEEN'S BAKERY, 2 Parnell Street, Ennis. Tel: (065) 24356. Contact: Mr A. Mulqueen. The bakery sells gluten free bread and diabetic cakes to order. Best of all visit for the Dublin Gur Cake — two of the bakers trained in the capital.

OPEN SESAME, Parnell St, Ennis. Wholefood shop with organic vegetables.

QUINSLOW DELICATESSEN, 24 O'Connell Street, Ennis. Tel: (065) 20246. The Deli sells Kilshanny cheese and Limerick County Pickle amongst other meats, cheeses and tins.

COUNTY CORK

Cork is the food capital of Ireland. Nowhere else enjoys so many producers, growers, smokers, cheesemakers and restaurateurs whose discrimination and ability can be relied upon. The best smoked fish in the country comes from here; there are restaurants whose inventiveness is a joy, cheesemakers whose diligently-made farmhouse cheeses are original and distinctive. The traditional dishes of the area still survive: O'Reilly's shop in Cork's covered market sells only tripe and drisheen and the city's restaurants will often serve this enigmatic combination. You can buy salted ling; barmbrack is happily ubiquitous. Above all, there is a sense of enjoyment and indulgence towards food, helped by a feeling of abundance that is almost Mediterranean.

Happily, this wealth of food is not accompanied by any snobbery or artifice; Corkonians take their good fortune quietly but confidently, and show no diffidence when it comes to describing the food they enjoy. Growers, producers, sellers and restaurateurs will often tell you, in their delicious sing-song accents, that yes, there is another fellow elsewhere making similar food, but, well, he just isn't as good.

Often they are right (but not always!). You can travel through Cork and never encounter that blight of Irish food and cooking: mediocrity.

BALLINCOLLIG

MALTING COMPANY OF IRELAND
Ballincollig
Co Cork
Tel: (021) 871646
Contact: Phil Jones

Malt

Malt is the raw material from which both brewer and distiller work, and the Malting Company of Ireland is one of only three companies in the country who carry out this precious work. The Malting Co of Ireland supply to Irish Distillers in Midleton and the Bushmills distillery in Bushmills, as well as Murphy's brewery in Cork, Guinness in Dublin, Smithwicks in Kilkenny and the Ulster Brewery in Belfast. They use only Irish grown Barley.

Telephone for more details.

BALLINHASSIG

BILLY MACKESY'S BAWNLEIGH HOUSE
Ballinhassig
Co Cork
Tel: (021) 771333
Contact: Billy Mackesy

Restaurant

The first thing you discover when looking for Billy Mackesy's restaurant, is that it's not anywhere near its townland address of Ballinhassig. It's much closer to the Half Way Village (half way between Cork and Bandon). Bawnleigh is reminiscent, visually, of those sixties lounge bars. All the chairs and tables are heavy and brown, lightened slightly by fresh flowers and candles. It's a traditional sight, in an Irish sense. The furnishings are the same as you might find in any farm-house on the way, and as such it won't win any stars for decor. The next discovery, however, is the cooking: creative, modern, but catering to all the needs of a country who love good meat, potatoes and vegetables in large portions. We christened it nouvelle country cooking. Other bonuses are a good wine list and interesting, friendly and ultra-professional staff.

We advise that you telephone for more detailed directions. Open 7.30-11.30pm. Closed Sunday and Monday.

121

BANDON

BANDON VALLEY ORGANIC FARMHOUSE CHEESE
Teadies
Enniskean
Co Cork
Tel: (023) 47663
Contact: Liam
Chambers

*Farmhouse cows'
cheese*

Liam Chambers makes a semi-hard Leicester type cheese. He's been making it for five years, but he has only recently been awarded the Organic symbol. His cows are mostly Fresians, though he also uses milk from his Jersey cows also.

Leave Bandon on the Dunmanway Road (going in the direction of Bantry). Liam Chambers' farm is one mile before the village of Enniskean on the Bandon side. When you get to the area you are best advised to ask somebody passing. You can buy from the farm, and Liam distributes the cheese to local shops himself.

DILLONS
Timoleague
Bandon
Co Cork
Tel: (023) 46410
Contact: Isabelle Dillon
or Chris Harte

➥ *Pub/cafe*

Sandwiched between two pubs on the narrow main street of Timoleague, Dillon's bears no relation to its neighbours. Instead it is a pub in the continental style, with a bright, open atmosphere, a neat variety of wines, good tea and coffee, magazines and papers, and food from Otto Kunze's Dunworley Restaurant. Food available all day. Pub Opening hours.

Main Street of Timoleague.

DUNWORLEY COTTAGE RESTAURANT
Butlerstown
Bandon
Co Cork
Tel: (023) 40314
Contact: Otto Kunze

➥ *Restaurant*

Otto Kunze is dedicated to finding and using the best ingredients possible, and in his hands they are crafted into the finest recipes one could imagine. He works closely with the Organic farmers, using organic vegetables from the Cork Co-operative, and pork from Vicky Heslop. Much of the remainder of his ingredients is gathered from the seas and fields of the area. Nettle soup is one of his most notable concoctions, and his home-made salamis are the best in the country. He cold-smokes them in a room off the restaurant, and you can buy them to take away or order them by post. Otto also makes Dutch Frikadel sausages, which he sells to chippers around Cork including the Golden Grill in Bantry and the chippers in Kenmare and Castletownbere. Other of his products include Vanilla and Crab Apple Jelly and luscious Chocolate Truffles, which you can buy from him at the various shows and fairs he attends on behalf of the Organic Movement. But it is for the restaurant that Otto is to be most prized. The menu is full and imaginative. You can choose between duck, beef, pork and chicken, and accompany them with fabulous vegetable side dishes. You leave the restaurant not sure whether to be sorry that it's situated right at the end of the country, or delighted that such a wonderful place exists in the far flung hills that envelop it.

Ring for directions, the restaurant is well signposted. Open Wed-Sat 6.30pm-10pm. Sunday 1pm-8.30pm. Look out for the restaurant's annual pig party in late Summer.

UMMERA SMOKED PRODUCTS

Ummera House
Timoleague
Bandon
Co Cork
Tel: (023)
46187/49828
Contact: Anthony
Creswell

➡ *Smoked salmon, turkey, chicken and eel*

The seas and rivers of Ireland are the hunting grounds that give up wild salmon, whereupon the Creswells, who take only the very best, cure and oak smoke the bounty, and then sell it to you through the post. Ummera also smoke silver eel, chicken and turkey, and they have designed a smoked salmon sausage: "Ideal for cocktail parties, gives people something to talk about" said Mr Creswell Snr. You can buy Ummera products straight from the smoking house, by arrangement, or order through the post.

First on the right, over the hill, after the Protestant graveyard in Timoleague.

ROUND TOWER CHEESE

Bride View House
Enniskeane
Co Cork
Tel: (023) 47105
Contact: Nan and
Michael O'Donovan

Farmhouse cheese

Round Tower is a creamy, semi-hard, cows' milk cheese, which the O'Donovan's make by hand at Bride View House. They use their own raw milk which is pumped directly into the cheese room each morning. Then begins the process which, at the end of six to eight weeks produces this mustard-coloured waxed cheese. 'You have no worry if the milk is good' says Nan, and their milk is good. They distribute the cheese themselves selling it in Cork, Kerry and Waterford.

Turn right at Enniskeane (Bride View is signposted). Go straight on when the road turns sharply, Bride View is about three miles up this road on the right.

BANTRY AND THE SCHULL PENINSULA

At the head of Bantry Bay, sheltered by Whiddy Island and surrounded by the Caha Mountains to the north and the Maughanaclea hills to the east, you find the old market town of Bantry. You leave Bantry travelling up-hill, and can look back over the town and the bay. But though it's a feast for the eyes, there is no food shop or restaurant that would bring fame to the town. Even though Bantry is a seaside town, there is no fish shop (there is a van which delivers fish, and a small stall open 'till 11.30am), and much of the 'local specialities' come down from Cork.

DURRUS
Coomkeen
Durrus
Bantry
Co Cork
Tel: (027) 61100
Contact: Jeffa Gill

➤ *Farmhouse cows' cheese*

Jeffa Gill exports about half of her production of Durrus, a semi-hard surface ripened cheese made from raw milk. Her fresians graze on luxurious meadows, which means Durrus has a wonderfully rich complexity that improves with age. Visitors are welcome at the farm.

Go through Durrus on the Ahakista road, turn right at the Church of Ireland and head up the hill for about two and a half miles until you see the sign.

GLENLOUGH YOGURT
Enterprise Centre
Bantry
Co Cork
Tel: (027) 51051
Contact: Alan and Caroline Dare

Yogurt and distribution company

Glenlough produce an excellent yogurt in four varieties of flavour: plain, and with fruit and honey. The Dare's also operate a small distribution company, going up as far as Dublin with other local products. The yogurts are widely available.

Telephone for details.

MARY GRANT
Kilcrohane
Bantry

Mary Grant is known as a cheese-maker in this area, but you will only be able to find her cheese in the Blair's Cove Restaurant in Durrus; she does not

Co Cork
Contact: Mary Grant

Farmhouse goats'
cheese

produce on a commercial basis. If you're in Blair's Cove, do look out for the cheese. It's a lovely goat feta, flavoured with thyme.

See directions for Blair's Cove.

GUBBEEN
Gubbeen House
Schull
Co Cork
Tel: (028) 28231
Contact: Tom & Giana
Ferguson

★ *Farmhouse cheese*

A well-matured Gubbeen cheese is a most curious and gorgeous sight: its soft pinky brown rind folds to give it the appearance of a soft Burgermeister's hat. The taste is even more pleasing. A smoked version, the smoking done by Chris Jepson, is also made. Visitors are welcome at the farm, indeed this is the best chance to buy Gubbeen at its best. A wonderful, totally individual cheese.

Go through Schull and head towards Ard na Greine Restaurant but instead of turning right head on straight and you will come to Gubbeen House.

HAND CRAFTED KNIVES
Ballylickey
Bantry
Co Cork
Tel: (027) 50032
Contact: Rory Conner

Handcrafted Knives is a cottage industry operating from a small workshop at Ballylickey. Their range of hand-made kitchen knives includes a set of three in a leather wallet (boner, medium and small utility knives) which are made from ATS 34 stainless steel, manufactured especially for knifemaking, which they import from Japan. The handles are made from fibre-

126

Most cheese in Ireland is sold long before it reaches maturity. This is a pity as the symphony of flavours achieved after a little ageing can turn a good-tasting cheese into a great one.

Many cheese producers will sell mature cheese to you direct from the farmhouse, and others will post it. Sometimes it will cost a little extra, which is quite fair — like wine, aged cheese is an investment in taste.

These two cheeses are Gubbeens. The top shows the way it looks after a month, the bottom, three months, at which stage it is a perfect cheese. Eventually, if you leave it long enough, a well-made Gubbeen will just disappear, the two rinds meeting in the middle.

Hand-made kitchen knives.

laminated phenol composite, which is a hygienic and long-lasting substance (price £105). They also sell steak sets, a serrated knife with three-pronged fork with impregnated beech handles; a carving set (price £70) and what they call a 'pro' kitchen knife, a plain blade with a hard-wood handle. Blades come with excellent guarantees, delivery can be arranged, and the only proviso is that they don't accept orders for more than ten knives at a time. This, they say, is to preserve the quality of their craftwork.

Telephone for more details.

CHRIS JEPSON
Harbour Smoke House
Ballydevlin
Goleen

Chris Jepson's house, down in the harbour at Goleen, is cut off at high tide, so if you plan to buy any of his magnificent smoked salmon, check the tides first. Along with salmon he smokes Gubbeen cheese and

127

Schull
Co Cork
Tel: (028) 35283
Contact: Chris Jepson

➤ *Smoked products*

MANNING'S EMPORIUM
Ballylickey
Co Cork
Tel: (027) 50456
Contact: Val Manning

➤ *Foodshop*

OVER THE RAINBOW
Wolfe Tone Square
Bantry
Co Cork
Contact: Tanya Feely
or Deirdre Hardwick

Wholefood shop and cafe

PAUL SCHULTZ
Mill Beg
Coomhola
Bantry
Co Cork
Contact: Paul Schultz

Organic vegetables

Westphalian ham and is currently experimenting with lamb. You can buy smoked products at the house.

Telephone for detailed directions, and details of tides.

Manning's foodmarket is one of those places that gladdens the heart. Stocked with discrimination and featuring as many local products as possible, including all the Cork cheeses, Mrs Healy's Irish Whiskey Cake from nearby Gougane Barra, Follain jams and preserves from Coolea and the most wonderful traditional cheesecake from Ballydehob — Mrs Parson's. It also has a fair selection of wines. Val Manning organises The West Cork Food Fair each year at the shop.

The shop is on the N71 just north of Bantry.

Over The Rainbow is yet another of those small wholefood/health food shops which act as a retail outlet for local growers. Here you can buy the fresh organically-grown produce of Paul Schultz, from Millbeg, as well as local cheeses (look out for Ballingeary Goats' cheese) and free-range eggs.

Bantry town centre.

Paul Schultz runs a small vegetable-growing operation on his one-and-a-half acre holding. He grows enough to keep Over The Rainbow filled with a wide choice of organic vegetables the whole year around. Paul is anxious to build a special relationship with his customers, who are welcome to visit him and 'have a chat about the garden'.

Ask in Over The Rainbow for directions, or you can buy his produce there.

SEA VIEW HOUSE HOTEL
Ballylickey
Co Cork
Tel: (027)
50073/50462
Contact: Kathleen
O'Sullivan

Hotel with restaurant

Sea View is a charming, old style hotel owned by Kathleen O'Sullivan. The all-day bar menu includes platters of cheese or fish, and the restaurant serves Irish cooking that in the past made Irish hotels worth travelling to. Everything is fresh and the vegetables are beautifully cooked. The young waitresses administer in a quiet cossetting manner, and families of three generations go along for communion lunches, filling the place with a festive atmosphere.

Situated on the N71 into Bantry.

SHIRO JAPANESE DINNER HOUSE
Ahakista
Durrus
Co Cork
Tel: (027) 67030
Contact: Kei & Werner
Pilz

➡ *Restaurant*

This is the most extraordinary eating place in the country. The Ahakista is a grand house, formerly the Bishop's residence, and the interior is a pleasing clash of teutonic robustness and Japanese finesse. Kei Pilz is a Japanese artist who is the cook, Werner Pilz is a retired Luftwaffe pilot from Germany, who looks after guests. The food is the most splendid culinary art form: delicate tempura made from carved vegetables, fan shaped noodles, and fantastic prawns; pleasingly gelatinous sashimi, raw slivers of the fish Werner Pilz catches in the estuary; and Zensai, a collection of Japanese appetizers, including a rich fishy custard with a juicy pork meatball smothered within it. The meal, which encompasses many courses, ends with a rainbow of home-made ice cream: kiwi, strawberry, vanilla, grape and banana, garnished with delicate banana fritters and perfumed mandarin segments. Booking is absolutely essential. The restaurant comprises two rooms and two tables, and once the tables are booked (whether it be one person dining or, the maximum for each table, a party of seven) then the restaurant is full. Dinner 7pm-11pm. August gets booked out around June, so plan ahead.

The restaurant is on the road from Bantry into Ahakista.

WEST CORK NATURAL CHEESE

Bill Hogan used to make cheese in the very north of Donegal. He's now moved to the very south of the country, the Schull peninsula, where he makes two

129

Ardmanagh
Schull
Co Cork
Contact: Bill Hogan

Irish farmhouse cheese

gruyere-type cheeses: Gabriel, a hard cheese with a pushy flavour, and Desmond, a more mellow cheese, still quite hard. Both are superb for cooking.

Write for more details. The cheese is well distributed and you can buy it throughout the country.

BEARA PENINSULA

Drive down the Beara Peninsula on a hot day when the sunlight spangles off the sea and you will have to work very hard to think of a more beautiful part of the country. Tumbling hills, picturesque villages, a lazy and confident pace of life make this an area that calls out for superlatives.

ALLIHIES GLOBE ARTICHOKE CO-OPERATIVE
Reenatrisk
Beara Peninsula
Co Cork
Tel: (027) 73025
Contact: Tony Lowes

Globe artichokes

On the road from Allihies to Eyeries you will see signs alerting you to the presence and the sale of globe artichokes. Drive up the back-breaking slopes and falls of the road and you will be able to buy some of these aristocratic vegetables from Tony Lowes who is, in fact, the Allihies Globe Artichoke Co-Op all by himself. 'They do very well here' he says, his American accent undimmed by more than twenty-five years of living in Ireland. He calls his one-man operation a 'Co-op' because he hopes many more will see the potential of growing Globe Artichokes on the Beara Peninsula and that they will join him.

Follow the signs on the right hand side of the road as you drive from Allihies to Eyeries.

BALLINGEARY GOATS' CHEESE
Carrig
Ballingeary
Co Cork
Tel: (026) 47126
Contact: Aourt & Lick Versloot Koolen

Ballingeary Goats' Cheese is one of those elusive little cheeses that handsomely repays any effort to find it. A pale white cheese made in medium-sized tablets, it is sold by Aourt Versloot in Bantry every Friday, and you may be able to find it in Over The Rainbow (they keep it in the fridge — open it up and take a look). You can also buy the cheese from the Versloot Koolen's farm. But if in doubt telephone for

130

**Farmhouse goats'
cheese**

instructions.

Take the road from Ballingeary to Gougane Beara, coming from Ballingeary direction. Take the turning on the right hand side just before the parking area. Go up the road a few hundred yards and past a white bungalow, carry on a further hundred yards and you will see the sign saying 'Goats' Cheese'.

COOLEA CHEESE
Coolea
Co Cork
Tel: (026) 45204
Contact: Dick and
Helene Willems

*Farmhouse cows'
cheese*

Dick and Helene Willems have been producing their milk gouda-type cheese for nine years now and have seen their efforts rewarded with the prize of Best Farmhouse Cheese in 1983 and First prize in the 1984 and 1987 Spring Show. They also sell a herb variety of Coolea, for which they use eight different herbs.

Telephone for directions.

DAVE DURELL
Ballinacarriga
Garnish
Bantry
Tel: (027) 73083
Contact: Dave Durell
Garlic

Dave and Penny Durell grow garlic organically at their holding near the cable car on the Beara Peninsula. Most of the crop is bought by Munster Wholefoods, and some of it can be found in shops in Dublin. Some is sold to restaurants and friends. You can also buy from the house, though it's a good idea to telephone first. The drive down to the house is beautiful, and the garlic is much cheaper than imported garlic so it's worth the trip.

Telephone for directions. The Durell's garlic is for sale in Here Today, Magill's, Fitzers, and the Runner Bean in Dublin.

MILLEENS CHEESE
Eyeries
Beara Peninsula
Bantry
Co Cork
Tel: (027) 74079
Contact: Veronica and

Veronica Steele was the first in Ireland to make and market a farmhouse cheese, and twelve years on her Milleens cheese can be one of the best cheeses made anywhere, spoken of in the company of Reblochon, Camembert and Brie. It is a soft, washed-rind cheese, which we like best when it is almost weeping, and a perfect dinner course on its own. The Steeles welcome visitors to the farm, but telephone first.

131

Norman Steele

➡ *Farmhouse cows' cheese*

Turn left at the graveyard just past Eyeries, then take the second turning on the right — it is wise to ask at this point.

CAPE CLEAR

CLEIRE GOATS
Cape Clear
Skibbereen
Co Cork
Tel: (028) 39126
Contact: Ed Harper

Irish farmhouse goats' cheese and ice cream, goats' milk

The most southerly island of Ireland is Cape Clear. It is a magnet for sailors of all description as well as bird watchers, who come to see the bird observatory. It is also a magnet for those who like cheese. Ed Harper is blind, but that doesn't stop him making the delicious soft Cais Cleire, a semi-soft cheese made from the milk of his British Alpine goats. Nothing is added to the fresh cheese, apart from salt in the maturing process. Ed also makes a garlic flavoured goats' cottage cheese, which you can buy on the island, and in a few shops on the mainland in Baltimore, Skibbereen and, in the summer, Schull. If you visit the island you will be lucky enough to be able to buy Ed Harper's legendary goats' ice cream, which never makes it to the mainland.

You can buy Cais Cleire in Farm Produce, on Baggot St, Dublin. Norven's in Cork also sell it, as do various restaurants nationwide including Dunderry Lodge and Ballymaloe House. You can buy it from the farm, which is just West of the Church.

CARRIGALINE

CARRIGALINE COUNTRY MARKET
The GAA Hall
Crosshaven Road
Co Cork
Tel: (021) 882856 or 921089

Country Market

Probably the best Country Market in the country is in the east Cork village of Carrigaline. It runs from 10am-11am every Friday and producers use it to market their wares when production is in an embryonic stage. The market sells free-range chickens and eggs, fresh vegetables and cakes, farmhouse cheese, and their boast is that they will make, bake or grow anything to order.

Ask in Carrigaline for directions.

CARRIGALINE FARMHOUSE CHEESE
Merello
Leacht Cross
Carrigaline
Co Cork
Tel: (021) 372856
Contact: Pat O'Farrell

Farmhouse cows' cheese

The milk of fresian cows grazed on limestone land gives Carrigaline cheese its smooth, individual taste. A small operation with the emphasis on 'hand made', Pat O'Farrell and his wife lovingly take their cheese carefully from beginning to end, pressed for twenty-four hours, three days in brine and six weeks in the cold room before waxing. You can buy the cheese from the farm. It's distributed by Chieftain foods, who also portion and pack it. Pat is developing a new garlic and herb variety.

Turn left at the roundabout in Carrigaline (coming from Cork). At the graveyard and the Protestant church take the entrance on the left. Turn right at the corner and it is the third opening.

OWNABWEE PRESERVES
Ballynametagh House
Carrigaline
Co Cork
Tel: (021) 372323
Contact: Phil Thompson
Preserves

Over the last few years Ownabwee preserves, jams and chutneys have happily become available in more and more outlets throughout the country. Hampers can be ordered to suit specific requirements, and there is a selection of Christmas goods available including Brandy Butter.

Telephone for details.

CASTLETOWNBERE

CASTLETOWNBERE FISHERMANS' CO-OP
The Pier
Castletownbere
Co Cork
Tel: (027) 70045
Telex: 75181
Fax (027) 70194
Contact: Donal O'Sullivan

Fresh fish

There is an excellent fishermans' Co-op in the thriving port of Castletownbere. Here you can buy fresh fish soon after they've been landed.

On the pier at Castletownbere, Open six days a week, Sat until 12 noon.

CASTLETOWNSHEND

South East of Skibbereen there are some of the most beautiful villages to be found in Ireland, where painted stone houses sit on deep inclines that run into the sea. One such village is Castletownshend where you find the famous bar and restaurant, Mary Ann's Bar. Mary Ann's was founded in 1854 and its present owners are Fergus and Patricia O'Mahony (Tel: 028 36146). One of the unfortunate aspects of Mary Ann's is that it's difficult to hear an Irish voice. The bar is recommended by Pan Am and features in many of the British Guides. It is also expensive, charging restaurant prices for pub food. But given those drawbacks it is a beautiful pub in a beautiful village. At the end of the Main Street is Castletownshend pier where fishermen will sell you crabs and crayfish. Two other exquisite fishing villages nearby which offer the same service, if you choose the right moment to ask, are Union Hall, where a lot of fish are landed, and Glandore; the two sit on either side of Glandore harbour.

WOODCOCK SMOKERY

Gortbreac
Castletownshend
Co Cork
Tel: (028) 36232
Contact: Sally Barnes

Smoker of fish and some meat

Sally Barnes goes to endless trouble to ensure the quality of her fish, and the wood she uses to smoke it. 'Basically I'll smoke anything' she says. The business started as a smoking service for anglers, but through scarcity of wild fish amongst other things, it has developed, and now Sally seeks out different fresh fish straight from auction at the Castletownshend Fishermans' Co-Op. Sally never puts dye in her salmon, and seeks out timber that has no preservatives. Her fastidious demand for quality, ensures just that.

Telephone for more details.

CLONAKILTY

O'DONOVAN'S HOTEL
44 Pearse Street
Clonakilty
West Cork
Tel: (023)
33250/33883
Telex: (023) 34393
Contact: Tom
O'Donovan

*Hotel and pub with
small restaurant/cafe*

O'Donovan's Hotel and pub is run by Tom O'Donovan and his two sisters, the fifth generation of the family to have charge of this characterful establishment. O'Donovan's still boasts a style of hotel which has, sadly, become rare in Ireland, and a beautiful public bar. 'All the boards creak' says Tom 'but it lets me know who's around'. There is a magnificent polyphon in the tea rooms, and cabinets which house fascinating historical artefacts. Many hotels ignore history, but O'Donovan's is proud of its past, and the family photos reveal a multitude of ancestors. Do ask about Catherine O'Donovan ('Auntie Cat'), the first woman in Clonakilty to smoke in public and wear trousers.

Clonakilty town centre.

TWOMEY'S BUTCHERS
16 Pearse Street
Clonakilty
West Cork
Tel: (023) 33365
Contact: Edward
Twomey
Butcher specialising in
➡ *Black pudding*

Twomey's butchers dates back to 1889 and its fine tradition of black pudding has been extended even further, ever since Edward Twomey took over in 1976. Based on an old Harrington family recipe, the white pudding is delicious, but the black pudding is quite superb — the best in the country. All Edward Twomey's beef is supplied from local farmers with whom he has built up a relationship over the years, and he supplies to hotels and restaurants in Cork.

Clonakilty town centre.

CORK

CHETWYND IRISH BLUE
Castlewhite
Waterfall
Cork
Tel: (021) 543502
Contact: Jerry

Jerry Beechinor began to make cheese after he retired, and for the last year has slowly built up his production of Chetwynd, a soft, creamy blue cheese. Made from pasteurised milk, penicillium roqueforti is added at the same time as the lactic starter. After the cheese has been left overnight in moulds, it is salted on both ends, a process that continues for three days

135

Beechinor

Farmhouse cheese

before the cheese is washed, then pierced. It then spends four weeks in the moulding room to allow blue veining to develop, when the surface is cleaned and the cheese allowed to drain before wrapping. It can be eaten straight away, or stored for another four months, depending on preference.

You can buy Chetwynd at various supermarkets including Superquinn and Roches' Stores. Jerry does not sell from the house.

CORK COVERED MARKET
Cork City Centre

Market

Cork boasts a thriving market selling fish, meat and vegetables. The fish stalls are situated on the south side and sell mostly cod (smoked and filleted) and other white fish. Butchers and vegetable shops criss-cross throughout, and the stall holders remonstrate with you if you pick out your own vegetables. At the corner of Grand Parade you will find the Tripe and Drisheen stall (O'Reilly's, Contact: Stephen or Maurice O'Reilly Tel: (021) 966397). Otherwise look out for fresh farmyard ducks, free-range eggs, flowers and the wonderful Ballymaloe Potatoes. There is even a wholefood shop. The market is generally known as 'The English Market'.

Between Patrick Street, Grand Parade and Oliver Plunkett Street.

THE CRAWFORD GALLERY CAFE
Emmet Place
Cork
Tel: (021) 274415
Contact: Fern Allen

Restaurant

A recent offshoot of the mighty Ballymaloe enterprise and duplicating the same intuitive understanding and appreciation of good food. Situated in a rear ground floor room of the Crawford Gallery, it serves lunch six days a week (closed Sunday) and is open on Wed, Thurs and Fri from 6.30-9pm. Some of the art in the gallery is to be found on a plate.

Cork city centre.

GALVIN'S OFF LICENCES
37 Bandon Road, Cork

Galvin's import wines directly from Europe, and the three shops have a good variety of both old and new world wines. They open weekdays until 11pm,

Tel: (021) 275598
Watercourse Road,
Cork
Tel: (021) 500818
22 Washington Street,
Cork
Tel: (021) 276314
Contact: Barry Galvin

Wine Merchant

LEONIDAS CHOCOLATES
106 Oliver Plunkett
Street
Cork
Tel: (021) 276970
Contact: Rosemary

Belgian chocolates

THE LONG VALLEY
Winthrop Street
Cork
Tel: (021) 272144
Contact: Humphrey
Moynihan

Pub

NATURAL FOODS
26 Paul Street
Cork
Tel: (021) 277244
Contact: Wendy
O'Byrne

Wholefood shop and bakery

Sundays and Bank Holidays until 10pm. In addition to wine they stock a comprehensive selection of spirits, soft drinks and beers.

Cork city centre.

Even before they were available in Ireland, the reputation of Leonidas, the chocolates in the little gold boxes, was already established. Now you can buy them here. They're regularly imported from Brussels, and sold through the traditional continental window to the street.

Cork city centre.

This agreeable pub is staffed by serious-faced, white-coated women who conjure up delicious sandwiches with quiet aplomb. Crescending Italian operatic arias implode discreetly, the best background music you can get, as you romp through the salt beef, the home-baked ham, the lettuce, the onions, the egg and the tomatoes.

Cork city centre.

Natural Foods sell a cherry bun which has deservedly come to be known as the 'famous' cherry bun, but the bakery also produces excellent breads, especially the pouches of pitta bread (which they fill with salad for lunch) and their excellent rank sourdough, baked every Wednesday and Saturday. They sell organic vegetables on Thursdays, and local yogurts and cheese, as well as maintaining a comprehensive stock of pulses, legumes, herbs ,spices and so on.
Cork city centre. Open Mon-Sat 9.30am-5.30pm.

137

O'FLYNN'S BUTCHERS

36 Marlborough Street
Cork
Tel: (021)
275685/272195
Contact: John O'Flynn

Butcher

O'Flynn's smoke their own Kassler and beef — a Cork delicacy — in their Marlborough Street shop and have a stall in the nearby market where their business began. Other specialities are Spiced Beef, which is marinated in a wet spice mixture (rather than the Dublin version which is dry spiced), venison, including venison sausages and Irish veal. There is always a comprehensive selection of other cuts available including osso bucco. You can buy the Kassler through the post if you have an access or visa card.

Cork city centre.

RECIPE: KASSLER

Kassler is a German speciality of smoked loin of pork. It is so delicious that it's best served simply roasted. You can buy it either on the bone, or without bones. The benefit of getting it with bones is that they make an absolutely magnificent stock. Put the kassler on a rack and roast for 20 mins per pound in a 200 C, 400 F oven. There should be a half to three-quarters of a cup of water placed under the joint, so as to keep it steaming and moist. Some people suggest you cover with tin foil for half the cooking time, but if you have a small piece, this isn't absolutely necessary. You may like to roast potatoes around the pork as in a normal roast. Serve with steamed shredded red cabbage and an apple sauce.

QUAY CO-OP

24 Sullivan's Quay
Cork
Tel: (021) 967660

Restaurant, wholefood shop and bookshop

The Quay Co-op has a restaurant, a wholefood shop (which also sells organic wines) and a bookshop sharing its enjoyably ramshackle premises. The food in the restaurant is satisfying and cheap, following traditional wholefood/vegetarian/vegan lines: bakes, pizzas, salads etc. The shop is similarly familiar, but the bookshop has the odd surprise amidst standard agit-prop material.

Cork city centre.

DRIMOLEAGUE

FIG TREE COTTAGE
Upper Moynys
Drimoleague
West Cork
Contact: Kim
Waterman

Vegan/vegetarian guesthouse

Fig Tree Cottage is a pretty stone building overlooking a charming manicured garden. The whole effect is most surprising, situated as it is in the rugged hills around Drimoleague. Kim and her husband are vegetarians and provide shelter and a meal for those who want a complete break with cruelty-free minded organic growers. The cost is very low and both lunch and dinner can be arranged. You can even just call for a meal. They have no telephone, so try your chances, though, better still, write first.

Ask in Drimoleague, or write for detailed directions.

FERMOY

BALLYVOLANE HOUSE
Castlelyons
Co Cork
Tel: (025) 36349
Contact: Merrie and Jeremy Green

Country house with restaurant

The atmosphere in Ballyvolane is most relaxing, which is quite a feat considering both the splendour of the surroundings — complete with glaring portraits of ancestors looking down at you in the dining room — and the fact that a grisly double murder was once carried out in one of the bedrooms. The cooking is homely, but elegant, the atmosphere friendly, and the landscape a feast for the eyes with magnificent mature trees, gardens and places of historic significance.

Telephone for more details.

KANTURK

ARDRAHAN CHEESE
Ardrahan House
Kanturk
Co Cork
Tel: (029) 78099
Contact: Mary Burns

Farmhouse cows'

This semi-soft Gouda-type cheese is laden with flavour. It's made by Mary Burns, who's been making it for seven years. Most of the cheese is exported to France and Mary's husband drives to Paris each month. The cheese is made from the milk of their Fresian cows. It's sold in two sizes of two and nine pounds.

Take the Killarney road out of of Cork city. After about

twelve miles you come to an old creamery on the right hand-side. The road you want is actually the last right before the Creamery. Follow the road until you come to a cross roads and take the right turn. Keep straight until you come to the white gates and the sign Ardrahan House. They are happy to sell you the cheese direct from the farm.

KINSALE

Go to Kinsale at holiday time, or during one of the bacchanalian festivals which the town organises, and it can appear to be a place where everyone is a character, no one ever needs to sleep, the pubs never shut and nobody ever shuts up. This image attracts ever greater crowds every year, all determined to have the time of their lives in this non-stop, lively town.

This is only part of the story, of course. When the town reverts to normality, which is, anyway, usually two steps above normality anywhere else, you find that by midnight most folk are in bed and the pubs and restaurants have closed. This is actually a good time to stroll around the town — like many other places where the streets are narrow and the buildings of a decent human size, too many people thronging about gives a misleading impression of the place.

One fact which attracts the tourists and the trippers is the large number of restaurants and places to eat. 'A restaurant for every hundred citizens of the town' is the proud boast, and when you add to this the fact that most of them are good, it is a proud boast indeed. There is a Kinsale Good Food Circle which has thirteen members (Tel: (021) 772579). Each restaurant has its own distinctive character, and no one shines above all others. Thus, if you were to stay within the Good Food Circle, staying in Kinsale for a fortnight gives you a different place to eat every night, and a night off to recover. In fact, there are enough pubs and other places serving food to ensure that you can have lunch in a different place each day also. Competition ensures a certain level of ability, a fact which cannot, regrettably, be vouchsafed for the singers in the myriad pubs, who can be heard mercilessly murdering classic songs most evenings. All of this frenetic activity culminates each autumn in the Gourmet Festival held in the first weekend of October, following which the town, in its own way, hibernates for the winter.

THE OLD PRESBYTERY
Cork Street
Kinsale
Co Cork
Tel: (021) 772027
Contact: Ken and
Cathleen Buggy

B&B with restaurant

Ken and Cathleen Buggy have resisted the dull homogenisation which has swept over so many hotels and guest houses, and have created in the Old Presbytery a place of wonderful character and interest. Evening meals are cooked in the summer months, and Ken, who uses old copper pots and Mrs Beeton recipes, needs to know by 6pm who is eating as that's when the fresh fish shop closes.

Kinsale town centre.

MACROOM

MACROOM OATMEAL
Walton's Mills
Manor Villa
Macroom
Co Cork
Tel: (026) 41800
Contact: John Creedon

★ *Oatmeal*

People often remember exactly where they were when events of great historical significance took place: the assassination of JFK, the birth of their first child and so on. Thus it is with the first time you taste porridge made from Macroom Oatmeal. Smooth, dense with sweetness, it is a nectar of oats and a dish you could happily eat for the rest of your life. Look out for the white, red and yellow bags which, sadly, can only be found in the South and West of the Country.

Telephone for more details.

MALLOW

LONGUEVILLE HOUSE
Mallow

Longueville House is set in the valley of the River Blackwater. The atmosphere is informal, despite the magnificence of the Georgian mansion buildings, and

Co Cork
Tel: (022) 47156
Telex: 75498
Contact: Michael and
Jane O'Callaghan

➡ *Country house with*
restaurant

the opulence of the Presidents Restaurant with its
original Georgian conservatory. The cooking of chef,
William O'Callaghan, who trained with both
Raymond Blanc, at Le Manoir aux Quat' Saisons and
Marco Pierre White at Harveys, is a fine example of
the craft of excellent cooking.

Telephone for detailed directions.

MIDLETON

BALLYCOTTON FISH SHOP
Main Street
Middleton
Co Cork
Tel: (021) 613122
Contact: Anthony
Coffey-Walsh

Fishmonger

The Ballycotton fish shop opens from 9am to 6pm,
Monday to Saturday. Most of their fish is landed at
Ballycotton, and you can buy a number of varieties.
They also sell from their home at Carrigduff,
Ballycotton (Tel: (021) 646776: after the Protestant
church it is the third house on the right), and fish can
be sent, vacuum packed, through the post or by rail.

Midleton town centre.

THE BALLYMALOE COOKERY SCHOOL
Kinoith House
Shanagarry
Co Cork
Tel: (021)
646785/646727
Contact: Tim and
Darina Allen

➡ *Cookery school*

Ballymaloe Cookery school has been in operation for
six years and with Darina Allen's success as a
television cook and cookery writer ('Simply Delicious'
and 'A Simply Delicious Christmas' Gill & MacMillan,
Dublin 1989) the school's reputation is certain to
increase. Set amongst tastefully converted buildings,
the school features a variety of courses running from
three months to one day. Guest cooks visit each
season, including such famous names as Jane
Grigson and Madhur Jaffrey. Students may be
residential or non-residential.

Ask directions in Shanagarry.

BALLYMALOE HOUSE
Shanagarry
Midleton
Co Cork

Myrtle Allen has presided over Ballymaloe's
determination to achieve excellence for over twenty-
five years, and has seen her efforts rewarded with an
international reputation. Her kitchens are fed from
local suppliers and this, combined with understated

Tel: (021) 652531
Contact: Ivan & Myrtle Allen

★ *Country house with restaurant*

elegance and a judicious wine list, produces an inspirational result. The eggs are golden yellow, the porridge dreamy, the fish fresh, the lamb sweet, the vegetables used with imagination — there are few places in Ireland where one can eat so well. Myrtle Allen's book 'The Ballymaloe Cookbook' contains scores of fine recipes (Gill & Macmillan, Dublin).

Turn off the roundabout from the Midleton bypass (coming from Cork), taking the signs for first Shanagarry, then to Ballymaloe itself.

BALLYMALOE KITCHEN SHOP
Ballymaloe House
Shanagarry
Midleton
Co Cork
Tel: (021) 652531
Contact: Wendy Allen

➥ *Kitchen shop*

Ballymaloe Kitchen shop has a fine selection of utensils and essential kitchen tools that will last for generations. Much of the stock is imported from Europe. Look out for the wooden-handled knives and the stainless steel saucepans, amongst many other bits and pieces. Ballymaloe chutneys and jams, and local smoked salmon is also for sale as well as post cards, books and rather fetching gansies.

Situated in Ballymaloe House.

BALLYMALOE POTATOES
Ballymaloe Farmlands
Shanagarry
Midleton
Co Cork
Tel: (021) 652531
Contact: Rory Allen

Potatoes

Rory Allen's potatoes are for sale all over the Southwest. Look out for the large Ballymaloe bags, which can be divided, selling the spuds by the pound. The variety is Golden Wonder, and they are what we used to call 'balls of flour', with a dryness that is sadly no longer widespread.

Telephone for more details.

BRECON LODGE FOODS

East Ferry
Midleton
Co Cork
Tel: (021) 613122
Contact: Robert Nunn

Preserves

Brecon Lodge make a smooth and a grainy mustard as well as preserves and some unusual savoury jellies.

Ring for details.

BILL CASEY

Shanagarry Village
Co Cork
Tel: (021) 646955
Contact: Bill Casey

Fish smoker

Bill Casey smokes wild salmon in season, farmed otherwise. He tells us he prefers to use farmed salmon as it is more oily and less likely to be bruised. Much of his production is exported, but callers to the house can buy directly from him. His secret, he says, is in his choice of wood. He is only prepared to divulge that it isn't oak. His salmon is sometimes for sale in the Ballymaloe Kitchen Shop.

Bill Casey's house is the middle bungalow on the right hand side after the church in Shanagarry village.

JEAN FITZSIMMONS

East Ferry
Co Cork
Tel: (021) 652611
Contact: Mrs Fitzsimmons

Free-range chickens

Mrs Fitzsimmons supplies free-range chickens to Ballymaloe House, and will not let down anyone who wants to buy one.

Telephone for details.

THE MIDLETON DISTILLERY

Midleton
Co Cork
Tel: (021) 631821
Contact: Barry Crockett

Whiskey

Midleton whiskey vanished from the market years ago and has only re-appeared in a de-luxe form, costing approximately IR£48.00 per bottle in 1989. At the distillery they could only tell us that you can buy it duty free at Dublin Airport, but in T. Wallis & Sons (74 Main Street, Midleton Tel: (021) 631155) — a pub and off-licence that doubles as an undertakers — they had a bottle for sale. 'Very smooth' said the man

144

behind the bar.

Signposted from Midleton town centre.

MRS NORTHRIDGE

Sheenliss
Midleton
Contact: Mrs
Northridge

Ducks and free-range eggs

It took us a little time to find Mrs Northridge's farm, and when eventually we did, said 'We hear you keep chickens'. She looked up slowly from her work. 'No' she said solemnly, and our hearts sank. But, 'Tis Ducks' she added at last. Mrs Northridge is just one of a number of farmers' wives in the country who sell Aylesbury Ducks, and free-range eggs. Ask anywhere in the country and you may be lucky to find another Mrs Northridge.

Take the road opposite Ballymaloe House, driving up the hill and straight ahead at the crossroads marked 'Church and Tower'. Her house is the first on the left up a shingle drive.

THE PIER

Ballycotton Bay
East Cork

Fish

If you can drag your gaze away from the transfixing beauty of Ballycotton Bay and the lighthouse which dominates it, you will find fish for sale, straight from the boats. Catches come in twice in twenty-four hours, and the optimum time to purchase is usually around 2pm. Local knowledge will fill in the daily details.

Due south from the central point between Midleton and Youghal.

ROSSMORE OYSTERS

Atlantic Shellfish Co
Rossmore
Carrigtohill
Co Cork
Tel: (021) 883248
Contact: Colm Guerin

Native and rock oysters, mussels, clams, sea urchins

Rossmore oyster farm is set in a beautiful estuary found at the end of a stony, muddy wet lane which runs from the Midleton bypass. Colm Guerin brings the parent oysters ashore into large sea-water ponds. The larvae grow one eye and cling to empty mussel shells which are deposited in the pond. These are then transferred back to the estuary to mature for three years. When ready the oysters are packed and sent all over the world. Orders can be delivered anywhere in Ireland within twenty-four hours, and oyster-knives, an essential tool, can be supplied with orders. Visiting is difficult but the unspoilt beauty of

145

the estuary is unforgettable.

Telephone for directions.

ROSSCARBERY

**GILLIAN
BOAZMAN**
Rosscarbery
Co Cork
Tel: (023) 48407
Contact: Gillian
Boazman

Sausages

Gillian Boazman comes from Cumberland, in Britain, which may explain her appreciation of good sausages. She makes four varieties: traditional pork, spicy, tomato and basil, and pork and sage. She makes about 150lbs per week. No preservatives are used, so the sausages should be eaten quickly and cared for carefully (don't leave them on the back shelf of the car in the sun, for example). There's absolutely no problem eating them quickly. Other varieties are planned and Gill hopes to make pies in the future.

Telephone for details. You can buy them in Fields of Skibbereen, Careys in Bandon and Cantillons in Kinsale amongst other places.

SKIBBEREEN

The town of Skibbereen has entered into legend on account of an editorial in its newspaper 'The Skibbereen Eagle' in the early part of the century. As events in Russia hotted up, 'The Eagle' bravely declared that the Tsar should watch his step, because 'The Eagle' was keeping its eye on him. Alas, 'The Eagle' has vanished, so we cannot know just how the good people of Skibbereen feel about glasnost and perestroika.

ATLANTIC FRESH FISH

The Bridge
Skibbereen
Tel: (028) 22145
Contact: Nadine
Graillot

Fishmonger

Nadine Graillot has brought her native French discrimination to this tiny wooden shack, which sits on the bridge over the river Ilen in the centre of Skibbereen. All the fish is from the previous night's catch, and Nadine salts her own ling and cod, a Skibbereen traditional dish, which she suggests you cook in a provencal sauce.

Skibbereen town centre.

KEN AND CAROLINE BADDILEY

Glounthane
Skibbereen
Co Cork
Tel: (028) 28406
Contact: Ken and
Caroline

Organic farmer

Ken and Caroline are members of the West Cork growers' co-op, and sell some of their vegetables locally. Hudsons' Wholefood and Blair's Cove take some of their produce. They are experimenting with Shiitake Mushrooms, but this year's dry weather resulted in a poor crop. They're hopeful for next year, however.

Telephone for more details.

ELYSIUM HERB FARM

Tragumna Road
Skibbereen
Co Cork
Tel: (028) 21325
Contact: Rosari
O'Byrne

Herb butters, and yogurt dressing, also B&B with excellent cooking.

Rosari O'Byrne is yet another of those indefatigable women who manage to combine half a dozen jobs and do them all well. As well as growing and selling herbs and running a guesthouse, she makes flavoured butters including a wonderful tarragon butter (excellent for sauces) and a yogurt and herb dressing. Her guests at the house can enjoy the produce of her organic garden which includes asparagus beds. Her guesthouse is known for its excellent cooking. Her butters and dressings can be found in Fields in Skibbereen.

Telephone for directions.

147

FIELDS
26 Main Street
Skibbereen
Tel: (028) 21400
Contact: J.J. Field

Supermarket

Good supermarket, selling many locally produced products (sausages, country butter, cheeses, pates) alongside conventional supermarket produce. Fields also stock some interesting wines, and the shop has a bubbly atmosphere about it.

Skibbereen town centre.

KITCHEN GARDEN
27 North Street
Skibbereen
Co Cork
Contact: Hans and Jenny Maas

Restaurant and food shop

Hans and Jenny are Dutch and one of the specialities of their back of shop restaurant is Dutch Open Sandwiches. They also make pies, soups, pizzas and a daily 'special'. They operate a take-away service, which is especially popular for pizzas. The shop sells organic vegetables, salamis, preserves and wholefoods.

Skibbereen town centre.

WEST CORK ORGANIC FARMING GROUP

All over the country there are pockets of organic farmers who gather together and sell their beautiful crops to lucky restaurants and shops in the area. One such is the West Cork Group. The Chairman is Heiner Miller (Holyhill, Ballineen, Co Cork Tel: (023) 47667), and the Acting Wholesaler is Joe Barth (Toreen, Dunmanway, Co Cork). Members include Cornelius Conner (Manch House, Ballineen, Co Cork), Anthony Miller (Toreen, Dunmanway, Co Cork), John O'Donovan (Castleview House, Ballincollig, Co Cork), Manfred Wandel (Trawlebawn, Bantry, Co Cork), Jonathon Doig (Upper Froe, Rosscarbery, Co Cork), Billy Wolfe (Stuke, Ballydehob, Co Cork), Ken and Caroline Baddiley (Glounthane, Skibbereen). Vegetables change with the season, and you can buy them on Thursdays at Natural Foods, and throughout the week at Otto Kunze's Dunworley Cottage Restaurant amongst other places.

YOUGHAL

HENRY PONSONBY
Ballynatray
Youghal
Co Cork

If the idea of buying half a deer sounds intimidating bear in mind that Henry Ponsonby's deer are fallow deer which are half the size of red deer. He sells them in these large amounts wholesale from his door. You can buy smaller cuts at O'Flynn's butchers in Cork

148

Tel: (024) 97221
Contact: Henry
Ponsonby

Venison

(who also make them into excellent sausages). The season is from September to February.

Telephone for more details.

BANDON

MULRISE FOODS, Waterfall Road, Bandon, Co Cork. Prepared meats.

BALLINCOLLIG

HEALY'S HONEY, Ballincollig, Co Cork. Always look out for their wholly Irish honey, though you rarely see it.

BALLYDEHOB

FORTRESS FOODS LTD, The Fortress, Ballydehob, Co Cork. Tel: (028) 37281. Contact: Hartmut M. Eppel. Hartmut Eppel runs a distribution business and exports many Irish cheeses to Germany.

CORK

BORD FAILTE, Grand Parade, Cork, Co Cork. Tel: (021) 273251; Telex: 76131.

HANSENS LABORATORY IRELAND LTD, Sitecast Industrial Estate, Little Island, Cork. Tel: (021) 353500. Hansens are the first word in cheesemaking. They sell cheesemaking equipment, give advice and sell starter cultures, rennets etc. Anybody who makes cheese has some contact with Hansens.

IRISH ALE BREWERS LTD, Industrial Estate, Little-Island, Cork. Tel: (021) 354377

149

MURPHY'S BREWERY IRELAND LTD, 58 Leitrim Street, Cork. Tel: (021) 503371

DURRUS

BLAIR'S COVE, Durrus, Bantry, Co Cork, Tel: (027) 61127, Contact: Philippe & Sabine De Mey. The fame of Blair's Cove stretches the length and breadth of the country. It is a converted Georgian mansion and they make a feature of the two hundred and fifty year old courtyard. They also rent self-catering apartments. Look out for Mary Grant's goats' feta cheese. Ask in the locality of Durrus, which is just south of Bantry. Consistently recommended.

LEAP

ROURY FRESH FOOD, Ballyroe, Leap, Co Cork. Tel: (028) 33388. Contact: Deirdre and Ian McNinch. A husband and wife team selling tubs of pate to the home, or buckets of pate to shops and restaurants. Flavours are chicken liver, mushroom and cheese, smoked salmon. They also make salads.

LISAVAIRD

DOLOREE HOUSE, Lisavaird, Co Cork. Tel: (023) 34123. Contact: Joe Dolan, who makes garlic butter, coleslaw and potato salad for other restaurants and delicatessens.

MIDLETON

THE FARM GATE, Coolbawn, Midleton, Co Cork. Tel: (021) 632771. Organic vegetables, good cheese counter, bread, Brecon Lodge preserves and a restaurant at the back of the shop.

MITCHELSTOWN

HORGAN'S DELICATESSEN SUPPLIES LTD,
Mitchelstown, Co Cork. Tel: (025) 24410. Contact:
Michael Horgan, distributor of Irish cheeses, as well
as cooked foods to delicatessens. Also imports
cheeses and pates.

MONKSTOWN

HAVEN OYSTER FARM, Carrigmahon, Monkstown,
Co Cork. Tel: (021) 841068. Contact: Jamie Dwyer.
Suppliers of oysters to restaurants, pubs and parties.

OVENS

ALLIED FISHERIES, Bernwood, 19 Beverly, Ovens, Co
Cork. Tel: (021) 871791. Telex: 2498EI. Supplies
wholesale to the Dublin Fish Market and Restaurants
in Kinsale.

GRANGE CRAFTS PRESERVES, Ovens, Co Cork

SCHULL

ADELE'S, Main Street, Schull. Tel: (028) 28460.
Contact: Adele Connor. Consistently recommended.

SKIBBEREEN

BORD FAILTE, Town Hall, Skibbereen, Co Cork. Tel:
(021) 21766; Telex: 76067.

COTTAGE FOODS, Skibbereen, Goleen, Co Cork.
Tel: (028) 35283. Contact: Tony and Olwin
Fitzgibbon. Widely available garlic and herb butters,
also Dereenatra cheese, a soft cheese flavoured with
herbs. Tony Fitzgibbon also acts as a distributor for
other products.

MacEOIN HONEY, Kileena, Creagh, Skibbereen. Tel:

(028) 21779. Contact: Geroid MacEoin.

MILL HOUSE RESTAURANT, Rineen, Skibbereen, Co
Cork. Contact: Mr David Good. Tel: (028) 36299.
Seafood restaurant recommended locally.

COUNTY KERRY

DINGLE

The Dingle Dolphin has become the most celebrated attraction of recent times for those who head west from Tralee down the peninsula. But this intensely picturesque little town has much more to offer. Amongst its many bars do visit Dick Mack's (Green Lane, Dingle Tel: 065 51244) named after Richard McDonnell and now presided over by Oliver J. McDonnell. Here you can buy a pint at one counter and a pair of boots at the other, and get involved in a discussion as to whether Dingle enjoys eighty-four liquor licences, or is it thirty-seven?, or thirty-three?

Amongst Dingle's excellent selection of restaurants there is a good chipper — not surprising in a town where fresh fish is so much a part of the daily diet. Look out for Graney's Fish and Chip Shop.

TED BROWNE
Kilquane
Ballydavid
Dingle
Co Kerry
Tel: (066) 55183
Fax: (066) 55293
Contact: Ted Browne

Smoked salmon, crab claws and crab meat, cockle soup

Ted Browne smokes only wild salmon, which you can find in the shops in Dingle. You can also buy from the house, and if you are lucky this means you might see Ted slicing his smoked salmon by hand, a feat he manages with confident ease and consummate skill. The salmon is excellent, smoked for twelve hours using an oak mixture. Also good are his crab meat and crab claws which he sells frozen in 1lb vacuum packs. In the winter he produces cockle soup which is sold locally.

Go through Dingle and instead of turning onto the bridge for Ventry, go straight ahead for a few miles, then ask.

AN CAFE LITEARTHA

Dykegate Street
Dingle
Co Kerry
Tel: (066) 51388
Contact: Seoirse O
Luasa

Bookshop and cafe

Unusual combination of book shop and cafe, the only other example being in Dublin (see Winding Stair). Excellent selection of Irish titles, and a cup of coffee, or a snack to accompany your purchase.

Dingle town centre.

RECIPE:
CRAB CLAWS IN MILEEVEN'S HONEY VINEGAR

This recipe makes a sweet and delicious first course. Reduce half a cup of honey vinegar by boiling it frantically. It will caramelise to a tablespoon in a few minutes. Take off the heat and slowly stir in knobs of 1oz butter, melting each knob of butter before you add the next. In a frying pan fry a handful of crab claws in a little more hot butter until just warm. Put a spoonful of sauce on each plate and surround with a few crab claws, serve immediately. (Serves 2).

NOREEN CURRAN

Green Street
Dingle
Co Kerry
Tel: (066) 51398
Contact: Noreen
Curran

Smoked bacon, black pudding

Noreen Curran's smoked bacon, produced in small quantities on the premises, is already justly famous, and a feature of Dingle. She also makes cake-shaped, blood pudding. Fry the two together for breakfast and you have an unbeatable combination.

Dingle town centre.

DOYLE'S SEAFOOD RESTAURANT

John Street
Dingle
Co Kerry
Tel: (066) 51174

The Doyle's opened their restaurant in 1973 and have slowly amassed an impressive reputation, a cluster of awards, and a safe berth in all the major guide books. The reason why is obvious — everything about the restaurant is utterly professional, from the food to the service to the lunch or dinner. Stella Doyle gets fresh fish and knows how to cook it

Contact: John and
Stella Doyle

Restaurant

properly — lunch or dinner here is unlikely to be anything other than good. Try the smoked salmon prepared locally by Hans de Snoo, (The Wood, Dingle, Tel: 066 51157) and the goats' cheese made by Linda Cohu in Kenmare.

Dingle town centre. Open for lunch 12.30-2.15pm, Dinner 6-9pm.

EIRI NA GREINE
Main St
Dingle
Co Kerry
Contact: Eoin Duignan

Restaurant, bakery and wholefood shop

Eiri na Greine is a co-operative which has been functioning now for eight years. In addition to its shop, where you can buy good organic vegetables, it is both a Bakery and a reasonably-priced restaurant with a familiar whole-food slant.

Dingle town centre.

GARVEY'S BUTCHERS
Holy Ground
Dingle
Co Kerry
Tel: (066) 51397
Contact: Michael
Boland, Tom Garvey

Butcher

In these parts they will tell you that Kerry mountain lamb is different, and better, than any other lamb you might try. Garvey's specialize in lamb grazed on the Dingle mountains and reared by local farmers.

Dingle town centre.

THE HALF DOOR
John Street
Dingle
Co Kerry
Tel: (066) 51600
Contact: John &
Celeste Slye

Restaurant, Waterside wine bar

The Half Door is a quietly excellent restaurant. John Slye manages the front of house, and will remove one third of a bottle of wine for you if you want to drink something decent, but only want half a litre. Celeste Slye's cooking reflects a similar concern that customers should be warmly accommodated. They also own and cook for The Waterside Wine Bar, just opposite the pier in Dingle where the traveller can buy a packed lunch. Here you can find rarities such as good gravad lax, which is made locally by Hans de Snoo.

Dingle town centre. Lunch 12.30-2pm. Dinner 6-9pm.

155

LONG'S FISH SHOP AND RESTAURANT
Dingle
Co Kerry
Tel: (066) 51231

Fish shop and restaurant

Mr Flannery will happily fillet a fish on the spot for you in Long's pleasantly ramshackle shop opposite Dingle pier. He talks happily and eagerly about the goodness and freshness of his fish, but the variety is somewhat limited.

Dingle town centre.

O MATHUNA TEO
Emalugh West
Dingle
Co Kerry
Tel: (066) 51810
Contact: Paddy Mahony

Fishmonger

Situated on the left hand side of the road as you drive into Dingle on the Tralee Road, O Mathuna's is a sparkling new shop with an excellent selection of fish and shellfish.

Dingle town centre.

IAN McGREGOR
Ventry
Co Kerry
Tel: (066) 55183
Contact: Ian McGregor

Organic farmer

We stopped at the post office west of Ventry to inquire Ian McGregor's whereabouts and were given a detailed back-of-envelope map. In poly-tunnels on his windy land Ian manages to grow a wide variety of fruit, vegetables and herbs. 'Seeing as I don't know what I'm doing I grow everything', he says modestly, 'and if something fails it doesn't matter'. In season he gets many callers to buy his organically-grown produce; visitors are welcome. He also supplies local hotels and restaurants.

Ask directions in the Ventry Post Office.

156

KENMARE

The pretty tourist town of Kenmare is lorded over by the magnificent Park Hotel. This boasts one of the best restaurants in the country, but other places should not be overlooked. Kenmare's strategic location between the Ring of Kerry and the Beara Peninsula means that many travel through it as well as stay there. This gives the shops a thriving basis on which to build their trade and gives the town a rich holiday atmosphere even in the winter months.

AN LEITH PHINGIN
35 Main Street
Kenmare
Co Kerry
Tel: (064) 41559
Contact: Maria and Con

Restaurant

Slightly off-beat restaurant, with eccentricities in both food and service. Stick to the pasta cooked by Maria, who is Italian, and try some of their unusual wines.

Kenmare town centre. Open 12-6-11pm.

BILLY CLIFFORD
Killowen
Kenmare
Co Kerry
Tel: (064) 41127
Contact: Billy Clifford

Organic farmer

Billy Clifford grows a full range of organic fruit and vegetables which he supplies to local restaurants and hotels, and to shops such as The Pantry, Henry Street.

Telephone for details.

THE IVY LEAF RESTAURANT
Main Street
Kenmare
Co Kerry
Tel: (064)

The Ivy Leaf is pleasing both in character and cooking: terrines of splendid lightness and depth, dreamy smoked fish, excellent breads and intriguing soups. Francis Thoma concentrates on fish and vegetable dishes and executes his small menu with enviable skill.

157

41589/41296
Contact: Francis
Thoma

Kenmare town centre. Lunch 12.00-2.00. Dinner 6.30-9.30

Restaurant

LISETTE & PETER KAL

The White House
Tuosist
Kenmare
Co Kerry
Contact: Lisette & Peter

*Farmhouse cheese and
many other food
products*

You get no indication from their signpost of the level of industry and invention which characterises Lisette and Peter Kal. They make seven varieties of cheese, eggs, delicious goats' milk and yogurt, organic vegetables, fish (some of which they arrange to have smoked), pizzas, cheesecake, and wild mussels. They also hire bikes and organise boat trips for fishing. Lisette paints and sells embroidery.

The Kals' house is clearly signposted from the R571 running South West from Kenmare. Their cheese is on sale at the Pantry in Kenmare. The other produce can be bought at the house

THE PANTRY

30 Henry Street
Kenmare
Co Kerry
Tel: (064) 31320
Contact: Flika Small

➡ *Wholefood shop*

Flika Small's little shop is a bounty of good things: Capparoe goats' cheese, bread baked by her husband in the Ivy Leaf, vegetables from Billy Clifford and other growers, plus unusual features such as hand-picked mushrooms. This is a shop where philosophy and vetting excludes anything other than the best.

Kenmare town centre.

THE PARK HOTEL

Kenmare
Co Kerry
Tel: (064) 41200
Telex: 73905
Contact: Francis
Brennan

➡ *Hotel and*

Francis Brennan has collected so many awards for his hotel in Kenmare including accolades from Michelin and Egon Ronay, that one could forgive him for resting on his bounteous laurels. That he refuses to do so is what makes The Park so special. It is a place where no detail is left to chance, where each element is perfectly tailored to ensure the guest has a perfect stay. The cooking, under the charge of Head Chef Matthew Darcy, uses all the wisest techniques of nouvelle cuisine fused with a cuisine bourgeois *restaurant*

sumptuousness.

Kenmare town centre. Lunch 1pm-2pm, Dinner 7pm-9pm.

CON RIORDAN
Cahir
Kenmare
Co Kerry
Tel: (064) 41528
Contact: Con Riordan

Ducks and duck eggs

Con Riordan rears Aylesbury ducks and sells them privately for part of the year. Telephone for more details. He also sells eggs.

Telephone for more details.

KILLARNEY

CONTINENTAL SAUSAGES
Fossa
Killarney
Co Kerry
Tel: (064)
33069/31681
Contact: K. A. Weise
or Ann Myers

German butcher shop

Three miles from Killarney is a shop where Mr Weise produces a gargantuan variety of German meats: special Landlord sausages, mushroom sausages, a rough smoked pate with green peppers, kassler, conventional sausages, salamis, Westphalian ham, lean bacon, pork fat, meat loaf, mortadella and on it goes. He also bakes bread, and you can buy sauerkraut amongst other salads. No preservatives are used in any of the products.

Turn off the road that runs from Killarney to Killorglin, just three miles from Killarney. The butchers is on the right hand side as you drive west, on the corner of Aghadoe Heights.

PAUL & DOT HAYNES
Glandore Lake
Lauragh
Killarney
Co Kerry
Tel: (064) 83110
Contact: Paul & Dot Haynes

All varieties of shellfish

The Haynes' house faces one of the most beautiful views in Ireland, and when they're not at home admiring it they collect and sell all varieties of shellfish including mussels, oysters, clams, sea urchins, periwinkles, scallops, lobster, crab and shrimp. The only crustacea they don't work with are prawns. They supply throughout the area and will deliver orders if you are on their route. You can order in small quantities. Telephone first.

Drive through Lauragh village, and on your left you will see an old ESSO sign and a signpost for Glandore Lake. Follow the road and the Haynes' house is the first you come to on the lake shore.

SPILLANE SEAFOODS
Lackabane
Killarney
Tel: (064) 31320
(Lackabane)
Tel: (064) 32938
(New Street)

Fishmonger and fish distributor

Spillane's sell direct to the public from their shop in New Street, whilst at Lackabane they organise more widespread distribution and also smoke their own salmon.

Telephone for details.

LISTOWEL

BEAL LODGE FARM PRODUCTS
Beal
Asdee
Listowel
Co Kerry
Tel: (068) 41137
Contact: Kate Carmody

Farmhouse cows' cheese

Her Cheshire upbringing inspired Kate Carmody to make a British territorial-type cheese, and thus Beal Lodge Cheese was born. She matures it for around four months, and for the moment it is distributed only locally. The milk is from the farm's fresian cows, and is used unpasteurised. At present the cheese is wax-coated, but Kate wants to change this next year. The cheeses are made in 30lb slabs, which benefits the maturing process.

Telephone for up-to-date details of where you can buy the cheese.

RING OF KERRY

The peninsula running west from Killarney and Kenmare is beloved of tourists and travellers, but offers little for the food lover except some fine cheese, including the extra special Capparoe preserved goats' cheese. Fish can be bought at the pier in Portmagee at the fishermans' co-op. It is a good idea to ask about the availability of fish and shellfish locally.

CAPPAROE GOATS' CHEESE
Greenane
Blackwater
Co Kerry
Contact: The Hensel
family

Farmhouse cheese

This is a unique cheese — the only soft cheese sold in Ireland which is preserved in jars of olive oil. The Hensel family have used an old Israeli recipe for their soft cheese, which you can buy in The Pantry at Kenmare, and the local fairs. They use their own goats' milk, organic olive oil and organic garlic from their own garden. The cheese will last a year in the jar if you have the strength and fortitude to leave any of it uneaten.

You can buy the cheese in the Pantry in Kenmare, otherwise ask locally for the bicycling Germans.

WATERVILLE GOATS' CHEESE
Derryneaden
Mastergeehy
Co Kerry
Contact: Marian &
Hans Stoffberg

Farmhouse cheese

Marian Stoffberg keeps thirteen goats and makes the small round cylinders of Waterville Cheese every four to five days. Alongside the plain cheese there are three flavoured types: cumin, mustard and chives.

Turn right at the grotto in Waterville and then ask directions. You can buy the cheese from the house, or find it in Seancara in Tralee and in local shops during the summer.

WILD NATIVE OYSTERS

At the turn of the century there were fifty wild beds of Native oysters, ostrea edulis, being actively fished off the coast of Ireland. The oyster was the poor man's food and a dozen or so washed down with a pint of stout was the common order of the day. Oysters and poverty went hand in glove.

As we near the end of the century, the oyster has become the rich man's food par excellence, along with truffles and caviar. Bivalve fiends wait for September and the start of the oyster season, getting the Muscadet or the Chablis to just the correct chilled temperature before embarking on the tricky task of opening the little devils. But no amount of difficulty in prising open the shell will deter the oyster lover who is once bitten, forever smitten.

It is a cause for regret then that today there are only four native oyster wild beds being fished, all of them off the West Coast. The Tralee Oyster Fisheries Society Ltd is probably the last surviving significant natural producer in Europe. In the seventies they produced a mere six tons which had risen to one hundred and fifteen tons by 1988. Most of the oysters are exported to France where consumption of oysters in 1988 reached 100,000 tons. Details of the Tralee Society can be obtained from Michael Quinn at (066) 22555, or Mr O'Shea on (066) 23180.

The other wild beds are Clew Bay (Contact: Paddy Quinn, Tel: (098) 41273), Clarinbridge (Contact: Mrs Mary Mullins, Tel: (091) 96174) and at Kilkieran, Comhar Chumann Sliogrisc Chonamara (Contact: Mark Norman, Tel: (095) 32300).

Details of other oyster producers can be obtained from Aquaculture Ireland, P.O. Box 16, BIM Building, Crofton Road, Dun Laoghaire, Co Dublin. Contact: John Joyce. Tel: (01) 800078/843405.

TRALEE

Tourism has given a gloss and bustle to Tralee which masks the lack of good shops and restaurants. You have to look hard to find worthwhile things, but then you are rewarded. Look for Kieran O'Callaghan's bread, tripe, drisheen, various jams and jellies and local cheeses. O'Sullivan's Delicatessen, on The Mall, will stock most of these.

KERRY FARMHOUSE CHEESE
Coolnaleen
Listowel
Co Kerry
Tel: (068) 40245
Contact: Shiela Broderick

Farmhouse cheese

Shiela Broderick makes between five and six hundred pounds of cheese each week on her farm, using raw milk from her own fresians. The cheese is a cheddar type, usually with a waxed surface, though it can be made with a natural rind on request. Varieties include a powerful garlic and chives and nettle. Shiela occasionally makes country butter in her traditional wooden churn.

Thirteen miles along the Tralee/ Listowel Road you will see a sign for Lixnaw. Take the road on the right, go up the hill past two houses opposite each other. The Broderick's is the next painted entrance on the right. Cheese is sold from the house, or you can buy it in O'Connor's Delicatessen in Listowel.

RUTH'S WHOLEFOOD KITCHEN
76 Boherbue
Tralee
Co Kerry
Tel: (066) 22665
Contact: Ruth O'Quigley

Restaurant

Fresh spring water, organic vegetables from Sean Scollard's farm, delicious banana bread: Ruth O'Quigley's little restaurant on the road into Tralee enjoys the quiet confidence of its owner. You can also take food away, and packed lunches can be organised.

Tralee town centre. Open 10.50am-5.30pm.

AN GARRAI GLAS
Alderwood Road

Sean Scollard's fascinating organic holding is divided by the Alderwood Road, but this small farm produces an amazing variety of vegetables, fruits and even

163

Tralee
Co Kerry
Tel: (066) 26752
Contact: Sean Scollard

Organic farmer

teas. Sean grows garlic also, and is keen to have students (who can stay at the farm) who wish to study organic farming methods. Visitors can buy from the house, and if they're lucky can have a conducted tour. Be sure to ask about Sean's farm-made peat-based compost.

Take the Listowel Road out of Tralee, go past the ESB station on your right. You will then see signs for An Garrai Glas.

SEANCARA
Courthouse Lane
Tralee
Tel: (066) 22644
Contact: Scott or Phil

Wholefood shop

Excellent free-range eggs, bread baked by Kieran O'Callaghan (special requests gluten-free bread baked to order) good cheeses, lemon curd and organically grown vegetables can be found with all the other features of a wholefood shop.

Tralee town centre

FARRENFORE

MUNSTER WHOLEFOODS, Farrenfore, Co Kerry. Tel: (066) 64691/64692, Fax: (066) 64692. Suppliers of wholefoods from vanilla pods, to Chinese Wok instruments, to wholemeal flour, to pills to pulses, throughout Munster. Minimum order £200.

KENMARE

REME'S CUISINE, Kilmurry, Kenmare, Co Kerry. Tel: (064) 41162, Contact: Reme Benois. The Benois sell smoked salmon (Kileancha Salmon) and smoked trout (Kenmare Mild), and their fish, which comes from fish farms, is available nationally in supermarkets, as well as throughout Europe, and in America.

KILLARNEY

BORD FAILTE, Town Hall, Killarney, Co Kerry. Tel: (064) 31633; Telex: 73952.

GABY'S SEAFOOD RESTAURANT, 17 High Street, Killarney, Co Kerry. Tel: (064) 32519. Contact: Geert Maes. Open Mon 6-10pm, Tues-Sat 12.30-2.30pm, 6-10pm. Restaurant specialising in seafood. Consistently recommended.

TRALEE

BORD FAILTE, Aras Siamsa, Godfrey Place, Tralee, Co Kerry. Tel: (066) 21288; Telex: 73125.

CHEZ JEAN-MARC, 29 Castle Street, Tralee, Co Kerry. Tel: (066) 21377. French restaurant. Consistently recommended.

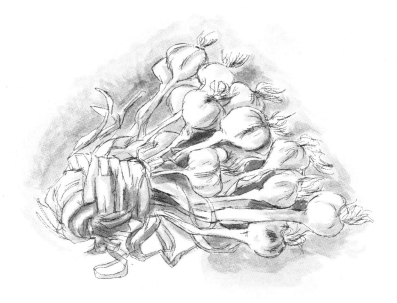

COUNTY LIMERICK

Limerick would hardly call itself a tourist town, but as the closest city to Shannon airport, it does see many visitors passing through. A number of good food products are made in this area, and there are two or three shops that would benefit any town. Limerick has a reputation for ham, and this is where one of Ireland's most famous brews, Irish Coffee, was first created.

DRUMCOLLOGHER

JONATHAN & BETTY SYKES
Springfield Castle
Drumcollogher
Co Limerick
Tel: (063) 83162
Contact: Jonathan or Betty

Venison

Jonathan Sykes farms both fallow and red deer. He is the secretary of the Irish Deer Farmers' Association, and can supply information regarding the other producers. He supplies local restaurants including the Mustard Seed in Adare, and also sells venison from the farm. It is best to ring beforehand to check that the particular cut of venison you require is available. Jonathan and Betty are also the authors of "The Irish Venison Cookbook", which you can buy for £3.95.

Ring for directions.

KILMALLOCK

GLEN-O-SHEEN
Ballinacourty

Matthew O'Brien makes Glen-o-Sheen from raw cows' milk, and ages it for a minimum of four months.

IRISH COFFEE

Irish coffee is synonymous with the Shannon region. Irish chef, Joe Sheridan, was the first to give this beverage to American movie stars, presidents and other notables when Shannon Airport first began its role as North America's gateway to Europe. This is his original recipe: Heat a steamed whiskey goblet; Pour in one jigger of whiskey; Add three cubes of sugar; Fill with strong black coffee to within one inch of the brim; Stir to dissolve sugar; Top off with whipped cream slightly aerated, so that it floats. Do not stir after adding cream, as the true flavour is obtained by drinking the hot coffee and Irish whiskey through the cream.

166

VENISON

Venison can be divided into 'cuts' in much the same way as beef, pork or lamb. For roasting you have the Shoulder, which can be boned and rolled, or roasted on the bone. The Haunch can also be roasted on the bone, or again, boned and rolled, and the Saddle cut is a prime roasting joint. For grilling or frying, Venison Chops come from the Loin, and you can also fry or grill Shoulder chops. You can cut 'steaks' from the Sirloin, the Fillet, the Topside, the Flank and the Silverside. Otherwise casseroles and pies can be made from the Shoulder meat or the Shin meat, and this meat can also yield Sausages, Burgers or Mince. Venison offal — Heart, Kidney or Liver — is also usable, though you rarely see it for sale or in restaurants. For more details and recipes buy the Sykes' Irish Venison Cook Book' (see above), or consult your butcher. Venison sausages can be bought in O'Flynn's Butchers in Cork City.

Glenroe
Kilmallock
Co Limerick
Tel: (063) 86140
Contact: Matthew and
Margaret O'Brien

It is a traditional cheddar, mild but with a distinguishing depth. The cheese is distributed mainly by Horgans, and is widely available. You can also buy from the farm where more mature cheese is available. The cheese is made in eight and fourteen pound truckles.

Farmhouse cows'
cheese

Take the road to Kilfinnan from Kilmallock, and when you come to the townland of Glenroe, Glen-o-Sheen cheese is signposted both on the road and at the farm.

LIMERICK

RENE CUSACK
Dock Road
Limerick
Tel: (061) 317556
Contact: Rene Cusack

Cusack's are a large-scale fish operation: they smoke fish, prepare it, and sell it over the counter. They buy fish from all over the country, and sell both wild and farmed. They supply to other shops, hotels and restaurants.

Fishmongers

Limerick city centre. Open: Mon-Fri 8.30am-5.30pm, Sat 8.30am-1pm.

EATS OF EDEN
Lower Cecil Street
Limerick

You will find local cheeses such as Cratloe and Inagh in Nancy Flexman and Rita O'Mahony's wholefood shop, as well as excellent sourdough breads and

167

Tel: (061) 49400
Contact: Nancy
Flexman or Rita
O'Mahony

Wholefood shop

LIMERICK FOOD CENTRE

Raheen Industrial
Estate
Limerick
Tel: (061)
302033/302035
Fax: (061) 301172
Contact: Reception

Food processing centre

FINE WINES

48 Roches' Street
Limerick
Tel: (061) 47784
Contact: John Blake

Wine merchant

Wm HOGAN BACON SHOP

74A Little Catherine
Street

wholesome brown and oat scones. There is also de Braam spring water, and on Saturday mornings do visit for Helga Friedmacher's organic vegetables (see Whitegate, in Co Clare).

Limerick city centre.

Shannon Developments have given Limerick Ireland's first ever food centre, a huge industrial estate which gives assistance to new food ventures. It offers a laboratory and a library, business accommodation and a processing hall where budding food processors can make a pilot batch of their product. This leads to occasionally tasteless, processed food, the odd failure, and a number of quality products.

Leave Limerick on the Cork/ Killarney Road — N20/N21 and you will find the Raheen Industrial Estate clearly signposted.

Italian beer, Lebanese Wine, Japanese Sake and a fine range of good European and New World wines make this off-licence an ideal place to find something unusual.

Limerick city centre.

Hogan's sell a variety of cuts of bacon and ham, the speciality of Limerick. The window is full of smoked or green rashers, hocks, and shoulders. The shop also sells cabbage.

LIMERICK SATURDAY MARKET

You will have to ask directions to the Saturday market: it's not far from O'Connell Street and held behind a walled yard, but none of the locals know of it as anything other than 'the market' and it has no formal address. You can buy Kilshanny cheese, home-made jams, bread, cakes, wonderful fresh-picked vegetables and assorted bric-a-brac. The Limerick banter is worth hearing. It was here we heard the best excuse for damp, and potentially mouldy onions: 'Sure, it was rainin' when I picked them'.

RECIPE: BACON AND CABBAGE

One of the most well-loved of Irish dishes is the traditional mixing of ham and cabbage. The ham is boiled and the rich salty stock is used to cook the cabbage. It's a marriage made in heaven. There are many different cuts of bacon to use. Some say the Gammon joint is the most tender, others opt for the shoulder, a long boiling cut. You can also use the collar, which is the continuation of the loin, and takes less time to cook, and, shorter cooking time still, you could use the breast — streaky bacon. The combinations are doubled, when you think of using smoked instead of pale. Some people recommend soaking cuts overnight, others say change the water once you bring it to the boil to remove the salt. The only thing to definitely watch is not boiling the meat too hard, as this makes it tough. You can vary the cabbage as the seasons change. In the winter the more hardy varieties need longer cooking. We think there can be nothing better than a fresh crinkly savoy, but Irish curly kale is also hard to beat. Serve with boiled potatoes, which can also be cooked in the ham juices.

Limerick
Tel: (061) 42542
Contact: William
Hogan

Bacon shop

Limerick city centre.

SPRINGFIELDS

Raheen Food Centre
Raheen Industrial
Estate
Limerick
Tel: (061) 302033
Fax: (061) 301172
Contact: Joan Hamilton

Fresh herb butters

Joan Hamilton makes a range of excellent herb butters using fresh herbs that she grows herself and fresh garlic. The flavours are: Garlic, Tarragon, Dill, Lemon and Parsley, and Mixed Herb. For the moment she is operating from the Limerick Food Centre, but she hopes to get her own premises soon. She generally supplies to the catering trade.

Telephone for more details.

ADARE

THE MUSTARD SEED, Adare, Co Limerick. Tel: (061) 86451 Contact: Dan Mullane. Much-prized by locals all the way to Limerick, both for its creative cooking, and its beautiful location in the picturesque village of Adare. Consistently recommended.

KILMALLOCK

LIMERICK COUNTRY PICKLE, Knockmore Grange, Kilmallock, Co Limerick. Contact: Patricia Merrigan.

LIMERICK

ADRINA KELLY, Limerick Food Centre, Raheen, Limerick, Tel: (061) 302033/302035, Fax: (061) 301172. Contact: Adrina Kelly. Homemade soups.

BORD FAILTE, The Granary, Michael Street, Limerick, Co Limerick. Tel (061) 317522; Telex: 42049.

LEONIDAS CHOCOLATES, O'Connell Mall, O'Connell Street, Limerick. Tel: (061) 45415. Contact: Gill. A branch of the famous Belgian Chocolate shop.

MORTELLS, 49 Roches' Street, Limerick. Tel: (061) 45457. A delicatessen in the front has Irish cheeses and neat-looking salads, as well as pasties and savouries. In the back, dinner is served from Mon-Sat, 6.30-10.30pm. Reservations to Brian.

JAMES MULLANY & CO, 283 Bedford Row, Limerick. Tel: (061) 45391. A good cheese counter and some decent bread amidst the more predictable deli products.

SHANNON

BORD FAILTE, Shannon Airport, Co Limerick. Tel:
(061) 61664.

COUNTY TIPPERARY

There is probably no other single construction in Ireland as impressive as the Rock of Cashel. The church dates originally from the thirteenth century; it was set on fire in 1495 and then again in 1647, abandoned and then re-edified before being abandoned again. For the last one hundred and twenty five years it has been a national monument. The rock dominates not only the neat town of Cashel, but also the surrounding countryside; it may be a ruin but it is a magnificent ruin, allowing the town to struggle up to the title of 'Cashel of the Kings'.

There is nothing else in Tipperary quite so grand, except perhaps the heather, when it is in bloom on the bogs. A mist of lilac and purple, it looks so inviting that it makes you want to lie down amongst it.

ARDFINNAN

NUJUICE
Main Street
Ardfinnan
Co Tipperary
Tel: (052) 66245
Contact: Robert or
William Nugent

Fresh fruit juice.

The Nugents squeeze their fresh fruit juices at night and deliver them first thing in the morning. They deliver door to door, and to hotels from Clonmel to Carlow. What you get is pure orange juice, nothing more, nothing less. It will last up to three days.

Telephone for details.

CAHIR

BALLYBRADO HOUSE
Cahir
Co Tipperary
Tel: (052) 66206
Contact: Joseph Finke

Organic flour

You can find and buy Ballybrado flour and organic oatmeal all over the country. Joseph Finke looks after the mill and the animals on the farm, whilst Richard Auler looks after the tillage. Ballybrado have recently allied to Brennan's Bakery in Dublin to produce an organic loaf — Brennan's Ballybrado Bread — which is sold in many shops and supermarkets. At the farm there is also a guesthouse, which is suitable for a

Organic oatmeal

couple and two children to stay in.

Telephone for further details.

CARRICK-ON-SUIR

JOHN JO DUNPHY
Currasilla
Grangemockler
Carrick-on-Suir
Co Tipperary
Tel: (051) 47087
Contact: John Jo
Dunphy

Organic farmer, vegetables and milk

Holder of the IOFGA symbol — vegetable grower and farmer. Potatoes and milk are in transition stage.

Telephone for more details.

CASHEL

MICHAEL HICKEY
Gortrua
Cashel
Co Tipperary
CLOGHEEN
Tel: (062) 72223
Contact: Michael
Hickey

Organic beef

Michael Hickey sells single suckled organic beef to various restaurants and private customers in the area. You have to order it in advance, and when the animal is ready you receive your order. There are no storage facilities at the farm. All beef is sold at under two years of age, and Michael sells it by the quarter, or by the half side.

Telephone for more details.

BAYLOUGH CHEESE
Mount Anglesby
Clogheen
Co Tipperary
Tel: (052) 65275
Contact: Dick and Ann
Keating

Every single aspect of the production of Baylough cheese is carried out by hand — a cheese making day will see Dick and Ann Keating put in eight solid hours of work. The cheese they make repays all their efforts: Baylough is proudly individual and one of those cheeses that people can't leave alone until it is all eaten. The Keatings age the cheese for twelve weeks and are fortunate in having pastures littered

Farmhouse cheese

with wild herbs for their fresian cattle to graze on. Along with the plain Baylough there are two other varieties: Garlic and Herb, and Fresh Herb. They are currently experimenting with a smoked cheese. You can buy the cheese from the farm.

The farm is just outside the village of Clogheen. Ring for accurate directions.

CLONMEL

EDMUND BURKE & SONS
O'Connell Street
Clonmel
Co Tipperary
Tel: (050) 22700
Contact: Mr Burke

Bacon and ham

Burke's shop on O'Connell Street in Clonmel has been in business for more than one hundred and twenty five years. It's a big, ungainly shop which specialises in bacon and hams amongst other meat products. Their green bacon is excellent — meat which you can fry and which doesn't then boil in its own added water. Or buy one of their hams and boil and bake and serve with cabbage for an everyday treat.

Clonmel town centre.

CORMAC LOGUE
Ballynamuddagh
Grange
Clonmel
Co Tipperary
Tel: (052) 38233
Contact: Cormac
Logue

Organic farmer

Holder of the IOFGA symbol, a vegetable grower. Cormac is also a member of the Clonmel Co-Op.

Telephone for more details. or buy his produce from the Fri and Sat market in Clonmel (See Over The Rainbow)

PATRICK AND ANGELA MULROONEY
Manganstown
Kilsheelan
Clonmel

Holders of the IOFGA symbol, farmers with a mixed farm. Part of the Clonmel co-op supplying potatoes, especially in the winter. Milk of transition standard.

Telephone for more details.

174

Co Tipperary
Tel: (052) 33196
Contact: Patrick and
Angela

*Organic vegetables,
tillage and milk*

**OVER THE
RAINBOW
THE HONEY POT
THE ABBEY CO-
OP**
14 Abbey Street
Clonmel
Co Tipperary
Tel: (052) 21457
(Abbey Rest)

*Wholefood shop,
organic vegetables,
restaurant*

This impressive organisation houses a wholefood shop, an excellent organic vegetable market, lasting from 10am-6pm on Fridays and Saturdays and a good restaurant run by a co-operative. The vegetables come from local symbol holders such as Peter Binder and Regula Chriisten of Carryduff, South Lodge, Carrick-on-Suir, and you can also find gorgeously aromatic herbs, free-range eggs and rarities like desiree potatoes. The restaurant has good wholesome food and does simple things like bread and cheese and a pot of tea simply and properly. Further information on local organic foodstuffs can be obtained here.

Clonmel town centre.

FETHARD

CASHEL BLUE
Beechmount
Fethard
Co Tipperary
Tel: (052) 31151
Contact: Jane and
Louis Grubb

★ *Farmhouse cows'
cheese*

Cashel Blue is hand-made from unpasteurised cows' milk, dry-salted by hand for two days, then pierced and kept at ten degrees centigrade for two weeks during which time the surface is washed. It is then wrapped in gold foil and further matured in a cold store. This careful production results in one of the finest Irish cheeses you can buy: a good Cashel Blue, perhaps a couple of months old, is a monstrously wonderful cheese — the blue well-balanced amidst the pale creaminess of the cheese, the whole a crescendo of tastes. Jane and Louis Grubb started off with an old beer vat they bought for fifty pounds in Clonmel. Now, happily, they are amongst the largest producers of farmhouse cheese and this is the cheese that can be found everywhere. You can buy from the farm, but only by appointment, and cheeses can be sent in the post.

Ring for more details.

JENNIFER WHYTE
Grangebeg
Fethard
Co Tipperary
Tel: (052) 23402
Contact: Jennifer
Whyte

Organic vegetables

Holder of the IOFGA symbol — vegetable grower. Members of the Clonmel Co-Op.

Telephone for more details.

MULLINAHONE

COMPSEY CREAMERY SOCIETY LTD
Mullinahone
Co Tipperary
Tel: (052) 53194
Contact: David
Mitchell

➡ *Yogurt, cottage and cream cheese*

Compsey Creamery yogurt has to be tasted to be believed. It is a thick, lush emulsion, packed with smooth effervescence, and served with a little clover honey it cannot be bettered as a dessert. Along with this glorious product, David Mitchell produces a range of cottage and cream cheeses which are perfect for cheesecakes, and supplies other dairies which sell Compsey products under their own labels.

Look out for the Compsey label but the cheeses are sold under the Greenhills label, as well as Avonmore and Marks and Spencer.

NENAGH

LAKESHORE FOODS
Coolbawn
Nenagh
Co Tipperary
Tel: (067) 22094

Lakeshore Foods was established by Hilary Henry in 1986, since when the company has seen its mustards march onto shelves in almost every shop in the country. There are six varieties of whole-grain mustard, including one with Irish whiskey, sold both in large angled pots and tiny little tubs. Because of their

Contact: Hilary Henry

Mustard

mildness they are particularly good for using in sauces.

Telephone for more details.

ROSCREA

ABBEY STONEGROUND WHOLEMEAL

Mount Saint Joseph
Abbey
Roscrea
Co Tipperary
Tel: (0505) 21711
Contact: The Cistercian
Monks

Wholemeal flour

Abbey Stoneground Wholemeal came to fame when Elizabeth David described it in 1977 as 'the finest flavoured 100 per cent stoneground wholemeal I have yet come across'. It does indeed have tremendous flavour, and despite being 100% wholemeal, and coarsely ground, it holds together well and gives you 100% success if you're making brown bread.

Telephone for further details.

TEMPLEMORE

CRANNAGH CASTLE

Templemore
Co Tipperary
Tel: (0504) 53104
Contact: Gillies
MacBain

Organic farm, organic gardening courses, hostel

Gillies MacBain farms organically and runs an Independent Hostel and an Organic Guesthouse. Five or six times a year he runs organic gardening courses at the castle — these are organised by Laura Turner (Tel: (01) 453853) and last around five days. You can buy any surplus vegetables Gillies produces at the Castle.

From the N7 turn west at Johnstown, the road is signposted to Templetuohy. Drive for about twelve miles, and at Templetuohy take the Loughmoe Road. After a quarter of a mile turn again to the right (also posted Loughmoe) After a mile you will see the house on the right hand side. Telephone for further details.

THURLES

COOLEENEY CHEESE

Cooleeney House
Moyne
Thurles
Co Tipperary
Tel: (0504) 45112
Contact: Breda Maher

Farmhouse cows' cheese

Breda Maher has been making Cooleeney, a camembert-style cheese, for three years now. She uses raw milk from her herd of fresian cows, and the cheese is usually sold when it is two to three weeks old. If, however, you want a more mature cheese, you can usually find them in Peter Ward's shop, Country Choice, in Nenagh. Breda also sells from the farm. Look out especially for the small Cooleeney which comes in an exquisite little wooden box which Breda makes also.

Cooleeney House is about three miles off the main N7 Dublin-Cork Road. Take the turning at Mary Willie's Roadhouse, on the right hand side of the road as you drive south, and go straight for three miles. It is a good idea to ring to check availability etc of the cheese.

DERRYNAFLAN CHEESE

Derrynaflan
Ballinure
Thurles
Co Tipperary
Tel: (052) 56406
Contact: Sheila
O'Sullivan

Farmhouse cows' cheese

Derrynaflan is a creamy, semi-smooth cheese made from raw cows' milk by Sheila O'Sullivan. It's usually aged for about three weeks — though this can be extended to up to two months. The cheese is widely available — it is distributed by both Horgans and the Traditional Cheese Company. It's a salted cheese with a natural rind.

The cheese is sold at Quinnsworth supermarkets. Telephone for more details.

TWOMILEBORRIS

LIATHMORE DAIRIES
Twomileborris
Co Tipperary
Tel: (0504) 44325
Contact: Donal Hayes

*Farmhouse cream
cheese*

Liathmore make a cream cheese with pasteurised milk, and call it Coolemore Cream Cheese. They make it in two flavours, plain, and garlic and herb. It's widely available around Tipperary, but they don't sell from the farm.

Telephone for more details.

CAHIR

BRAMLEIGH LODGE, Cashel Road, Cahir, Co Tipperary. Tel: (052) 41838 Herb Jellies.

W. TRAAS, Clonmel Road, Co Tipperary. Three miles from Cahir. Apples.

CASHEL

CHEZ HANS, Cashel, Co Tipperary. Tel: (062) 61177, Contact: Hans Peter Matthia. Restaurant at the base of the Rock of Cashel in an old church. Open for dinner Tues-Sat, 7pm-10pm. Consistently recommended.

COUNTY WATERFORD

Many people know Waterford on account of its glass. Fewer know of it because of Blaas, a round white roll with a crispy crust that can be found throughout the county. It's an unusual item, insofar as it has not travelled beyond the county boundaries — most Irish specialities are quickly ubiquitous. Otherwise, the high price of land and houses has meant that one finds few of the cottage industries here which thrive elsewhere. This is a tidy, neat county where people keep their hands clean.

Sadly, many visitors to the 'sunny south east' know only of Tramore, the resort south of Waterford city. Choose instead the pretty, settled places like Lismore, bustling Dungarvan, or beautiful Dunmore East.

BALLYMACARBRY

VICKY HESLOP
Tooracurragh
Ballymacarbry
Co Waterford
Tel: (052) 36304
Contact: Vicky Heslop

*Organic pork
sausages, vegetables*

Vicky Heslop keeps organic free-range saddleback pigs on her holding in a luscious valley in Co Waterford. Her farm is a perfect unity between pigs, goats and a donkey, who clear her land, allowing her to grow organic vegetables which she sells locally. You can buy pork and kid meat from her, and best of all she makes delicious sausages: plain and herb.

You can buy from the farm. Telephone for details.

DUNGARVAN

RING
Gortnadiha House
Ring
Dungarvan
Co Waterford
Tel: (058) 46142
Contact: Eileen and

The big, orangey cylinders of Ring cheese can be seen in most parts of the country. It's a lovely full, almost spicy cheese with an intense, complex taste and melting texture. As with most cheese, the older it is the better it gets. Tom and Eileen Harty make the cheese from the raw milk of their Fresian cows. They age it for five months before it is sold.

Tom Harty

Farmhouse cows' cheese

You can buy the cheese from the farm, as well as numerous shops throughout the country. Telephone for directions.

DUNMORE EAST

THE SHIP
Dunmore East
Co Waterford
Tel: (051)
83141/83144
Contact: D & L
Prendiville

Pub with restaurant

This restaurant is one of a rare type in Ireland: inexpensive, informal, relaxed and good. The discretion and good taste shown by the Prendivilles runs right through from the furnishings — barrel seats, polished tables without cloths, discreet bars — to the wine list, one of the most intelligent and selective small lists you will find. The food includes excellent bisques and unusual combinations such as fish mousse sandwiched between tortillas, good fresh fish simply pan fried, and pork stuffed with wild mushrooms. Vegetables range from hearty local varieties like marrow, to the rather more ethereal, like bok choy.

Dunmore East town centre.

KNOCKANORE

KNOCKANORE CHEESE
Ballyneety
Knockanore

Eamonn Lonergan uses raw cows' milk from his farm to make Knockanore, a very pale, creamy, semi-soft cheese. The cheese is aged for between sixteen and twenty weeks, when it leaves the farm. It is, says

THE PORT AT DUNMORE EAST

Such is the fame of the fishing port of Dunmore East that you expect, when you first visit, to find a sprawling mess of corrugated-roofed buildings and a rank smell of decomposing fish. Instead, thanks to a vigilent harbour master, the port is neat and well-contained, adding to, rather than stealing from the quaintness of the village. But, if you want to buy fresh fish, George Roche is your only man, we were told: there is no selling from the boats. Roche's is on the right hand side as you drive down the hill to the pier, and keeps fairly standard business hours, so don't expect to buy fish either late at night or early in the morning.

Co Waterford
Tel: (024) 97275
Contact: Eamonn
Lonergan

Farmhouse cheese

LISMORE

MRS GARDNER
Eenaknockhan East
Lismore
Co Waterford
Tel: (058) 54071/54084
Contact: Mrs Gardner

Smoked foods, Jacob sheep

SYBILLE KNOBEL
Kilmoura
Lismore
Co Waterford
Tel: (058) 543415
Contact: Sybille Knobel

Baby Beef

PASSAGE EAST

CHEZ FLAVIEN
The Farleigh Pub
Passage East
Co Waterford
Tel: (051) 82536
Contact: Flavien Poirier
➥ *Restaurant*

Eamonn, particularly suitable for cooking. You can buy from the farm.

Telephone for directions.

Along with rearing Jacob sheep which she sells by the half carcass, Mrs Gardner smokes a wide variety of fish including salmon, mackerel, eel and cod's roe. The salmon is from the local Blackwater river. You can telephone to arrange orders which is the only way the products are available apart from the annual Wexford Festival at the end of October. She can arrange for the sheep to be butchered according to specification — one notable fact is that they have a very low bequerel level.

Telephone for more details or to arrange orders.

Sybille Knobel rears calves on grass and milk — the animals are suckled until the day they are slaughtered — which results in animals that are a cross between baby beef and veal. Ballymaloe House is one of her customers, but she is also happy to sell privately and can arrange for the meat to be prepared for the freezer.

Telephone first to check availability.

Burgundy comes to Passage East! Flavien Poirier cooks boeuf bourguignonne exactly as you hope it will be cooked, not a steaming stew of meat and carrots, but a compact assemblage of tastes and textures, each perfectly related to the other. With fish his understanding is even more astute, each thing perfectly cooked in daring French sauces. Vegetables are perfect and gratin dauphinois an invitation to be a glutton. Desserts are dreamy concoctions. The wine list is a fine selection of specially imported French varieties. This is genuine French provincial cooking in the Irish provinces.

Situated over the Farleigh pub in the centre of Passage East. Passage East can be approached by road from Waterford or by a continuous car ferry service from Ballyhack in Wexford. Dinner only, from 7.30pm.

WATERFORD

BRENNER'S PORK SHOP
28 Barronstrand Street
Waterford
Tel: (051) 70450
Contact: Ger Brenner

Pork butcher

Brenner's was established over sixty year's ago, and little in the shop has changed since. The sausages both look and taste the way sausages used to taste: peppery, long knotted tubes of meat that burst if you don't prick them. The black and white puddings are good, and so is the often derided hazlett. Don't expect a modern style antiseptic butcher with all the cuts neatly displayed as if they have never been part of any beast; in this shop great slabs of shoulder sit beside the sausage machine, and the butchering takes place in the front of the shop.

Waterford city centre.

CHAPMAN'S DELICATESSEN
61 The Quay
Waterford
Tel: (051)
74938/76200
Contact: Mr
Prendergast

Food shop and restaurant.

Chapman's is, simply, the best shop in Waterford. You can buy almost everything good the county and its surroundings offer: Lavistown sausages, Dunmore Eastern Curry Paste, fine free-range eggs, salmon and mackerel, cheese from Compsey Creamery and, best of all, freshly ground coffee which is roasted on the premises. The staff exude both knowledge and courtesy: if you bring in salmon they can arrange to have it smoked for you. Well-made pate and ice-cream make this an indispensable place. There is also a restaurant at the back of the shop.

Waterford city centre.

183

FULL OF BEANS
9 George's Court
Waterford
Contact: Ian & Sonia
McLellan

Wholefood shop

This small shop in the modern George's Court complex is notable for the organic vegetables the McLellan's grow themselves: what they can offer varies with the season, but peas, lettuce, courgettes and beans are summer staples. There is also excellent wholemeal bread — made by a professional baker using both a recipe and flour from the McLellans. Goats' milk yogurt from Coolfinn Farm, Ann Smyth's yogurt from Dunmore East as well as the predictable array of wholefoods. Vegetables are usually in on Tuesdays and Fridays.

Waterford city centre.

KILKENNY HERBS
High Street
Waterford
Tel: (051) 70213
Fax: (051) 77542
Contact: Joseph Kiely

Specialist restaurant services

Kilkenny Herbs is, in fact, a company supplying a great deal more than herbs. Joe Kiely supplies French barbery ducks, including Magret de Canard, fois gras — both fresh and in terrines, whole duck, breast of duck, etc. He supplies wild mushrooms: morels, cepes, or boulets. He will get you guinea fowl, filo pastry or vanilla pods, escargots, kumquats or saffron. As well as all this there are the herbs: basil, chives, chervil, lovage, all culinary herbs that either grow in this country, or come in from Israel. He sells directly to restaurants and supermarkets, and you will find his herbs in the Dublin corporation market at N.J. King, Keatings, or Begleys. The company is unique in supplying edible flowers all year round.

Telephone for more details.

DUNMORE EAST

BORD FAILTE, 41 The Quay, Waterford, Co. Waterford. Tel: (051) 75788.

PAUL CHEDGY, Coxtown, Dunmore East, Co Waterford. Tel: (051) 83130. Holder of IOFGA symbol, selling fruit.

DUNMORE EASTERN CURRY PRODUCTS: Exotic curry pastes which you can find in old marmalade jars for sale in Chapman's in Waterford Town, where you can get more details.

DUNMORE EAST NATURAL YOGHURT, Contact: Ann Smyth, Lisselan, Dunmore East, Co Waterford. Tel: (051) 86115.

GLENCAIRN

ELIZABETH KINGSTON, Ballymartin House, Glencairn, Co Waterford. Tel: (058) 56227. Holder of IOFGA symbol. Fruit and vegetable grower.

GRANNAGH

EDWARD PURCELL, Grannagh, Co Waterford. Tel: (051) 76438. All manner of equipment for beekeepers.

PORTLAW

MICHAEL SHANAHAN, Coolfinn Farm, Portlaw, Co Waterford. Tel: (051) 87314. Farm in transition to IOFGA symbol — look out for excellent yogurt which can be bought in Full of Beans, and also goats' milk.

WATERFORD

CHERRY'S BREWERIES LTD, Mary Street, Waterford. Tel: (051) 74963.

LEONIDAS CHOCOLATES, Broad Street Centre, Waterford. Tel: (051) 70533. Contact: Angela.

Ulster

COUNTY ANTRIM

Sweeping glens, a mottled and occasionally magnificent coastline, rolling pastures and sprightly bogland interspersed with frowsy towns and the sprawl of Belfast means that County Antrim offers a huge panoply of scenery and sights. The excellent roads mean that the traveller can, if he or she is daft enough, miss all of it and by-pass place after place, but it is best to stray from the M-roads and waddle around the coast and through the Glens. Everyone knows about the Giant's Causeway, but the county has much more to offer, above all a complex and stubborn character, as well as a pleasingly incoherent accent which increases in character as you head east.

BALLYCASTLE

GLENSHESK DAIRIES
67 Whitepark Road
Carnmoor
Ballycastle
Co Antrim
Tel: (026 57) 62743
Contact: John McKinley

Cream cheese, yogurt dessert, fromage frais

Glenshesk Dairies' soft cheese is a pleasingly smooth, mild-flavoured emulsion that comes in a variety of flavours: Garlic, Spring Onion, Pineapple, Hazelnut, and Natural. As well as the tubs of cheese, which can be found in many shops and wholefood stores, Glenshesk make a yogurt dessert with fruit and, best of all, fromage frais with fruit, a meltingly gorgeous dessert concoction.

Telephone for details.

WYSNER MEATS
18 Ann Street
Ballycastle
Co Antrim
Tel: (026 57) 62373
Contact: Roland Wysner

Customers have given Wysner's sausages one of the supreme accolades: they have compared them to the late lamented and much missed Hafner's sausages of Dublin. Awards given to Roland include the Champion of Champions of Great Britain, and he has picked up numerous prizes for his black pudding. Look out for the beef sausages made by Roland's daughter Jackie, and ask to see the black pudding made in the shape of a bottle of Black Bush with a shamrock made of tongue running through it.

Ballycastle town centre.

BELFAST

So much demolition and building has been carried out in Belfast in recent years, that it can be difficult even for locals to find their way around. But along with the neat new post-modern architecture there is a more relaxed atmosphere to the city than could be found a decade ago; the restaurants and pubs are busy and even if the city still empties after working hours some pockets of life remain, especially around the University and Shaftesbury Square.

BELFAST RESTAURANTS

The visitor to Belfast who is puzzled by just how the citizens of this city have managed to survive twenty years of 'the troubles' need go no further than the restaurants and pubs of the capital to get an answer. People in Belfast have made the equation between eating good food and having a good time and while there is not yet a great deal of the former, it is easy to find a great deal of the latter.

The bistro La Belle Epoque, on Great Victoria Street (Tel: (0232) 323244, open Mon-Fri 5pm-12.30pm, Sat 6pm-11.30pm), is a niftily reconstructed premises with a touch of fin de siecle depravity about it. It is, as bistros should be, pleasingly democratic, and showcases Northerners and their famous devotion to a good time.

Much of the rest of the city's food is like this: a grab-bag of foreign fare that has squeezed out any indigenous cooking. The only place you will find true Ulster food is in Ulster houses; it is not for restaurant menus and has never been elevated to anything other than the domestic kitchen. In the vacuum created by this diffidence, the world and its chef has moved in.

So for good French bistro fare, try La Belle Epoque.

Something more straightforward can be found in The Strand, half a mile away on the Stranmillis Road (Tel: (0232) 682266. Open: 11.30am-11.30pm, Mon-Sat). Here ageing couples court away the afternoon amidst the office lunchtimers and visiting coffee drinkers. It's predictable food, chewy chilli, well-defined vegetarian lasagne, cheesy croquettes and teasing dishes wrapped with filo pastry, and it's open all day.

You can get Tapas in Hammill's on Botanic Avenue (Tel: (0232) 332626, Open 10.00am-11.30pm), but it's Costa del Sol Tapas rather than the real thing. Those who want Italian tend to opt for Ciros or Speranza (Tel: (0232) 230213, on Great Victoria Street. For Indian food head for the Ashoka on the Lisburn Road (Tel: (0232) 660362, Open Mon-Thurs 5.30-11.30pm, Fri-Sat 5.30-12 midnight, Sun 5.00-10.30pm) and for Chinese food try The Welcome House on the Stranmillis Road (Tel: (0232) 381359, Open Mon-Fri, 12-2pm & 5.30-11.30pm, Sat-Sun 5.30-11pm).

If you want to step back into history head for the glorious Crown Liquor Saloon, opposite the Opera House. It's a stupendous architectural monolith that serves stew, champ, and oysters. Otherwise go around the corner to the Linen Hall Pub, a more tamely reconstructed version of the past. (Tel: (0232) 248458, Open for food 12pm-2.30 Mon-Sat). There is old-fashioned cordon bleu in Restaurant 44, near the Ulster Hall (Tel: (0232) 244844, Open Mon-Fri 12-3pm and 6.30-11.30pm, 6-11.30pm Sat). But the jewel in Belfast's crown is Roscoff, in Shaftesbury Square an eating house of thorough excellence.

DIRECT WINE SHIPMENTS
5/7 Corporation
Square
Belfast
Co Antrim
Tel: (0232)
238700/243906
Contact: Kevin
McAlindon

*Wine importers and
merchants*

Direct Wine Shipments work from an appropriately
musty, dusty building near Belfast docks, which
transforms wine buying into something of an
adventure. They are agents for the wines from Spain
made by Miguel Torres, but have wide-ranging
selections from all the European countries, especially
Bulgaria. Good older French vintages can be found,
and the staff are friendly and knowledgeable. There
is a second shop at 18 Abbey Street, Coleraine (Tel:
(0265) 2113/4031) and associated shops are
Duncairn Wines at 555 Antrim Road, Belfast (Tel:
(0232) 370694) and Downtown Shopping Centre,
Downpatrick, Co Down (Tel: (0396) 3392). The shop
at Corporation Square is open from 9.30-5.30pm
Mon-Fri, and from 10-1pm on Saturday.

In the docks area of Belfast city centre.

ROSCOFF
7 Lesley House
Shaftesbury Square
Belfast
Co Antrim
Tel: (0232) 331532
Contact: Paul and
Jeannie Rankin

➥ *Restaurant*

Spanking new, deliciously fashionable and with an
assurance in its cooking that is almost unique in
Northern Ireland, Roscoff is an exciting and ingenious
restaurant. The decor is California crossed with
surrealism, and the food an expertly delivered
variation of post-nouvelle cuisine: melting confit of
duck, minced balls of veal with thin ribbon pasta,
cuspy red pepper gateau are some of the starters.
Main courses include monkfish on a bed of wild rice,
crisp chicken and splayed breast of duck, with
desserts an extravagance built from simple
foundations such as caramel, strawberries and home-
made ice cream. The wine list could perhaps be more
discriminating, but otherwise everything at Roscoff is
perfect.

Belfast city centre, near the University.

SUPERMAC
Newtownbreda
Shopping Centre
Saintfield Road
Belfast 8

Supermac was the first of the large-scale supermarkets
in Northern Ireland, and today it is distinguished by
being more selective and receptive than any of the
other multiples. There is an excellent cheese counter,
organic lamb from Brackfield Farm, Organic

192

Tel: (0232) 491176
Contact: The Manager

Supermarket

Vegetables grown by the Hawthornes in County Derry and even Organic bread. Most of the food from small producers throughout the North can be found here: look out for the fromage frais with fresh fruit from Glenshesk dairies, Adelboden bread and Caora and Boley Hill cheeses. The staff are extremely helpful.

At the top of the Saintfield Road on Belfast's Outer Ring.

SAWERS LTD
Unit 7
Fountain Centre
Belfast 1
Tel: (0232) 322021
Contact: The Manager

*Fishmonger and
delicatessen*

Fresh fish and shellfish, good counters of both cheese and cooked meat, country butter and a wide assortment of delicatessen products. Upstairs in the Fountain Centre you can find a decent kitchen supply shop if you want to splash out on smart kitchenware.

Belfast city centre.

ARCADIA
378 Lisburn Road
Belfast
Tel: (0232) 666779
Contact: Mr Brown

Delicatessen

A narrow shop packed with good things. A good cheese counter with cheeses from North and South, cooked meats, including pastrami, many types of salami and a healthy selection of pates both home-made and imported. Bells coffee is also for sale. There is another decent deli on Botanic Avenue: Canterbury and Dyke is just up from the train station and has a good array of fruit and veg.

Near the top end of the Lisburn Road, on the left hand side as you drive towards the King's Hall.

BUSHMILLS

OLD BUSHMILLS DISTILLERY
Bushmills
Co Antrim
Tel: (026 57) 31521
Contact: The Tour Dept
for arranging tours,
and the Public Relations
Exec. for general
enquiries

Whiskey

The Distillery organises tours and tastings of their splendid whiskies during the week. Long a favourite haunt of crazed students day-tripping from Queen's University in Belfast, it's a good chance to absorb both history and the potent spirit distilled here. Try the pleasingly cloying Black Bush, the sharper Bushmills whiskey and the pricey Bushmills Malt.

Telephone for details.

LISBURN

GREENS FOOD FARE
23 Bow Street
Lisburn
Tel: (0846)
662124/662641
Contact: The manager

Delicatessen

Delightfully old-fashioned, labyrinthine shop that sells everything you could need. Good eggs, including duck eggs and quail eggs from Firgrove Quail, (40 Ballymachedan Road, Moralin, Craigavon Tel: (0762) 323149, Contact: Derek & Lynne Patterson), local vegetables including some organic produce, Cottage Pride preserves from Allistragh in Armagh and so on, all arranged in a pleasingly ramshackle way. Look out also for the Thorntons sweet shop a few doors down from Greens: excellent toffee.

Lisburn city centre.

PORTGLENONE

OUR LADY OF BETHLEHEM ABBEY
Portglenone Co Antrim
Tel: (0266) 821473
Contact: Father Jim
Conlon

Flour, oatmeal and

'We bought the digester in order to farm organically', said Father Jim of their machine which runs a mysterious cycle from cow slurry to sweet smelling compost. The side product of the machine is that it helps to heat the Abbey to which the farm is attached. It also warms the grain that is ground to make Abbey Corn flour, and porridge oats. Slats underneath the cattle collect the slurry and scrape it down into the Digester. Here the heady cocktail of hen slurry, rotten *organic compost*

potatoes and silage effluent is slewed together into the massive drum. A series of pipes under what they call the 'Bishop's Hat' sweeps the bacteria through the machine every ten minutes. The bacteria nibble away at the solids until the whole thing is 'digested'. The offshoot of gas fills a balloon, and the solids and liquid matter are separated and composted to make Concentrated Compost, a Turf Dressing and a Mulch which is composed partly of tree bark. They are working on a multi-purpose compost, but are trying to make one without using peat (substitutes could be dried animal blood and more tree bark). Abbey Corn wheat, organically grown, both coarse and finely ground is available, along with Abbey Corn Pinhead Oatmeal, in many wholefood shops through-out the North. At the Abbey it is sold in the craft shop along with a little recipe leaflet, and some country butter.

Telephone for details.

PORTRUSH

RAMORE RESTAURANT
The Harbour
Portrush
Co Antrim
Tel: (0265) 824313
Contact: John & Joy
Caithness, George &
Jane McAlpin

Restaurant

Stylish and very busy restaurant in the unlikely location of Portrush, which is otherwise a town of chippers, candy-floss and decaying Victorian buildings. The Ramore is probably the best-known and most oft-awarded, eating place in Ulster and some of their food can be thrilling: intense pigeon breast on springy kale cabbage puddled in a chocolate jus, feuillette of morels, a chocolate souffle that is simply breathtaking. But occasionally technique triumphs over taste. The wine list is good, and includes the famous Rothschild/Mondavi Opus One at £65.50, but many of the diners seem addicted to the house white. There is also a wine bar, open during the day, attached to the complex.

Overlooking the harbour at Portrush.

TOOMEBRIDGE

LOUGH NEAGH FISHERMENS' CO-OPERATIVE SOCIETY

Toomebridge
Co Antrim
BT41 3SB
Tel: (0648) 50618
Telex: 747465
Contact: Chief
Executive, Father
Kennedy; Secretary/
Manager, Pat Close

Eels

In season you can see an efficient troop of men catch, grade, pack and transport both brown eel and silver eel. This most mysterious fish is a prized delicacy in Holland and Germany where most of the Lough Neagh catch ends up, smoked and packed into neat little trays. The Co-Op is the largest eel fishery in this part of Europe, and almost all of its catch is exported. Of local people, secretary/manager Pat Close told us, only the Chinese community value this most quixotic of foods, a pity because all you need to do to a fresh eel is to fry it slowly in its own oil, in a pan, turning occasionally for about one hour, to have a most delicious meal. Serve it hot or cold with horseradish.

Coming into Toome from the town of Bellaghy, the Co-Operative building is just on the left before the bridge.

BALLYNURE

LODGE FARM PRODUCE, Legaloy, Ballynure, Co Antrim. Country Butter.

BELFAST

BORD FAILTE, 53 Castle Street, Belfast BT1 1GH. Tel: (0232) 327888, Telex: 74560.

EQUINOX, Howard Street, Belfast, Co Antrim. Lots of nifty Rosenthal china and Italian art objects for you to fall in love with.

NORTHERN IRELAND TOURIST BOARD, 48 High Street, Belfast, BT1 2DS. Tel: (0232) 231331

LISBURN

NORTHERN IRELAND GOAT CLUB, Chairman: Peter

Woods, 37 Lisnoe Road, Lisburn, Co Antrim. Tel: (0849) 663565. Will know producers of goats' milk, etc, though not a producer himself.

PAUL SCOTT, Secretary, Ulster Organic Producers, 41 Warren Gardens, Lisburn BT28 1EA, Co Antrim.

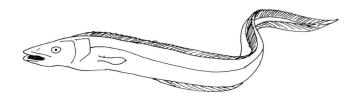

COUNTY ARMAGH

Neat orchards with rows of well-behaved trees sagging with red-speckled apples have always been the hallmark of County Armagh. The second, less pleasing characteristic is the fortress-like nature of the towns and villages. Heavily fortified with an overpowering security presence, the stranger in this area can feel totally alienated and unsettled just driving around. Add to this the aggravated metropolis of Craigavon and you realise that Armagh is a place where one is wisest to stay in the countryside.

To counter this the town of Armagh is a charming, settled place, dominated by the sharp spires of the cathedral. Its compactness and easy familiarity with history give it a unique flavour. The other rich aspect of Armagh's history, the apple, has declined in flavour and variety. You can buy from many of the growers and there are copious numbers of signs inviting you to do so as you drive along, but trying to find something unusual seems just about impossible.

HOCKLEY

BRUCE AND GRACE CLUNY

Meadow Farm
23 Drumilly Road
Hockley
Co Armagh
Tel: (0762) 870667
Contact: Bruce and
Grace

Organic farmers

The Cluny's farm part-time, so their produce is only available from the farm. In their gorgeous Victorian walled garden they have beetroot, cabbage, spuds and some honey — though Grace Cluny tells us that the enormous volume of sprays used by farmers to protect their apple crops, in fact kills the bees. Some of the varieties of apples in the Cluny's garden cannot now, sadly, be identified, but this only makes the fruit more intriguing. In their greenhouse they also have peaches, wonderfully luscious, indulgent fruit which drench you as you bite into them, and they also grow grapes.

Drumilly Road is seven miles from Portadown on the road to Armagh. Meadow Farm is behind the Hockley Lodge Old People's Home — use the same entrance but go left at the park. Ring first to check availability of produce.

MOUNTNORRIS

BOLEY HILL CHEDDAR

Mountnorris
Co Armagh
BT 60 2TZ
Tel: (0861) 57209
Contact: John and
Elizabeth Magowan

*Farmhouse cows'
cheese*

Boley Hill is a splendid, rich cheddar cheese which, thanks to being aged for six months, has a complexity and fullness that you never find in a conventional cheddar. John and Elizabeth Magowan currently make about 150lbs of this raw milk cheese each week. It is the only farmhouse cheddar produced in the North: when John approached the Milk Marketing Board about making a cheese 'they did not know what to do with me', he says. The Magowans distribute the cheese themselves at present. The mountain which is drawn on the label of the cheese is Slieve Gullion.

You can find the cheese in Arcadia on the Lisburn Road in Belfast, Greens of Lisburn, The Gourmet in Warrenpoint and in shops in Newry, Armagh and Banbridge. Telephone for more details.

ALLISTRAGH

COTTAGE PRIDE, Plum Preserve. Allistragh, Armagh.
Excellent preserves found throughout the province.

ARMAGH

FINE FOODS, Scott Street, Armagh. Contact: Mrs
Brownleigh. An interesting delicatessen.

ONLY NATURAL, Abbey Lane, Armagh. Contact: Pat
McKenna. Compact wholefood shop.

CRAIGAVON

FIRGROVE QUAIL, 40 Ballymacbredan Road,
Maralin, Craigavon, Co Armagh, BT67 OQU, Tel:
(0762) 323149, Contact: Derek and Lynne Patterson.
Quail and Quail eggs.

COUNTY CAVAN

In Cavan the roads are lumpy and bumpy and you pitch and toss much like the small hills that nip and tuck into the landscape. The county only really finds itself when you enter into the lakeland territory, for here it becomes suddenly a reflective, introverted place. Off the main roads you find a land that seems to be always hiding amidst itself — away from the main thoroughfares you can seem quickly to be strolling in a wilderness, miles from civilisation.

In Cavan there are more pigs per square mile than anywhere else in Europe. Sadly, you never see these sympathetic, intelligent animals out in the fields — the pork industry here is conducted behind closed doors.

BAWN BOY

NICO BARTSCH
Tirnawannagh
Bawn Boy
Co Cavan
Tel: (049) 23461
Contact: Nico Bartsch

Honey

Nico Bartsch exports much of the honey she collects from her bee hives, but some can be found locally in Cavan.

Telephone to find out if there is any honey for sale and for directions.

BELTURBET

CORLEGGY FARMHOUSE GOATS' CHEESE
Belturbet
Co Cavan
Tel: (049) 22219
Contact: Michael and Silke Cropp

➡ *Farmhouse goats' cheese*

Most of Silke Cropp's cheese is exported, but you will occasionally see it in Dublin or in Back to Nature in Cavan town, or in the Londis Supermarket in Belturbet. It's a most distinctive, beautiful cheese with a natural rind which comes in three flavours — plain, fresh herbs and green peppercorns. The cheeses are made with a vegetarian rennet and no salt is used — only the rind is salted. Silke uses raw milk from her herd of sixty goats who graze only on grass. Each cheese is decorated with both the distinctive Corleggy label — a maternal goat leaning on an old-fashioned

Free-range eggs, ducks, pork, kid, goats' milk

plough — and an IOFGA symbol. Silke and Michael recommend that you impale a piece of their cheese on a stick and toast it in front of a fire until it bubbles, but Corleggy can be enjoyed any way — it is a gorgeous cheese. The Cropps also sell free-range eggs, ducks, and both pork and kid meat, sold by the half carcass, and goats' milk. Cheese and eggs can be bought from the farm and if you visit you can see happy pigs rooting around in the yard.

In Belturbet take the road on the right as you enter the town — it runs down to the river — at the bridge turn left and continue for about one-and-a-half miles until you see the sign for Corleggy Cheese.

COOTEHILL

JOHN AND MARIE McCANN
Mountain Lodge
Cootehill
Co Cavan
Tel: (049) 30238
Contact: John and
Marie McCann

Ducks and geese

The geese reared by the McCanns in Cootehill are one hundred percent free-range and are never fattened. They keep about four hundred geese wandering their fifteen acre holding. Their ducks are allowed outside after five weeks, when they have developed enough down to stop them catching pneumonia. If you want a free-range duck it is necessary to specify this as John and Marie also do non free-range. They hope to have the IOFGA symbol in about one year. You are welcome to buy at the farm, where you can also buy duck eggs.

Six miles from Virginia, on the Virginia/Cavan road, the farm is just off the right hand side. The geese can be bought in Superquinn, Sawers in Chatham St. Dublin, and Doyle's of Dalkey.

KINGSCOURT

DUN A RI FARMHOUSE CHEESE
Kingscourt
Co Cavan

This attractive gouda-type cheese comes in both young and mature versions, the latter providing a pleasant complexity compared to the friskiness of the young cheese. Patrick Burns and Geurt Van de Dikkenburg also make flavoured varieties — look out

Tel: (042) 67342
Contact: Patrick Burns
and Geurt Van de
Dikkenburg

*Farmhouse cows'
cheese*

VIRGINIA AND RYEFIELD
Ryefield House
Virginia
Co Cavan
Tel: (049) 47416
Contact: Anne Brodie

*Farmhouse cows'
cheese*

for the tart garlic and red pepper, and the chive. The cheese is widely available and you can buy from the house. Groups can also visit the cheeseroom if you make an appointment first.

In the long main street of Kingscourt, head for the houses across the road from Mackens hotel — you will see the Dun a Ri stickers on the windows.

Anne Brodie's cheeses are the only farmhouse cheeses from the south which are widely available in the North of Ireland. They are also amongst the most distinctive — the black plastic overcoats on both the logs and the tiny individual cheeses mark them out anywhere. Ryefield is a colourful orange mature cheese, Virginia is a mild, low-fat cheese. You can buy them from the farm.

In Virginia, take the road to Kell's. You will come to a new stretch of road, with articulated lorries on the left — take the road on the right, go for one mile and you will see the sign on the right saying Ryefield House.

BELTURBET

FRED MULLER, Tirliffin, Milltown, Belturbet, Co Cavan. Tel: (049) 34260. Fred Muller specialises in cooking for dinner parties, and can accommodate a maximum of ten people. Booking needs to be at least twenty-four hours in advance, to allow Fred to catch and prepare dishes like smoked pike. Telephone for more details. Consistently recommended.

CROSSDONEY

BERT AND IRIS NEILL, Lisnamandra, Crossdoney, Co Cavan. Tel: (049) 37196. Bed and breakfast establishment with a legendary reputation for breakfast. Four-and-a-half miles from Cavan, on the Killeshandra Road. Consistently recommended.

COOTEHILL

STONEGROUND OATS, Bunnoe, Cootehill, Co
Cavan. Contact: Owen Foy. Consistently
recommended.

COUNTY DERRY

Derry's famous walls may have repelled all manner of invaders in the past, and continue to be used as a symbol of resistance, but the town has surrendered to imitation architecture. The centre of Derry city is a sad confusion of inappropriate buildings, many of them populated by inappropriate shops. The Northern Irish passion for ever-wider smoother roads has meant that away from the pedestrianised centre there are only motorway wastelands.

Despite this the people of Derry retain their celebrated patience and affability. More than twenty years of 'the Troubles' has not altered the fact that Derry people look at life in a straightforward way. Life continues to revolve around getting your work done and then having a good time.

COLERAINE

CHOPS AND CHANGE
Church Lane
Coleraine
Co Derry
Tel: (0265) 43141
Contact: Mr Cunningham

Butcher

Northerners have an irresistible urge to make puns out of shop names. You end up with titles like the Krusty Kitchen, selling bread, or Nick's Plaice, selling fish. Chops and Change, you will not be surprised to read, is a butcher. In fact they specialise not in chops, but in sausages. They sell nine varieties: pork and fresh chive, steak, Cumberland, oriental, lamb and mint, lean pork, pork, and garlic.

Beside the Church in the centre of Coleraine.

KITTY'S OF COLERAINE
Church Lane
Coleraine
Co Derry
Tel: (0265) 42347
Contact: Mr David Irwin
Patisserie

This is both a bakery and a coffee shop. Specialities of the patisserie counter include filled croissants, pizzas, vol au vents, cakes, meringues, filled rolls and sandwiches.

Beside the Church in the centre of Coleraine.

DERRY

JOHNNY B'S
59 Victoria Road
Derry
Tel: (0504) 41078
Contact: Mark
Caithness

Wine bar/restaurant

Flash designer interior, hip photographs, a full bar and a cheap lunch. Sister of the more famous Ramore Restaurant in Portrush, Johnny B's is a good place to while away the early afternoon. You can buy wholesome fast food: Satays, real burgers, decent salads, and excellent beers. It's also open in the evening. Upstairs is the more formal Bell's restaurant, which is often booked for weddings.

On the Strabane Road out of Derry, just before the town of New Buildings. Open Mon-Sat 12.30-2.30pm, 5.30-10pm, Sun 5.30-9pm.

LEPRECHAUN RESTAURANT
23 Strand Road
Derry
BT48 7BJ
Tel: (0504) 63606
Contact: John McAlister

Coffee shop

This is a place to get a good breakfast, a good cup of coffee, light filled bridge rolls, cakes and pancakes. In the front of the shop there is a bakery selling traditional white and brown soda bread along with all the other aerated Ulster bread.

Derry city centre.

KILLALOO

DAVID HAWTHORNE
Brackfield Farm
Killaloo
Co Derry
Tel: (0504) 301243
Contact: David
Hawthorne

Organic grower, organic lamb

David Hawthorne's excellent organic lamb can be found in the Supermac Centre in Belfast, where it is pre-packed and sold across the counter. You can also buy the lamb, which must be ordered in advance from the farm — a local butcher cuts, packs and labels and you can collect an order from the farm. David also grows potatoes, turnips and spinach.

You can find these in Mother Earth in Newtownards, the Fruit Shop, Great James' Street in Derry, and the Harvest Store on the Culmore Road. The potatoes can now also be found in the Stewart's supermarkets. Brackfield Farm is on the main Glenshane Road from Belfast to Derry. Eleven miles after Dungiven there is a sign for the Ness Country

Park on the right hand side. Turn down that and the house is immediately on the left behind the church and the Primary School.

COLERAINE

DIRECT WINE SHIPMENTS, 18 Abbey Street, Coleraine, Co Derry Tel: (0265) 2113/3021

DERRY

BORD FAILTE, Foyle Street, Derry, Co Derry. Tel: (0504) 369501.

FIORENTINI'S, 47 Strand Road, Derry. Tel: (0504) 260653. Italian-style cafe where you can buy cappuccino and espresso as well as ice cream and sandwiches.

COUNTY DONEGAL

Donegal town takes its Gaelic name from the Viking invasions, literally: Dun na nGall, or Fort of the Foreigners. Even though the town has for hundreds of years been reuinited with its neighbours, there is still a feeling of foreignness about the place. The county is separated from its Ulster neighbours by the border, and separated from its neighbours in the Republic by being geographically part of Ulster. This schizophrenia is further confused by the feeling, when you are there, that you are in the heart of Ireland, in all of its sins and plenty of its graces.

Visitors from around the world are drawn to the magnificent mountain ranges tumbling into deep desolate loughs. The landscape can be forbidding even in a warm summer. It is in Donegal that you will hear sean nos singing, ballads and the sound of the harmonica.

The tradition of talking and socialising over a long evening has given Donegal not only interesting pubs, but a series of confident restaurants, where you will always be given a good meal. But you get the feeling that this comes about more to fill a social need than a culinary one. There are few producers of good food; apart from the fish from its western coastline the ingredients used in the restaurants come from the South, and from Britain via Northern Ireland. We even came across one restaurant that got its vegetables from the daily Belfast market.

BALLYSHANNON

CREEVY PIER HOTEL
Ristorante Larianella
Creevy Pier
Ballyshannon

There can be no better lunch than a bowl of home-made pasta and a glass of red wine; both are available in the Creevy Pier Hotel. Giovanni Archetti is an Italian, cooking Italian food in Donegal. It's an explosive combination, but it works. The pasta is not

Co Donegal
Tel: (072) 51236
Contact: Giovanni
Archetti

only home-made, it's cooked and served al dente, with sauces based on fresh ingredients. They also specialise in West Coast seafood.

Take the Rossnowlagh Road out of Ballyshannon, and the restaurant is signposted about five miles along the road. The restaurant and hotel are open from 1 June-31 Sept. Lunch 12.30-2.30pm; dinner 7-11.30pm.

DANBY RESTAURANT
Rossnowlagh Road
Ballyshannon
Co Donegal
Tel: (072) 51138
Contact: Gerry Brittan

Restaurant

The Danby restaurant is part of a modestly grand old house with a view over the Erne estuary and the Sligo mountains, which, on a good evening, is breathtaking. The food is a delicate form of country house cooking, incorporating kidneys, wild duck, and challenging combinations like monkfish, wrapped first in sorrel, then baked in a home-made pastry. Gorgeous Creme Brulee, a reasonable wine list and reasonable prices.

Take the Rossnowlagh Road out of Ballyshannon at the top of the hill, and you will see the restaurant, clearly signposted, about half a mile on the left hand side. Open: Tues-Sat, 7-10.30pm.

BUNDORAN

CONROY'S GERMAN/IRISH CLUB
Seafront
Bundoran
Co Donegal
Tel: (072) 41280
Contact: Mike Conroy

Restaurant specialising in
➥ *Smoked Salmon*

Conroy's is a club frequented by visiting Germans, and, given the restrictions of entry, it's a wonderful place to have dinner. There is a small bar selling Guinness on draught as it really should taste, and in the back there is a tiny unpretentious restaurant. The speciality of the house is their home-smoked wild Irish salmon. It's smoked over wood bought locally: the oak shavings from coffins. The restaurant sells seafood, all absolutely fresh, and simple. Mike Conroy has a lovely story of some German visitors scrutinising him as he ate bacon and buttered turnips, and then one by one asking for bacon and buttered turnips for their dinner. The restaurant has continued

209

in this tradition. Irish food served as it should be and given its proper status. The result is wonderful.

Ring for more information. The restaurant is situated on the seafront in Bundoran.

LANDHAUS RESTUARANT
Bundoran
Co Donegal
Tel: (072) 41915
Contact: Gunter &
Gabi Spielmann

Restaurant

The Landhaus is a charming German restaurant, with the priceless personality of Gabi Spielmann to make you feel welcome and at home. The cooking is spicy and rich, in true German style. The atmosphere is of people having a good informal night out; a gem of a place where you are sure to have a good evening.

Take the road out of Bundoran going towards Sligo, and the restaurant is set back on the old Southern road at the village of Tullaghan. Open 6.30-11pm. Closed Tuesdays.

DONEGAL

DONEGAL COUNTRY MARKET
St John Bosco Hall
Donegal
Co Donegal

Market

Home-baked cakes and bread, fresh vegetables, goats' milk and cheese, and occasional knick-knacks. Be sure to go early.

Donegal town centre. Fridays, Opens 10am.

FOODLAND
The Diamond
Donegal
Co Donegal
Tel: (073) 21006
Contact: Philip
O'Rourke

Food shop

A most striking feature of the Foodland shop is the cheese counter. Philip O'Rourke has been given awards by the National Dairy Council, and the display he arranges each day is a testament to the fine variety and quality of Irish farmhouse cheeses.

Donegal town centre.

FAHAN

RESTAURANT ST JOHN'S
Fahan
Co Donegal
Tel: (077) 60289
Contact: Reg Ryan

Restaurant

Reg Ryan and his talented staff run a special restaurant using ingredients from the Inishowen peninsula and beyond. The food is robust and uncomplicated, with occasional touches of finesse to make it interesting. A good wine list at competitive prices to satisfy Northern customers who are lucky enough not to have to pay Southern taxes.

On the Main Street at the southern end of Fahan.

GLENCOLUMBKILLE

GLEN-COLUMBKILLE FOLK VILLAGE
Glencolumbkille
Co Donegal
Tel: (073) 30017
Contact: Christina Daly

Tea rooms and food shop

Glencolumbkille has done its best to draw visitors away from the Continent by not only building rental cottages, but also reproducing an ancient working village, with museums and craft shops. Part of this is a little tea room serving home-baked bread and scones, salads and home-made soup. They sell home-brewed wine — heather, fuchsia or seaweed — and jars of butterscotch, marmalade, Irish honey, and sometimes country butter.

The village is clearly signposted as you enter the village which is on the Western Peninsula past Killybegs.

KILLYBEGS

DONEGAL FISHERMAN'S CO-OP
Killybegs Harbour
Killybegs
Co Donegal
Contact: Thomas Dorrian

Fresh fish

You can buy fish straight from the boats, via a cubby-hole marking the entrance to the port. Killybegs is the largest fishing port in Ireland, and one of the biggest in Europe. Gigantic tankers hover around the coastline waiting to take fish to Nigeria, Japan and Europe. There is, sadly, little left for Killybegs.

The Pier at Killybegs.

BURTONPORT

THE PIER, Burtonport, Co Donegal. Ask for details from the Burtonport Fisherman's Co-op if you want to buy fresh fish.

CARNDONAGH

BEV DOHERTY, Galwilly, Glentogher, Carndonagh, Co Donegal, Tel: (077) 74581. Bev Doherty sometimes sells goats' milk and goats' cheese from the farm, when they have a surplus. They also sell some organic vegetables in the summer, but are very small scale, so ring first.

LETTERKENNY

BORD FAILTE, Derry Road, Letterkenny, Co Donegal. Tel: (074) 21160; Telex: 42049.

KELLY & CO LTD, Port Road, Letterkenny. Tel: (074) 21348. Wholesale wines and spirits, but you can buy by the bottle.

RATHMULLEN

THE WATERS' EDGE, Rathmullen, Co Donegal, Tel: (074) 58182/58138, Contact: Pauline and Peter. Situated far in the North of Donegal is the award winning Waters' Edge restaurant. Open 7.30-11pm and Sunday lunch until 2.30pm. Consistently recommended.

COUNTY DOWN

It is the loughs which give County Down its beauty. The southern coast of Belfast Lough, the crunchy indents of Strangford Lough, the rolling elegance of the north coast of Carlingford Lough, have all particular and different attractions. Elsewhere the small towns can seem ordinary in comparison — private places that appear to have little interest in the visitor. The food culture is secret and conservative, and often conforms to the old adage: when it is good, it is very very good, but when it is bad it is awful.

ANNALONG

ROBERT COUSIN LTD
Hanold House
Annalong
Co Down
Tel: (039 67) 68643
Contact: Robert Cousin

Smoked game and herring

The Cousins have operated a family business in the harbour at Annalong for generations. They produce smoked herring and export ninety percent of it to the Italian market, but they also supply pheasant, partridge, quail, chicken, turkey, duck, goose and guinea-fowl, and smoke a wide range of game and poultry in both an old chimney kiln and a modern smokehouse. The factory is currently being expanded in time for 1992 and there are plans for a shop.

You can find the factory by turning down to the harbour at the road opposite the walled church in Annalong: at the bottom of the road turn left and Cousin's is on both sides of the road.

GLASSDRUMMAN HOUSE
Annalong
Co Down
Tel: (03967) 68585
Contact: Tom Guest

Restaurants, guesthouse, specialist food shop

'Simple excellence' is the motto Glassdrumman House use to describe themselves and, happily, they live up to it. The Gallery Restaurant serves pleasing, straightforward food all day, and there are two further restaurants, The Kitchen Garden, open from 7pm each evening and 12.30pm on Sunday for lunch, and Memories, open only on Saturday evening (booking essential) where a seven course meal is served. But of especial interest is the Farm Shop selling an exotic mixture of charcuterie and patisserie. Here you will find excellent walnut bread, elegant pate, marbled Aberdeen Angus beef, hams, jams, eggs and a collection of vegetables from the garden of the house. There is also a gift shop which sells hand-made chocolates and other craft items. There are bedrooms with a single room currently costing £45 stg and a double £65stg, in Glassdrumman Lodge, two miles from the house.

Glassdrumman House is just north of Annalong, and well signposted.

BANGOR

THE AVA BAR & OFF LICENCE
132 Main Street
Bangor
Co Down
Tel: (0247) 465490

Off licence

The Ava is a busy pub with an excellent off-sales attached. Their selection of wines is the most discriminating, and the best value, you will find in the province.

Bangor town centre

BANGOR MARKET

The great weekly ritual of Bangor life is the Wednesday morning market, which arranges itself in the squares off Main Street. A riot of Northern garrulousness, it is great crack, but somewhere to go for fun rather than food. 'Look at the size of those melons, ladies!' shrieks one stallholder, and the crowds peer curiously. Other stalls have names like Krusty Kreation (selling pies) and there are wonderful long-haired Sikhs flogging clothes and barking away in Belfast accents. Stout women sell you everything your pet could ever need or want.

Occasionally you will see local honey being sold from the back of a car, but head into the centre of the market where you will find Paddy's chickens and two good fish counters: Angus Cochrane from Ardglass; and George S. Cully from Portavogie who features exotica such as squid and eel. Replicas of Bangor market can be found throughout the Province: there is one in Belfast near the Law Courts, every Friday.

DAVID BURNS
112 Abbey Street
Bangor
Co Down
Tel: (0247) 270073
Contact: David Burns

Butcher

David Burns is a 'Traditional Butcher' making sausages, and selling good meat. He begins the process by ensuring that the cattle graze on good salty pastures on the Ards Peninsula and slaughtering in a traditional manner, which gives the meat better keeping qualities. All the beef is then hung for at least three weeks, or longer if you order in advance. David is a Champion of Champions sausages maker; he makes a variety of flavours, including a vegetable sausage, and the trophies he has won line the shop. Lamb is hung for ten days, leg of lamb, fourteen. He presses ox tongue, and roasts beef. At Christmas you can buy his wonderful salt beef. He will cut meat in a continental style if you ask for it, and is experimenting with sales of Angus beef, a more marbled cut, which you can order if you prefer.

Bangor town centre.

DROMORE

CAORA CHEESE
DRUMILLER
CHEESE
15 Leapoges Road
Dromore
Co Down
Tel: (0846) 692211
Contact: John and

John McBride and his mother produce the only sheeps' milk yogurt you will find in the country, a deliciously intense product with a unique taste. From their sheeps' milk they also produce the excellent Caora cheese, a pale-coloured medium-soft cheese which comes in a black plastic overcoat, and Drumiller Feta Cheese and Garlic and Herb soft cheese. The sheeps' milk, they point out, is closer to

215

Mary McBride

Farmhouse cheeses,
sheeps' milk yogurt

human milk than is cows' milk, and therefore ideal for allergy sufferers; it has a good balance of vitamins and minerals. You can buy the cheese in Superquinn in Dublin, in Supermac and a number of wholefood shops in Belfast and Greens in Lisburn, amongst many other delicatessens.

Telephone for more details.

RECIPE:
GREEK COUNTRY SALAD WITH DRUMILLER FETA CHEESE

3 tabs olive oil; juice half lemon; one small green pepper; 2-3 inches cucumber; 5 ozs Drumiller Feta Cheese; handful of parsley; handful of black olives; three tomatoes; 1 head of lettuce (Cos, or Irish Iceberg). Peel and slice the cucumber, slice the pepper and the tomato, crumble the cheese into cubes. Leave olives whole. Mix oil and lemon juice in the bottom of a salad bowl, place the other ingredients on top and toss carefully.

GROOMSPORT

ADELBODEN LODGE
Groomsport
Co Down
Tel: (0247) 464288
Contact: Margaret and Denis Waterworth

Restaurant, bakery

Adelboden Lodge encompasses a Restaurant, a country kitchen and a bakery. The restaurant is charmingly unpretentious and comfortable, and so it is with the food. Hearty portions of chicken, steaks, and vegetables are characterised by ingenious touches which lift them far above the ordinary. The chutneys from the country kitchen come in all flavours: banana and raisin, apple and date, or tomato. But it is the highly original variants on a standard wholemeal loaf which best reveal Margaret Waterworth's sense of invention. Date and Walnut; Guinness and Malt; Garlic and Herb all melt into the satisfying richness of a wholemeal loaf. Margaret is also working on an organic loaf.

Adelboden Lodge is clearly signposted just outside Groomsport on the road to Donaghadee. You can buy the bread from the restaurant and also in local shops, Belfast Delicatessens and Greens of Lisburn. Open Tues-Sat 5-7pm high tea, 7pm-11.30pm Dinner.

HOLYWOOD

THE IONA SHOP AND RESTAURANT
27 Church Road
Holywood
Co Down
Tel: (02317) 5655
Contact: Bartjan and
Heidi Brave

Restaurant, wholefood shop

Lurking behind the crafts in the front of the Iona shop is a splendidly discriminating selection of organic vegetables and cheeses, some from as far away as County Clare, and breads. Lurking above the shop is an equally discriminating restaurant where Bartjan Brave conjures up wonders from a tiny open galley. Pigeon is defiantly pink, pate coarse and full and there is an emphasis on imaginative vegetarian food: a terrine of special nuts on a silky mushroom sauce; a pasta teased through with grated fresh vegetables. You can bring your own wine.

Shop open: Mon-Sat 9.15am-5.30pm, Closed Wednesday. Restaurant open: 10-12am coffee, 6.30-10.30pm dinner, Tues-Sat. Holywood town centre.

MOIRA

McCARTNEY'S FAMILY BUTCHER
56/58 Main Street
Moira
Co Down
Tel: (0846) 611422
Contact: George
McCartney

Butcher

George McCartney's shop is garlanded with framed scrolls describing awards his legendary sausages have won, and in the window there are trophies further attesting to his skills. The shop has been a family business for over a century, and for the last couple of years has been the Champion of Champions among sausage makers in the U.K., successfully defending the award in 1988. Seventeen types of sausage are produced here, from Traditional Pork to Lamb sausages with mint, and they are all superb. Beef is hung for three weeks before it is sold,

217

and the various types of prepared meats are delicious. George also makes black pudding and prepared cuts for barbecuing in the summer.

Moira town centre.

NEWRY

ARTHUR McCANN LTD
Victoria Bakery
Castle Street
Newry
Co Down
Tel: (0693) 2076/2919
Contact: Christopher McCann, MD

Bakery

Though McCann's produce the complete range of bakery bread, the jewel in their crown is a rich, fruit-filled barm brack which people are quick to declare the best they have ever eaten. Look out also for their potato bread which is meltingly real, and their Guinness porter cake. They have been in business since 1837 and when you try their bread you will understand how their business has been maintained.

Telephone for details.

NEWTOWNARDS

MOTHER EARTH
13 Frances Street
Newtownards
Co Down
Tel: (0247) 814542
Contact: Patricia Miller

Organic food shop

Patricia Miller's little shop near the square in Newtownards is full of organically produced foods, free-range eggs, potatoes grown by John Hoey in Glengormley, a full range of fruit and vegetables, local honeys such as Bracken Hill Bramble Honey, as well as more familiar pulses and flours. To ensure supplies Patricia has to bring some foodstuffs from England, but otherwise the shop is a focus for locally grown foods. In season look for the cherry tomatoes from the Hilton Organic Gardens, in Scotshouse, County Monaghan: they're magnificent.

Newtownards town centre.

CUAN SEA FISHERIES LTD
Sketrick Island
Killinchy

Cuan Sea Fisheries is a subsidiary company of the Guinness empire. Jasper Parsons rears Pacific Oysters in Strangford Lough and specialises in Shore-to-Door delivery: they can have orders for oysters delivered

218

Newtownards
Co Down
Tel: (0238) 541461
Contact: Jasper Parsons

Oysters, fresh and prepared

within twenty-four hours. They also sell small amounts from the factory, which you find by turning left as you drive onto Sketrick Island. (If you turn right you will end up at Daft Eddie's pleasantly insouciant pub, where the bar food is good value and the view a feast.) As well as fresh oysters, Cuan prepare them in various ways: au gratin, mornay, in Guinness batter and both as cocktail oysters and angels on horseback. These are frozen and you can buy them in Supermac in Knockbreda and Greens of Lisburn.

Turn left after the bridge onto Sketrick Island, which juts out just outside Killinchy.

WARRENPOINT

THE GOURMET
The Square
Warrenpoint
Co Down
Tel: (06937) 74089
Contact: Claire
McCann

Delicatessen

Claire McCann's shop has a good cheese counter and some rare cooked meats such as Kassler, a smoked pork. Most of the familiar deli products are here, and there is decent bread to be found also. At the back of The Gourmet is a small restaurant/tea shop.

BANGOR

HUMBLE PIE, 28 Dufferin Avenue, Bangor. Tel: (0247) 466572. This is a restaurant that operates a take away service for parties of up to fifty. All the pies, tarts and quiches are freshly made and come with coleslaw and crisps.

DROMORE

"THE MAGGIMIN" B&B, 11 Bishopswell Road, Dromore, Co Down, BT251ST. Tel: (0846) 693520. Contact: Mr & Mrs W. Mark. A charming B&B where you can find a real Ulster fry for breakfast.

KILLINCHY

NICK'S PLACE, 18 Kilmood Church Road, Killinchy, Co Down. Tel: (0238) 541472. Open Tues-Sat, 7.30-11pm. Consistently recommended.

NEWTOWNARDS

THE MING COURT, 63 Court Street, Newtownards, Co Down. Tel: (0247) 811760. Open Mon-Fri, 12-2pm & 5.30-11.30pm; Sat 12.30-11pm; Sun 12.30-11.30pm. Consistently recommended.

SAINTFIELD

THE BARN, 120 Monlough Road, Tel: (0238) 510396. Open Tues-Sat 7.30-11pm. Restaurant. Consistently recommended.

COUNTY MONAGHAN

Monaghan has a strong agricultural culture which sits side by side with a busy business sense. A part of Ulster, it seems resolutely northern, determined to avoid frippery. Produce from this county is to be found both north and south of the border, and it's here that we found the sweetest tomatoes, and the most delicious apples.

HILTON ORGANIC GARDENS

Scotshouse
Co Monaghan
Contact: Marion Clarke
and Sean Love

Organic farmers

The first time you eat a tomato by Sean and Marion you think you have never eaten a real tomato before. Sharp with a tartness that mass-produced tomatoes never achieve, it is hard not to simply eat an entire box of them. Other produce includes snap peas, french beans, homeguard and British queen potatoes, cucumbers, parsley, leeks and lettuce. Marion and Sean also grow disappearing varieties of apples like Beauty of Bath, Laxtons Superb and Grenadier cooking apples.

A price list is available on request and delivery can be arranged. You can find the tomatoes and much of the other produce of Hilton Gardens in Patricia Millers shop, Mother Earth in Newtownards, Co Down and the Iona in Holywood, Co Down. There is no telephone so write for details.

EMYVALE

FERNDALE QUAIL, Emyvale, Co Monaghan, Tel: (047) 87578. Contact: Niall Wall.

WHERE TO STAY

Finding a bed for the night in Ireland, is the same as finding a bed in any other country — it's fraught with possibilities and potential difficulties. Standards can vary throughout the country.

However there are organisations to help you, once you know what you're looking for. First you have to decide the level of accommodation you can afford in your price range. The cheapest alternative is to carry a tent and bicycle from one camping sight to the next. Often these sites are situated in the most picturesque locations in the country, so it's a pleasant option. If you don't own a tent, or don't want to go to the bother of dragging one all over the country, then a lot of these camping sites have Mobile Homes for hire, which again can work out to be surprisingly cheap. The problem with them is that in the summer the best ones book out quickly, and in winter, when you have your pick, they are often damp and chilly. If you can get one then just open all the windows, bring along some music and a bunch of flowers, and they can be really quite acceptable. They're always fully equipped, and there's enormous benefit in spending your holiday self-catering. Bord Failte publish a booklet listing all their participating caravan and camping sites: CARAVAN AND CAMPING PARKS. It costs £1.50, and it also lists places where you can hire touring caravans and camping equipment.

The next step up the price rung is to rent a self-catering cottage. Again Bord Failte publish a booklet: SELF CATERING, and it's a guide to all participating self catering establishments in Ireland and costs £2. Very often these cottages are well equipped, quaint, and some even have traditional thatched roofs. Best of all they have fully equipped kitchens which allow you to discover the finest local ingredients and cook them when they are at their very best.

You can call into numerous homes in Ireland and be given a bed and some breakfast. They are always well signposted, and you will always find room. The standard varies enormously, some of these places are extremely luxurious and exceptional value for money. Others are rather dowdy, and the breakfast greasy and shoddy. Always ask to see the room, and don't be afraid of refusing and looking somewhere else, as there will be plenty of alternatives. Use the Bord Failte book GUEST ACCOMMODATION (price £2) if you want a list of addresses.

GUEST ACCOMMODATION also lists the accommodation in the next price range: Hotels, and Guesthouses. A Guesthouse is something between a B&B and a family hotel. They are usually exceptional, combining family hospitality with a guaranteed level of comfort, and you can find more information in their booklet, BE OUR GUEST. Hotels, however, can be rather bland in Ireland. They're the places to go if you want to remain anonymous. There are a small number of glorious exceptions to this rule. The only difficulty is that they usually have glorious prices to match.

You can also find details of Irish Farmhouse Accommodation in the GUEST ACCOMMODATION booklet, so it's certainly worth the £2 that it will cost you at any Bord Failte office.

Another excellent booklet, costing only the price of a stamp, is the IRISH ORGANIC FARM GUESTHOUSES, which you will receive if you write to: Gillies Macbain, Cranagh Castle, Templemore, Co Tipperary, Tel: (0504) 53104. In these houses you can be assured of being given organic food, sometimes freshly picked from their own gardens.

THE HIDDEN IRELAND, is a new publication which you can get from the offices of Ryanair, Tel: Ireland: (01) 774422, Britain: 0800 567890, or from Bord Failte, or: The Secretary, The Hidden Ireland, P.O. Box 2281, Dublin 4 Tel: (01) 686463. This is an exceptional booklet listing B&B, or weekly board, accommodation in houses of particular architectural character, atmosphere and luxury. Prices can also be very reasonable, though you pay more as the luxury increases.

THE IRISH COUNTRY HOUSES AND RESTAURANTS' ASSOCIATION (ICHRA) publish their Blue Book, listing all participating houses and restaurants. Again, most of these are of exceptional quality. You can get the Blue Book in Bord Failte offices, as well as direct from ICHRA, Contact: The Secretary, Ardbraccan Glebe, Navan, Co Meath, Ireland. Tel: (046) 23416, Fax: (046) 23292.

If it's unimaginable luxury you are looking for, then there is a specialist travel agent, ELEGANT IRELAND, at 15 Harcourt Street, Dublin 2. Tel: (01) 751665.

The agency was set up with the intention of helping people find a holiday of real quality, often very expensive, and including chauffeur-driven cars, helicopters, luxury castles to rent, fully-staffed mansions, yachts, and their like. But don't think you need only go if you have a lot of money to spend; even on a limited budget in Ireland you can afford a greater proportion of luxury than you would imagine.

ON THE ROAD

The time when you need the sustenance of good food most, is often when you're travelling. Unfortunately this is usually when you are least likely to find it. When the town or the road is strange, you are busy working, or you are experiencing the fraught tension of a family holiday, that's when you are at the mercy of the food industry, and it doesn't always come to your rescue.

If you're looking for a good meal, you could do worse than follow the road haulage truckers. When you start to look you'll find little cafes dotted all over the country with easy access to a car park. Sometimes you need hardly leave your car at all. On the road between Innishannon and Bandon in Co Cork there's a Dutch man who keeps a mobile van on the side of the road. Here you can buy genuine Dutch Frikadels, made by Otto Kunze in Dunworley Cottage. If you're in Co Waterford there's a trucker's food van just as you come into Dungarvan on the N25. But the king of the roadside vans is in Co Kildare. Barry McDonnell runs a tight ship at 'Mother Hubbard's', a semi-permanent mobile kitchen on the N4 just as you approach Kinnegad from the Dublin side. In all of these you can expect no more and no less than a good sausage sandwich, a cup of tea, or maybe a freshly fried burger. You know exactly what you're going to get, so you won't be disappointed.

Rather more permanent establishments are found on all major roads. If you are driving from Dublin to Belfast, then most of the roadside cafes are to be found adjacent to the border. Others are the Frying Irishman, just past the turnoff to Baldonnel on the Naas Dual Carriageway, going towards Naas, in Co Kildare; the Good Buddy just outside Moate in Co Offaly, or the rather more feminine Transport Cafe, just as you drive into Gorey on the Dublin/Wexford Road. Here you can start off with breakfast at 7.30am, and eat a la carte all day, and Elizabeth Sheehan will provide you with eggs, chips, fish and burgers.

If you can't keep up with the truckers, then ask the advice of friends who know. We did and these are some of their recommendations:

We have two friends with a house in Sligo and a house in Dublin. If they travel between the two they always stop in Longford (it's just about half way).

If they're travelling in the morning they buy sausage rolls from Herterichs butchers of 38 Ballymahon Street, if they're coming back at night they buy chips from Luigi's, from further down the main street. Both are the real thing and recommended by all who try them. There's another Luigi's in Monasterevin and we can vouch that they also sell good chips.

We asked some other friends who travel around the country distributing books, and here are some of the restaurants they recommend: Con's Public House, Mullingar, Co Westmeath; Geoff's Bar, Michael Street, Waterford, Co Waterford; Ormond Cafe, Dungarvan, Co Waterford; Langton's Bar, Kilkenny, Co Kilkenny; The Crawford Gallery, Cork, Co Cork; lunch in the Arbutus Lodge, Cork, Co Cork; the Glassialley's, Drawbridge Street, Cork, Co Cork; Baxter's, Lavitt's Quay, Cork, Co Cork; The Huguenot, Cork, Co Cork; the Riverrun, Limerick, Co Limerick; Matt The Thrasher Pub, Birdhill, Co Limerick; Mac Donagh's, Quay Street, Galway, Co Galway.

Everybody we asked recommended The Sportsman's Inn, Cullahill, which is just south of Portlaoise, on the Dublin/Cork Road.

Finally, Irish Rail produces some of the best railway food in Europe. Each meal is cooked individually on the train, there's no cooked/chilled/cooked airline package food here. Best of all is the breakfast on the Dublin/Cork train. The menu is large, the portions are large, drink plenty of tea, and Cork will arrive too soon.

THE IRISH COUNTRY HOUSES AND RESTAURANTS ASSOCIATION

There has been a quiet but insistent revolution in the catering ranks of Ireland. Previously restaurants battled it out with faceless hotels for culinary garlands, both regarding anyone with an amateurish approach as a non-starter.

But organisations like the Irish Country Houses and Restaurants Association (ICHRA) have carried out a sort of Country House putsch, and it's to these grand old houses, many of whose owners have had no previous culinary training, that those who march on their stomachs turn to if they want a good meal in the country.

All the houses and restaurants in the organisation are managed by their owners, who are there to greet you, and look after you during your stay. The Country Houses provide you with Bed and Breakfast, ranging in luxury from the majestic Park Hotel, or Marlfield House, through to more humble, but nevertheless still exceptionally comfortable mansions. Often they have access to golf courses or fishing and they are usually set amongst beautiful scenery. The restaurants often specialise in dishes formed from ingredients grown in the cook's garden, and again these vary from the eccentric to the splendid.

The Irish Country Houses and Restaurants Association Blue Book, giving details of price, is available from all Bord Failte offices, or from Hilary Finlay, Ardbraccan Glebe, Navan, Co Meath, Tel: (046) 23416, Fax: (046) 23292.

The following is a list of all those in the Association.

COUNTY CARLOW

STEP HOUSE, Borris, Co Carlow. Tel: (0503) 73401/73209, Contact: Breda Coady (Miss). Restaurant only.

COUNTY CLARE

MAC CLOSKEY'S, Bunratty House Mews, Bunratty, Co Clare. Tel: (061) 364082, Contact: Gerry and Marie MacCloskey. Restaurant only.

GREGANS CASTLE HOTEL, Near Ballyvaughan, Co Clare. Tel: (065) 77005, Fax: (065) 77111, Contact: Peter and Moira Hayden. Country House and Restaurant.

COUNTY CORK

AHERNE'S SEAFOOD BAR, 163 North Main Street, Youghal, Co Cork. Tel: (024) 92424/92533, Contact: the Fitzgibbon family. Restaurant only.

ARD NA GREINE INN, Schull, Co Cork. Tel: (028) 28181, Contact: Frank and Rhona O'Sullivan. Country House and Restaurant.

ASSOLAS COUNTRY HOUSE, Kanturk, Co Cork. Tel: (029) 50015, Fax: (029) 50795, Contact: the Bourke family. Country House and Restaurant.

BALLYLICKEY MANOR HOUSE, Bantry Bay, Co Cork. Tel: (027) 50071, Contact: Mr & Mrs George Graves. Country House and Restaurant.

BALLYMALOE HOUSE, Shanagarry, Midleton, Co Cork. Tel: (021) 652531, Telex: 75208, Fax: (021) 652021. Contact: Ivan and Myrtle Allen. Country House and Restaurant.

BLAIRS COVE, Durrus, near Bantry, Co Cork. Tel: (027) 61127, Contact: Philippe & Sabine De Mey. Restaurant only.

LONGUEVILLE HOUSE, Mallow, Co Cork. Tel: (022) 47156/47306, Fax: (022) 47459, Telex: 75498, Contact: Michael & Jane O'Callaghan and family. Country House and Restaurant.

COUNTY DONEGAL

RATHMULLAN HOUSE, Rathmullan, Co Donegal. Tel: (074) 58188, Contact: Bob and Robin Wheeler. Country House and Restaurant.

ST ERRAN'S ISLAND, Donegal Town, Co Donegal. Tel: (073) 21065.
Contact: Brian and Carmel O'Dowd.

COUNTY DERRY

BLACKHEATH HOUSE, 112 Killeague Road, Blackhill, Coleraine, Co Derry,
BT51 4HH. Tel: (0265) 868433, Contact: Joseph and Margaret Erwin.
Country House and Restaurant.

COUNTY GALWAY

CASHEL HOUSE HOTEL, Cashel, Co Galway. Tel: (095) 31001, Telex:
50812, Fax: (095) 31077, Contact: Dermot and Kay McEvilly. Country
House and Restaurant.

CURRAREVAGH HOUSE, Oughterard, Connemara, Co Galway. Tel: (091)
82312/82313, Contact: Harry and June Hodgson. Country House only.

DRIMCONG HOUSE RESTAURANT, Moycullen, Co Galway. Tel: (091)
85115/85585, Contact: Gerard and Marie Galvin. Restaurant only.

ROSLEAGUE MANOR, Letterfrack, Co Galway. Tel: (095) 41101/41102,
Telex: 50906, Contact: Anne & Patrick Foyle. Country House and Restaurant.

COUNTY KERRY

DOYLE'S SEAFOOD BAR & TOWNHOUSE, John Street, Dingle, Co Kerry. Tel:
(066) 51174, Contact: John and Stella Doyle. Restaurant and Townhouse.

THE PARK HOTEL, Kenmare, Co Kerry. Tel: (064) 41200, Telex: 73905, Fax:
(064) 41402, Contact: Francis Brennan. Country House and Restaurant.

COUNTY KILDARE

DOYLE'S SCHOOLHOUSE RESTAURANT, Castledermot, Co Kildare. Tel:
(0503) 44282, Contact: J.W. Doyle. Restaurant only.

MOYGLARE MANOR, Moyglare, Maynooth, Co Kildare. Tel: (01)

286351/286405/286469, Telex: 90358, Fax: (01) 285405, Contact: Mrs Norah Devlin. Country House and Restaurant.

COUNTY MAYO

ENNISCOE HOUSE, Castlehill, Nth Crossmolina, Ballina, Co Mayo. Tel: (096) 31112, Telex: 40855, Contact: Ms Susan Kellet. Country House only.

MOUNT FALCON CASTLE, Ballina, Co Mayo. Tel: (096) 21172, Telex: 40899, Contact: Mrs C. Aldridge. Country House and Restaurant.

NEWPORT HOUSE, Newport, Co Mayo. Tel: (098) 41222/41154, Telex: 53740, Contact: Kieran & Thelma Thompson. Country House and Restaurant.

COUNTY SLIGO

COOPERSHILL HOUSE, Riverstown, Co Sligo. Tel: (071) 65108, Fax: (071) 65466, Telex: 40301, Contact: Brian and Lindy O'Hara. Country House only.

REVERIES, Rosses Point, Sligo. Tel: (071) 77371, Contact: Damien Brennan and Paula Gilvarry. Restaurant only.

COUNTY WEXFORD

MARLFIELD HOUSE, Gorey, Co Wexford. Tel: (055) 21124/21572/22241/21849, Telex: 80757, Fax: (055) 21572, Contact: Ray and Mary Bowe. Country House and Restaurant.

COUNTY WICKLOW

HUNTER'S HOTEL, Rathnew, Co Wicklow. Tel: (0404) 40106, Contact: Mrs Maureen Gelletlie. Country House and Restaurant.

THE OLD RECTORY, Wicklow, Co Wicklow. Tel: (0404) 67048, Contact: Paul and Linda Saunders. Country House and Restaurant.

RATHSALLAGH HOUSE, Dunlavin, Co Wicklow. Tel: (045) 53112/53343, Contact: Joe and Kay O'Flynn. Country House and Restaurant.

TINAKILLY HOUSE, Rathnew, Co Wicklow. Tel: (0404) 69274/67227, Fax: (0404) 67806, Contact: William and Bee Power. Country House and Restaurant.

COUNTRY MARKETS

Country Markets Ltd was founded by the Irish Countrywomen's Association in 1946. Over the last forty years energetic housewives have been occupying draughty halls throughout the country selling their excellent home-made foods.

The markets traditionally last a couple of hours, but be sure to always arrive early, otherwise all the best produce will be long gone.

Free-range chickens, home-baked cakes, country butter, farmhouse cheese, buttermilk, fresh cream, home-grown vegetables, freshly-baked bread, jams, chutneys and fresh flowers are just some of the items you are likely to find.

Enquiries regarding Country Markets Ltd to Mary Coleman, Secretary, Country Markets Ltd, Swanbrook House, Morehampton Road, Dublin 4, Tel: (01) 684784. Each individual market will have a Board and sometimes a telephone number to which orders and enquiries can be addressed.

Arklow, Co Wicklow, Masonic Hall, Sat, 10.30am
Arva, Co Cavan, Parochial Hall, Fri, 10.30am
Bagenalstown, Co Carlow, Kilcarrig Street, Sat, 9.30am
Bailieboro, Co Cavan, Community Centre, Sat, 3pm
Balbriggan, Co Dublin, Town Hall, Fri, 9.30am
Ballina, Co Mayo, Market Square, Fri, 10am
Ballincollig, Co Cork, Community Hall, Fri, 9.30am
Ballyjamesduff, Co Cavan, Community Hall, Fri, 11am
Bandon, Co Cork, South Main Street, Fri, 2pm
Bansha, Co Tipperary, Glen Road, Fri, 9am
Blanchardstown, Co Dublin, St Brigid's Community Centre, Fri, 10am
Blessington, Co Wicklow, Main Street, Sat, 2.30pm
Boyle, Co Roscommon, Bridge Street, Fri, 10.30am
Cahir, Co Tipperary, Community Hall, Fri, 8.30am
Carrickmacross, Co Monaghan, Arus na Gloumann, Fri, 11am
Carrick-on-Shannon, Co Leitrim, Gaiety Cinema, Fri, 2pm
Carrigaline, Co Cork, GAA Pavilion, Fri, 10am
Castlepollard, Co Westmeath, Local Cinema, Fri, 10.30am
Cleggan, Co Galway, Market House, Wed, 11.30am (summer only)
Cobh, Co Cork, Ramblers' Hall, Fri, 10.30am

Culmore, Co Derry, Black Hut, Sat, 10.30am
Donegal, Co Donegal, Methodist Hall, Sat, 11am
Douglas, Co Cork, ICA Hall, Thurs, 2pm
Duleek, Co Meath, Parish Centre, Fri, 10.15am
Dungarvan, Co Waterford, O'Connell Street, Fri, 10.30am
Ennis, Co Clare, Friary Hall, Fri, 9am
Enniscorthy, Co Wexford, IFA Centre, Fri, 9.30am
Fethard, Co Tipperary, ICA Hall, Fri, 9am
Fermoy, Co Cork, Youth Centre, Fri, 3pm
Fingal, Co Dublin, The Old School, Sat, 11am
Gorey, Co Wexford, Parish Hall, Sat, 9.30am
Granard, Co Longford, Market House, Fri, 10.50am
Kells, Co Meath, Market Premises, Fri, 12noon
Kilkenny, Co Kilkenny, Market Yard, Fri, 9.30am
Killarney, Co Kerry, St Mary's Parish Hall, Fri, 11am
Kiltiernan, Co Dublin, Golden Ball, Sat, 10.30am
Kinnegad, Co Westmeath, Old Schoolhouse, Fri, 10am
Laytown, Co Meath, Alfies Restaurant, Fri, 9.30am (summer only)
Limerick, Co Limerick, Augustinian Hall, Fri, 9am
Longford, Co Longford, Main Street, Fri, 11am
Mallow, Co Cork, Dromahane Community Centre, Thurs, 7pm, , , St James'
Hall, Fri, 2.30pm
Manorhamilton, Co Leitrim, Gilbride's Main Street, Sat, 11am
Midleton, Co Cork, Mart Canteen, Fri, 2.30pm
Monaghan, Co Monaghan, St Macartan's Hall, Fri, 9.30am
Mountrath, Co Laois, Macra na Feirme Hall, Fri, 2.30pm
Mullingar, Co Westmeath, Parochial Community Centre, Fri, 10.30am
Naas, Co Kildare, Town Hall, Fri, 10.45am
Navan, Co Meath, The Banba Hall, Fri, 1.30pm
Nenagh, Co Tipperary, Dun Muire, Castle Street, Fri, 1.30pm
New Ross, Co Wexford, 1, The Quay, Fri, 9am
North Wicklow, Co Wicklow, St Patrick's Hall, Kilcoole, Sat, 10.30am
Oldcastle, Co Meath, Masonic Hall, Fri, 10.30am
Ramelton, Co Donegal, Town Hall, Fri, 11am
Rathdowney, Co Laois, Community Centre, Fri, 2pm
Ravensdale, Co Louth, Community Centre, Sat, 11am
Riverstown, Co Sligo, Community Centre, Fri, 10am
Roscrea, Co Tipperary, Abbey Hall, Fri, 2.30pm

Skibbereen, Co Cork, Scouts' Hall, Fri, 2.30pm
Slane, Co Meath, Parish Hall, Fri, 11am
Sligo, Co Sligo, Market Yard, Sat, 10am
Strandhill, Co Sligo, Dolly's Cottage, Wed, 3pm (summer only)
Thurles, Co Tipperary, Confraternity Hall, Fri, 3pm
Toomevara, Co Tipperary, Toomevara Hall, Fri, 2pm
Tralee, Co Kerry, Barrack Lane, Thurs, 2.15
Trim, Co Meath, Town Hall, Fri, 2.30pm
Tullamore, Co Offaly, The Shambles, Fri, 2pm
Tullycross, Co Galway, Marian Hall, Renvyle, Tues, 7.15pm (summer only)
Valentia Island, Co Kerry, Farreneigh, Sat, 3pm (summer only)
Waterford, Co Waterford, Alexander Street, Fri, 9am
Wexford, Co Wexford, The Bull Ring, Fri, 9.30am

USEFUL ADDRESSES

DEPARTMENT OF AGRICULTURE AND FOOD, Agriculture House, Kildare Street, Dublin 2. Tel: (01) 789011, Fax: (01) 616263, Telex: 93607.

ARTICLE NUMBER ASSOCIATION OF IRELAND, Confederation House, Kildare Street, Dublin 2. Tel: (01) 779801, Fax: (01) 777823, Telex: 93502, Contact: The Secretary. This is the issuing authority for the 'Article Number' or 'Bar Code', those little black lines on the side of any packeted item.

AN BORD BAINNE (Irish Dairy Bord), Grattan House, Lower Mount Street, Dublin 2. Tel: (01) 619599, Fax: (01) 612778, Telex: 93615.

AN BORD BAINNE LABORATORIES, Moorepark, Fermoy, Co Cork, Tel: (025) 31399.

BORD IASCAIGH MHARA (BIM), P.O. Box 12, Crofton Road, Dun Laoghaire, Co Dublin. Tel: (01) 841544, Fax: (01) 841123, Telex: 93237. Responsible for the overall development of the fishing industry.

COMPANIES REGISTRATION OFFICE, Dublin Castle, Dublin 2. Tel: (01) 718811

CORAS BEOSTOIC AGUS FEOLA (CBF), Elm House, Clanwilliam Court, Lower Mount Street, Dublin 2. Tel: (01) 685155, Fax: (01) 687521, Telex: 93370. The Irish Livestock and Meat Board.

CORAS TRACHTALA TEO (CTT), Merrion Hall, Strand Road, Sandymount, Dublin 4. Tel: (01) 695011, Fax: (01) 695820, Telex: 25227. Irish Export Board.

DUBLIN CHAMBER OF COMMERCE, 7 Clare Street, Dublin 2. Tel: (01) 614111/764291, Telex: 90716, Fax: 766043.

DUBLIN CORPORATION MARKET, Little Green Market, Dublin 7. Tel: (01) 730681.

EARTHWATCH, Harbour View, Bantry, Co Cork. Tel: (027) 50968.
Environmental organisation, to watch and protect.

DEPARTMENT OF ENERGY, FOREST AND WILDLIFE SERVICE, 25 Clare
Street, Dublin 2. Tel: (01) 715233. Game Licences Tel: 615666.

FEDERATION OF IRISH BEEKEEPERS, Monkstown Park College, Dun
Laoghaire, Co Dublin.

FOOD FROM FRANCE, Marine House, Clanwilliam Place, Dublin 2. Tel:
680137. Part of the French Commercial office promoting French food and
wine.

FRESH FRUIT AND VEGETABLE INFORMATION CENTRE, Upper Mount Street,
Dublin 2. Tel: 614105

AN FORAS AISEANNA SAOTHAIR (FAS), Head Office, Carrisbrook House,
Ballsbridge, Dublin 4. Tel: (01) 603722, Fax: (01) 687138, Telex: 91331.
The Training and Employment Authority.

FOIR TEO, 25/28 Adelaide Road, Dublin 2, Tel: (01) 764484/608722, Fax:
(01) 611670, Telex: 90829. State-sponsored aid for Industry.

GREENPEACE, 44 Upper Mount St, Dublin 2. Environmental organisation.

GUARANTEED IRISH LIMITED, 1 Fitzwilliam Place, Dublin 2. Tel: (01)
612607. An independent company controling the use of its symbol, a large g
with an i through its middle. It is funded by manufacturers who use the symbol.

DEPARTMENT OF HEALTH, Hawkins House, Dublin 2, Tel: (01) 714711, Fax:
(01) 786074, Telex: 33451.

DEPARTMENT OF INDUSTRY, COMMERCE AND TRADE, Kildare Street,
Dublin 2, Tel: (01) 614444, Fax: (01) 762654, Telex: 93478.

INDUSTRIAL DEVELOPMENT AUTHORITY (IDA), Wilton Park House, Wilton
Place, Dublin 2. Tel: (01) 686633/688444/602244, Fax: (01) 603703.

INTERNATIONAL FUND FOR IRELAND, Department of Foreign Affairs, 80 St Stephen's Green, Dublin 2. Tel: (01) 780822.

IRISH CONSUMER RESEARCH, ICR Ltd, 24 Ely Place, St Stephen's Green, Dublin 2. Tel: (01) 764961/760751, Contact: Colm Carey or Leslie Collins. Expertise in Consumer Attitudes, In-home Product Trials, New Product Development, Advertising Strategy Development etc.

IRISH GOODS COUNCIL, Ireland House Trade Centre, Merrion Hall, Strand Road, Sandymount, Dublin 4. Tel: (01) 696011, Fax: (01) 696251.

IRISH ORGANIC FARMERS AND GROWERS ASSOCIATION (IOFGA) Springmount, Ballyboughal, Co Dublin. Tel: (01) 433051, Contact: Nicky Kyle. Farmers and growers can apply for their symbol proving that they have grown or reared their produce organically.

IRISH QUALITY ASSOCIATION, Merrion Hall, Strand Road, Sandymount, Dublin 4. Tel: (01) 695092, Fax: (01) 695820, Telex: 93678. Issues the Quality Mark — 'Q'.

IRELAND FUND, 16-20 Cumberland Street South, Dublin 2. Tel: 714677.

KLEE PAPER, P.O. Box 2266, Clonshaugh, Dublin 17, Tel: (01) 483114. Recycled paper.

DEPARTMENT OF THE MARINE, Leeson Lane, Dublin 2, Tel: (01) 615666, Fax: (01) 789527, Telex: 91253.

MARKET RESEARCH BUREAU OF IRELAND LTD, 43 Northumberland Avenue, Dun Laoghaire, Co Dublin. Tel: (01) 804661, Contact: Aine O'Donoghue/Barry Jones. Product Research and Testing, Consumer Characterisation Surveys and Distributive Surveys carried out for the food industry.

MARKET RESEARCH NORTHERN IRELAND LTD, 39 Malone Road, Belfast BT9 4RX, Northern Ireland. Tel: (084) 661037/8/9, Contact: Mandy McNeill/Robin Harrison.

NATIONAL DAIRY COUNCIL, Grattan House, Lower Mount Street, Dublin 2. Tel: (01) 619599, Fax: (01) 612778, Telex: 93615.

NATIONAL FOOD CENTRE, Dunsinea, Castleknock, Co Dublin. Tel: (01) 383222. Research and Development for the food industry.

NATIONAL STANDARDS AUTHORITY OF IRELAND (NSAI), Eolas, Glasnevin, Dublin 9, Tel: (01) 370101, Fax: (01) 379620, Telex: 25449.

THE PATENTS OFFICE, 45 Merrion Square, Dublin 2. Tel: (01) 760431.

RESTAURANT ASSOCIATION OF IRELAND, 67 Upper George's Street, Dun Laoghaire. Tel: (01) 806056.

REGISTER OF BUSINESS NAMES, Dublin Castle, Dublin 2. Tel: (01) 718811.

RGDATA, Rock House, Main Street, Blackrock, Co Dublin, Tel: (01) 887584, Fax: (01) 832206, Telex: 90521. Representing independent supermarkets, grocers and off-licences. Trade magazine, Retail News.

THE CENTRAL STATISTICS OFFICE, Earlsfort Terrace, Dublin 1. Tel: (01) 767531

TEAGASC, 19 Sandymount Avenue, Dublin 2, Tel: (01) 688188, Telex: 30459, Fax: (01) 688023. The Agriculture and Food Development Authority. An amalgamation of what used to be known as ACOT and AFT.

UNIVERSITY COLLEGE CORK, Faculty of Dairy and Food Science, Cork. Tel: (021) 276871 Ext 2393, Fax: (021) 277194.

UNIVERSITY COLLEGE DUBLIN, Department of Industrial Microbiology, Belfield, Dublin 4, Tel: (01) 693244 Ext 1512, Fax: (01) 694409, Telex: 32693. Department of Agriculture Tel: (01) 752116.

UNIVERSITY COLLEGE GALWAY, Shellfish Research Laboratory, Carna, Co Galway, Tel: (095) 32201, Fax: (095) 32205, Telex: 50800.

WORKING WEEKENDS ON AN ORGANIC FARM (WWOOF) c/o Annie Sampson, Crowhill, Newgrove, Tulla, Co Clare.

WINE PROMOTION BOARD OF IRELAND, 33 Clarinda Park West, Dun Laoghaire. Tel: (01) 804666. (Also known as Wine & Spirit Association)

USEFUL PUBLICATIONS

ALTERNATIVE IRELAND DIRECTORY, 24 Sullivan's Quay, Cork, Co Cork.

BOOKS FOR COOKS, Blenheim Crescent, London, Tel: (031) 221 1992. Will seek out cookery books that are in or out of print and send them by post to Ireland.

BAKERY WORLD, Jemma Publications Ltd, 22 Brookfield Ave, Blackrock, Co Dublin. Tel: (01) 886949 (Bi-monthly).

CHECKOUT, Vesey Publications Ltd, 22 Crofton Road, Dun Laoghaire, Co Dublin. Tel: (01) 808415. (Monthly).

COMMON GROUND, Annaghcor, Castlebaldwin, Co Sligo. Tel: (071) 65301. Includes the newsletter of IOFGA: c/o Murt Flynn, Poulmaloe, Whitechurch, New Ross, Co Wexford. Tel: (051) 88454. Subscriptions: Pat Beggan, Smutternagh, Boyle, Co Roscommon. Environmental magazine.

CO-OP IRELAND, Tara Publishing Co Ltd, Poolbeg House, 1 Poolbeg Street, Dublin 2. Tel: (01) 719244. (Monthly)

ENVIRONMENT IRELAND, 27 Fortfield Terrace, Upper Rathmines, Dublin. Tel: 976957. Environmental magazine.

FOOD IRELAND, Tara Publishing Co Ltd, Poolbeg House, 1 Poolbeg Street, Dublin 2. Tel: (01) 719244. (Monthly).

FOOD & PACKAGING DIRECTORY — IRELAND, Kompass Ireland Publishers Ltd, Connaught House, 44 Upper Mount Street, Dublin 2. Tel: (01) 612907/785798, Fax: (01) 766282, Telex: 30259.

IN DUBLIN, 15 Lower Baggot Street, Dublin 2. Tel: (01) 615555/615303. Contact: Maureen Gillespie. Magazine detailing what's on in the capital, including food.

INDUSTRIAL DEVELOPMENT AUTHORITY PUBLICATIONS, Wilton Park

House, Wilton Place, Dublin 2. Tel: (01) 686633, Fax: (01) 603703. 'A Future in Food' and 'Your Own Business'

IRELAND OF THE WELCOMES, Baggot Street Bridge, Dublin 2. Tel: (01) 765871. Contact Dr Peter Harbison. Bord Failte magazine with articles on all aspects of Irish culture, including food.

IRISH EXPORTERS HANDBOOK, INTRODUCTION TO EXPORT FOR THE SMALLER FIRM, CTT MARKET REPORTS. All from Coras Trachtala Teo, (The Irish Export Board), Merrion Hall, Strand Road, Sandymount, Dublin 4. Tel: (01) 695011.

IRISH HOTELS & CATERING REVIEW, Jemma Publications Ltd, 22 Brookfield Ave, Blackrock, Co Dublin. Tel: (01) 886946. (Monthly).

THE IRISH MARKET — FACT AND FIGURES, Wilson Hartnell Advertising and Marketing Ltd, 12/13 Leeson Park, Dublin 6. Tel: (01) 978822.

THE IRISH MEAT JOURNAL, Tara Publishing Ltd, Poolbeg House, 1 Poolbeg Street, Dublin 2. Tel: (01) 719244.

MARKETING GUIDE TO NORTHERN IRELAND, Ulster Television, Havelock House, Ormeau Road, Belfast BT7 1EB, Tel: (084) 328122.

MARKETING OPINION, 12 Magennis Place, Dublin 2. Tel: (01) 719896. (Monthly).

MASTER BUTCHER, Glencairne Associates, 82 Upper George's Street, Dun Laoghaire, Co Dublin. Tel: (01) 800470/407250. (Bi-monthly).

RETAIL NEWS, Tara Publishing Co Ltd, Poolbeg House, 1 Poolbeg Street, Dublin 2. Tel: (01) 719244. (Monthly).

SHANNON DEVELOPMENT PUBLICATIONS, Shannon Free Airport Development Company Limited, Limerick Food Centre, Raheen, Limerick, Co Limerick. Tel: (061) 302033, Telex: 70140, Fax: (061) 301172

THOMS DIRECTORY, 38 Merrion Square, Dublin 2. Tel: (01) 767481. An annual directory listing manufacturing and retail businesses in Dublin.

TODAY'S GROCER, FM Publications, Ashton, 6 Martello Tower, Dublin. Tel: (01) 809466.

ULSTER CATERING & LICENSING REVIEW, Jemma Publications (NI) Ltd, 151 University Street, Belfast BT7 1HH, Northern Ireland. Tel: (084) 231634.

ULSTER GROCER, Jemma Publications, (NI) Ltd, 151 University Street, Belfast BT7 1HH, Northern Ireland. Tel: (084) 231634.

VINTNERS' WORLD, Jemma Publications Ltd, 22 Brookfield Ave, Blackrock, Co Dublin. Tel: (01) 886946. (Monthly).

IRISH WINE BUYERS' GUIDE, Rosney House, Albert Road, Glenageary, Co Dublin. Tel: (01) 841611.

FOOD INDEX

GOATS' CHEESE

SHEEPS' CHEESE

DAIRY PRODUCTS

Carrowholly Quark 20
Co-Op Shop, Quark 15
Compsey Creamery Yogurt 176
Copsewood Yogurt 107
Corleggy Goats' Milk 201
Cottage Foods 151
Doherty, B, Goats' milk products 212
Doloree House, Garlic Butter 150
Dunmore East Natural Yogurt 185
Dunphy, J J 173
Elysium Herb Farm 147
Fuchs, A, Goats' Milk 17
Glenlough Yogurt 125
Glenshesk Dairies, Yogurt and
Fromage Frais 189
Kal, L & P, Goats' Yogurt Drink 158
Lodge Farm Produce 196
McCambridge's Ice Cream 69
Northern Ireland Goat Club 196
Old McDonnell Yogurt 109
Shanahan, M 185
Springfields Flavoured Butters 169

DRINKS

Academie Du Vin 67
Adam's Salesroom 67
Ava Off Licence 214
Bailey's Irish Cream 67
Ballygowan, Spring Water 68
Bewleys, Coffee and Tea 47
Boland's Wine Market, Wine
Importers 69
Bunratty Mead 118
Bushmill's Distillery 194
Callaghan Vintage Wines, Wine
Importers 69
Cassidy Wines, Wine Importers 69
Cheeseboard, The, Wine Importers 50

Cherry's Breweries 185
de Braam, Spring Water 90
Dillon, E & Co, Wine Importers 69
Direct Wine Shipments 192, 207
Dolan, P & Co, Wine Importers 69
Ecock Brothers, Wine Importers 59
Findlater's, Wine Importers and Wine
Merchants 69
Fine Wines, Wine Importers 168
Fior Uisce, Spring Water 12
Fitzgerald's, Wine Importers 70
Galvin's Off Licences 136
Gilbey's of Ireland, Wine Importers
70
Glenisheen Spring Water 113
Grants of Ireland, Wine Importers 70
Greenhills Wines and Spirits, Wine
Importers 70
Guinness, A 68
House of Wine, Wine Importers 70
Hotel & Restaurant Suppliers, Wine
Importers 70
Iber Wines, Wine Importers 70
Irish Ale Brewers 149
Kelly & Co, Wine Importers (Dublin)
70
Kelly & Co, Wine Importers (Dublin)
212
Kilkenny Spring Water 79
McArdle Moore & Co 86
McCabe's, Wine Importers 70
Malting Company of Ireland 121
Midleton Distillery 144
Mitchell's, Wine Importers and Wine
Merchants 70
Market Winery 59
Murphy 's Brewery 150
Nujuice 172
O'Brien's Fine Wines, Wine Importers
and Wine Merchants 70
O'Malley's Post Office 23

FISH AND SEAFOOD

Tralee Oyster Fish Society 162
Woodison, N 32

FREE-RANGE EGGS

Co-Op Shop 15
Corleggy 201
Drumbawn Farm 109
Joachim Hess 11
Kilcullen, A 29
King's River Community 79
Nolan's 61
Northridge (Mrs) 145
Peter's Herb Farm 16
Riordan, C 159
Thompson, J 27
Sea View Farm 29
Wood Martin, E & D 34

MEAT, MEAT PRODUCTS, BUTCHERS AND POULTRY

Aillwee Caves Salami 113
Ballyshemane Deer Farm 108
Best, James & Co 47
Boazman, G 146
Brennan's Pork Shop 37
Brenner's Pork Shop 183
Browne, G 25
Buckley, FX, Butchers 48
Burke, E & Son 174
Burns, David, Butchers 215
Chops and Change 205
Continental Meat Centre 84
Continental Sausages 159
Corleggy 201
Couper, D 95
Curran, N 154

Den Heyer, W, Sausages 6
Dunn's 52
Eldridge, R 26
Erlich's, Kosher Butchers 49
Ferndale Quail 221
Firgrove Quail 200
Fitzsimmons, J 144
Fuchs, A, Kid Meat 17
Gardner, Mrs 182
Garvey's Butchers 155
German Salami Company 86
Gokis Meats 94
Halal Group 49
Halal Meat Shop 49
Hanlon Ltd, 68
Hawthorne, D 206
Herterichs Butchers 227
Heslop, V 180
Hess, J 11
Hickey, M 173
Hick, J, Butcher 55
Hogan, Wm, Bacon Shop 168
Howard, G 115
Kieran's Brothers 83
Kilcullen, A 29
Knobel, S 182
Lavistown, Sausages 76
McCartney Butchers 217
McCann, J & M 202
McGeough, E, Butchers 11
Miklas, W & M 77
Mullins, W 13
Mulloy, T Ltd 61
Mulrise Foods 149
Multiyfarnham Deer Farm 94
Nolan's, General Store 61
Northridge (Mrs) 145
O'Flynn's 138
Ponsonby, H 148
Riordan, C 159
Roesler, U 103

249

PRESERVES AND HONEY

SMOKED PRODUCTS

VEGETABLES, HERBS AND VEGETARIAN FOOD

GENERAL INDEX

CATERERS

COOKERY CLASSES

DISTRIBUTORS

RETAIL FOOD SHOPS

FOOD WHOLESALERS

PUBS

RESTAURANTS

RECIPE INDEX

FUTURE EDITIONS

All entries in the Irish Food Guide are published free of charge. An updated edition will be published if there are sufficient new entries to merit it. Anyone with information to be listed should contact , in writing, the publishers, Anna Livia Press, 21 Cross Avenue, Dun Laoghaire, Co Dublin.

Please include the full names of the products supplied, as well as the address (with directions), telephone number and a contact name to be printed with the entry.

NOTES

NOTES